Defying the Tomb

Defying the Tomb

*Selected Prison
Writings and Art of
Kevin "Rashid" Johnson*

*featuring exchanges
with an Outlaw*

KER
SPL
EBE
DEB
2013

Defying the Tomb: Selected Prison Writings and Art of Kevin "Rashid" Johnson, Featuring Exchanges With an Outlaw

ISBN 978-1-894946-39-1
Published in 2010 by Kersplebedeb, second printing 2013
Copyright © Rising Sun Press

Cover artwork by Rashid
Cover and interior design by Kersplebedeb

To order copies of the book, contact:
        Kersplebedeb
        CP 63560, CCCP Van Horne
        Montreal, Quebec
        Canada
        H3W 3H8
        www.kersplebedeb.com
        www.leftwingbooks.net

Kevin "Rashid" Johnson is a New Afrikan Communist prison organizer and intellectual in the United States and one of the founders of the NABPP-PC (New Afrikan Black Panther Party–Prison Chapter). His writings, and updates on his situation, can be found on his website at www.rashidmod.com.

As Rashid is frequently transferred, in order to write to him please check out the rashidmod.com website or write to Kersplebedeb to receive his most up-to-date address.

ON RASHID'S SPLIT WITH THE NEW AFRIKAN BLACK PANTHER PARTY AND RECONSTITUTION AS THE REVOLUTIONARY INTERCOMMUNAL BLACK PANTHER PARTY:

On December 29, 2020 I and the entire outside membership of the New Afrikan Black Panther Party (NABPP) split with Shaka Zulu and Tom Watts, who were the only remaining outside members of the NABPP, to form the Revolutionary Intercommunal Black Panther Party (RIBPP).

This split followed several months of struggle against conduct of Shaka that was found problematic by members of the Party, and the United Panther Movement (UPM), the NABPP's principal mass organization.

Shaka had been released from prison during January 2019, and was able with the help of others to develop a small group of UPM activists and several promising community service programs in Newark, NJ where he lived.

Shaka was found to be leading this collective in a commandist manner and without supervision or accountability of himself to the NABPP's Central Committee, in violation of Party rules and principles. As struggles were made against this conduct, numerous complaints began surfacing from UPM members and others against further problematic conduct of Shaka's, including his abuse of women, misappropriation of funds donated by and raised from the people for Party programs, and so on, and his systematic evasion of criticism and accountability for this conduct.

Also challenged was Tom's role as a Euro-Amerikan, who persisted in dominating and controlling the NABPP, while inducing Shaka to portray it publicly as led by Blacks. Tom also persisted in issuing controversial documents in the name of the CC and Politburo with my name signed to them, that had not been collectively agreed upon, in violation of Democratic Centralism. I resigned from the CC and Politburo in protest over these practices.

To confront these practices, I called for a meeting of all Party members and the election of a new CC in place of the the existing self-appointed one. To avoid this meeting, to hold on to their positions of power, and in direct violation of the Party's internal democracy, Tom threatened to have me expelled if the meeting was held, and then convinced Shaka to join him in liquidating the entire outside NABPP membership.

The meeting of all outside NABPP members still took place on December 29th. At that time all attendees agreed unanimously to split with Shaka and Tom and reconstitute as the RIBPP, with an elected provisional CC, that unlike the NABPP, included several women Comrades. A few days later the new Party's CC met with the outside UPM, the majority of whom agreed to leave with the RIBPP to serve as its principal mass organization and to reconstitute under the name Panther Solidarity Organization (PSO).*

The RIBPP still maintains all of the line and ideology of the NABPP; the only change is in the name of the organization and in separating from those two members.

— — — — —

* I wrote several articles describing these events in greater detail and political perspective, which can be read online, specifically: "Let's Get This Party Started: On the Split in the NABPP and Founding of the RIBPP" (http://rashidmod.com/?p=2910) and "In the NABPP ('Tom Watts' Party') When the People Criticize the Leadership the Leadership Liquidates the People" (http://rashidmod.com/?p=2908).

Dedicated to the People, to the veterans and fallen warriors of our centuries-old liberation struggle, to the first wave Black vanguard Black Panther Party, and to our martyred comrade, Hasan Shakur. It ain't over yet! The struggle continues!!

All Power to the People!!

Each generation must, out of relative obscurity, discover its mission, and fulfill it or betray it.

Frantz Fanon

Table of Contents

RASHID
7-07₀₆

FOREWORD

by Russell "Maroon" Shoats

On being asked to write a foreword for this book, and after reading the manuscript, I became excited about contributing my views about the author's writings, ideology, life and work within the ongoing struggle for Black self-determination and against the universal plague of capitalism, that has advanced to the stage of a global fascist empire. Having been directly involved in similar efforts for close to 40 years, these are issues I care a lot about, and have also learned something about.

I've been in prison since 1972, when I was convicted of participating in a retaliatory attack on a Philadelphia police station in 1970. That action was in response to the ongoing killings of local Black youth, and the generalized murderous suppression of the Black Movement for Self-Determination, and of the Black Panther Party (BPP) in particular. Having then been a member of an armed clandestine unit of the Black Liberation Army (BLA), or Afro-American Liberation Army – which were one and the same – we operated as the offensive arm of the BPP and of our movement in general.

My excitement was due to my belief that the work that our author and his close comrades are doing is pivotal to our ongoing struggle, leaving me very encouraged by these efforts. Yet, when I was earlier invited to join their fledgling New Afrikan Black Panther Party–Prison Chapter (NABPP–PC), I declined. Now I know that sounds contradictory, and maybe a product of the ego, not wanting to follow younger comrades who were not even born when I first got involved in our struggle … But at 63, with no immediate prospects of voluntarily being released from prison, Hell, I've been in 23 hour lock-down for over 25 years, and serving "over" two natural life sentences – plus I've ducked so many police bullets, nightsticks and jailhouse shanks, as well as suffered through the deaths of so many comrades, relatives, associates and friends, until I've long ago submerged my ego to a stronger desire to just continue to soldier on in "whatever" capacity I can; knowing that such a never-say-die attitude provides its own ego gratification, as well as provides encouragement and inspiration to help fuel our fight.

Ancestor Harriet Tubman used to say: "Go free or die!" Over time I've come to see that, as she did; freedom from pride of place, deriving satisfaction from adhering to a cosmic set of ethics.

No, I'll explain why I declined their offer later on. But back to why the author's efforts are so important.

More than anything else, the author is interjecting some much needed revolutionary anti-capitalist views and class analysis into our contemporary efforts. Moreover, he's doing a lot of homework so that he can understand and pass on lessons learned by others who have also fought against this problem, helping him to better explain and struggle against various economic, political, and social phenomena that continue to vex many who desire and work towards revolutionary change. In fact, it has been so for millennia.

In *Civilization or Barbarism,* Cheikh Anta Diop informs us that as far back as three thousand or more years ago, the rebels against despotic rulers of ancient Egypt were never able to achieve their goals due to their inability to fully understand the various class strata that under-girded that society. More directly, the true forerunners of the NABPP–PC's efforts would be best perceived as beginning with the kidnapping and enslavement of their Afrikan Ancestors from that continent, while modern capitalism was in its infancy. And ever since that time, there has been an *internal ideological struggle* taking place between various elements and factions of the Afrikans affected, both on the Afrikan continent and throughout the Diaspora. That struggle deals with how best to achieve freedom from slavery, as well as self-determination in the economic, political, social and cultural spheres; with the ending of slavery being the only aspect easily agreed upon.

In truth, similar struggles were also being waged against many of the same forces by *other peoples* – on other continents. In political and social matters Afrikans – everywhere – wanted as much control and say over their lives as possible. Coming from societies where for centuries they had developed traditions that ameliorated much of the strife and antagonisms between classes – mainly due to their ability to reject too much down pressure from the upper classes by simply migrating throughout the vast continent – their political and social institutions relied more on *consciousness building* than anything else. This held true even amongst the large empires like Ghana, Mali, Songhai and the Ashanti: and even more so amongst the smaller states and the stateless societies found amongst the Ibo, Twa (pygmy), Sans (bushmen), Khoisan, Bantu and Niger/Congo peoples of west and southern Afrika. All of these were areas that provided the most kidnapped peoples who were enslaved in the Diaspora.

In economic matters, however, we return to where our author is so important. The forerunners of his NABPP–PC in the Diaspora found a robust mercantilism – which their enforced labor fueled – that evolved over the centuries into mature capitalism/imperialism, the likes of which were unknown earlier: especially amongst their Afrikan Ancestors! Thus, instinctively, the need to exert ever more demands on the Afrikans, who tenaciously held onto remnants of their traditional communal institutions and practices, caused many hard pressed individuals and groups to try to come up with ways to try to *synthesize* their efforts to achieve freedom and self-determination within a capitalist framework. While others began to examine what certain Europeans who were wrestling with similar forms of capitalistic exploitation – like Karl Marx and Fredrich Engels, and later V.I. Lenin – were discovering. And that was their determination that capitalism – at bottom – was a predatory system that needed to be abolished.

We can clearly examine this struggle between liberationists in the New Afrikan Diaspora by studying the clash amongst the leaders and followers of Marcus Garvey's United Negro Improvement Association and African Communities Leagues (UNIA–ACL) and the African Blood Brotherhood, led by Cyril Briggs, who were confirmed Marxists. Garvey, although it's not generally known, organized and led the first and *only* Global Pan-Afrikanist Movement, with *millions* of members in both hemispheres. Garvey's economic ideas and inspiration was derived from Booker T. Washington's

"Black capitalism," which was best manifested through his Tuskegee Institute in the then segregated US South.

Yet, Garvey was still a staunch Black Nationalist and Global Pan-Afrikanist, and was *also* an active and firm supporter of the Russian Bolshevik Revolution, as well as the Irish Republican Army's fight against British imperialism. In fact, after the Russian Communist Party controlled Comintern adopted the Black Belt Thesis – the basis of today's New Afrikan Independence Movement's efforts to win a homeland in five Southern states – a position Garvey never championed; (since his primary efforts were directed towards winning the continent of "Africa for the Africans" while still supporting "Democratic Rights" for other Afrikans throughout the Diaspora); Lenin still directed the Comintern to recognize Garvey and the UNIA–ACL as the *main force* amongst Blacks in the US, and to deal with them and not the Marxist African Blood Brotherhood! For all obvious reasons, which I'll return to.

The ABB for their part were *never* able to win a mass following, and eventually merged its all-Black following with the multi-racial Communist Party USA. Both the UNIA–ACL and the ABB/Communist Party USA were eventually suppressed and sidelined, while the ABB/CPUSA continued to have a clearer understanding than the UNIA–ACL and the groups it inspired about capitalism's faults.

A much-maligned individual from that period and ideological struggle is W.E.B. Dubois. Nevertheless, he still came closer than his contemporaries, (and most of us today), to synthesizing the different aspects *needed* for the Global Afrikan Struggle for Self-Determination and Freedom. And although he and Garvey had different leadership styles, and Dubois' growing rejection of capitalism – that eventually led him to becoming a Marxist – (coupled with the US and European governments' interference and instigation of a feud), he was also a thoroughgoing Global Pan-Afrikanist, and also clearly understood the need to help Afrikans regain their sense of self-worth that the *bastardization* of their collective cultural heritage had cost them.

Although he's best known for co-founding and tirelessly working in the NAACP, (causing most to assume he was a champion of integration), his work in that organization was directed towards what even the die-hard Black Nationalist Marcus Garvey recognized: democratic rights must be fought for *throughout* the Afrikan Diaspora. Indeed, Dubois was such a firm Pan-Afrikanist, for decades most Pan-Afrikan congresses were chaired by him, and a number of later heads of Afrikan states were there mentored by him. Furthermore, he headed a delegation of both Afrikan Continental and Diaspora Afrikans to Europe to pressure those powers to give up their protectorate over former German Afrikan colonies, (after the latter were taken following Germany's defeat in WWI), and turn them over to a Pan-Afrikan government; which was not successful. Finally, after having his passport – taken during the anti-Communist witch-hunts during the McCarthy era – returned, he accepted President Kwame Nkrumah's invitation to live in Ghana and to help restructure Ghana's textbooks and educational structures, along Afrikan-centric lines.

Next, we witness the Civil Rights Movement never really dealing with these questions, although A. Philip Randolph and a few others had a long history of espousing Socialist ideas. Thus, it was Malcolm X's evolution and travels that led him to recognize that many countries and peoples across the world were fighting against colonialism, and most were also looking to Russia and/or China, or coming up with their own forms of socialism. Although his own ideas and evolution was cut short by his assassination, Malcolm X's stature had already planted the seeds of a revival of the Garvey/ABB ideological struggle.

Consequently, the next major group to join this debate was the Revolutionary Action Movement – (RAM is how it's best known). RAM was led by Maxwell Stanford and a few other key male and female members, most interestingly from behind the scenes there operated the longtime Marxist husband and wife team of *Racism and the Class Struggle* renown, James and Grace Lee Boggs. RAM's main inspiration, however, was Robert F. Williams, who authored *Negroes with Gun,* and was then in exile – after being forced to flee underground – and whose travels allowed him and his family to meet and work with Socialist leaders and report on the activities of their socialist/communist/ujamma inspired countries, ("Ujamma" is a Ki-Swahili word that translates into "Collective Work and Collective Economics").

Secondarily, RAM's championing of *Revolutionary* National-ism – to distinguish it from the *narrow* Black (capitalist) National-ism handed down from Garvey – was followed by Oakland's Black Panther Party for Self Defense, (which for short will be referred to as the "original BPP"). Although the *true* original Black Panther Party was a Civil Rights Era group out of Alabama called the Lowndes County Freedom Organization, who had the *dual* name Black Pan-ther Party, derived from their flag having a black panther on it.

Moreover, around the same time, (the mid-1960's), literally hundreds of smaller local groups began to pop up throughout the Northeast, Midwest, and all the way to the Rocky Mountains and on the West Coast. Most of these groups had avowedly revolutionary nationalist, anti-capitalist and pro-socialist political-economic views, but were not exhibiting much, if any, of the Garvey/Pan-Afrikan sentiments – except in the cultural arena – until the original BPP's exiled cadre reintroduced them.

Accordingly, the Civil Rights Movement could clearly be distinguished from the *new* Black Liberation Movement by their different political, economic, social/cultural views, with the latter exhibiting a *rudimentary* Afro-centric understanding. Other than Garvey's RED, BLACK and GREEN Liberation Flag, however, just about all of his other cultural advancement ideas were forgotten.

With the defeat of that stage of the Black Liberation Struggle, however, socialist ideas and programs were mostly sidelined, although a few pockets remained amongst formations like the Republic of New Afrika (RNA) and associated revolutionary nationalist and Pan-Afrikanist groups, as well as having a token place amongst a few multi-racial Marxist groups. Representing the former was a valiant effort to educate both *prisoners* and outsiders about socialist ideas, by what would eventually be known as the Crossroads Collective, headed by Atiba Shanna.

Most of the imprisoned and *identified* revolutionary nationalists were progressively being isolated for long periods, during which their organizing, educating and proselytizing was eventually so limited that eventually reactionary and counter-revolutionary ideologies and practices took over the prison – and communities; since similar counter-revolutionary trends were also occurring out there. The fallout from the defeat created a backlash that opened the door for individuals and groups to begin to champion a *defeatist* ideology that centered on the omnipotence of the *white man* and "his" malevolence towards Blacks and their inability to stand up to such – as witnessed by our half-successful Civil Rights and Black Power gains – thus, it was argued, it's better to try to learn to live under their rule and according to their ideas.

So *education* was again supposed to lead Blacks to their salvation, (through Affirmative Action programs). Otherwise, a deep-seated paranoia set in about trusting one's own judgment concerning *anything* that had any input by the white man, even if presented with solid evidence, like Marx's damnation of capitalism. Consequently, those still committed to seeking Self-Determination for Afrikans in the Diaspora, (in particular), began to vacillate by seeking a *third way* between socialism and capitalism, (because most known socialist doctrines seemed too "white"), or flat-out proposed variations of capitalist-based programs: à la Booker T. Washington and Marcus Garvey.

I must *confess* that I've personally been through such spells, and I know how hard it is to break out of such self-imposed periods of insanity. After all, when someone points out something that's directly in front of your face, and you still refuse to accept it, then you're nuts!

An old-timer told me when I first got in the Movement, he said: "I'll assist you in understanding these new concepts, but if you won't believe your own eyes, then I can't help you." And the sad thing is that amongst these rejecters are some of our otherwise best minds and most dedicated people. Indeed, the trauma produced by the oppression in this white supremacist, patriarchal, anti-human, monopoly capitalist, "anti-existence empire" is enough to cause any of us to lose our bearings! Hopefully not permanently.

Compounding that was the reintroduction of capitalism throughout the Socialist world, leaving racism and all of the other ills in place. Nevertheless, how can a strata of near experts in all of the social sciences and the evolution of societies and systems, long believe that a Marx, Engels or Lenin can be so shrewd as to have one agree with their analysis about capitalism's weaknesses, yet follow through and act against what is *collectively* agreed upon is some kind of plot by these "diabolical" whites? And I hasten to add that these were *not* new ideas and concepts to them. I know from personal experience that at one time Marxist-Leninist-Maoist doctrines were mandatory reading amongst all within the Black Revolutionary camp. But like Morpheus told Neo in *The Matrix*, "There's a difference between knowing the path and walking the path."

My excitement, as you'll see from reading the correspondence between the author and his comrade Outlaw, is due to the way he helps clarify any number of these thorny issues, while still showing how various theoretical concepts developed by Marx, Engels, Lenin, Mao, Cabral and company can be used to help us analyze various economic, political and social questions. Using Dialectical and Historical Materialism (DM and HM), like the ABB, George Jackson, Atiba Shanna and a few others were good at doing; more so because our author's grasp of the DM and HM nomenclature and fundamentals is free flowing and readable. So much so that while reading his manuscript, I found myself back in the classroom, as if Atiba, George, Nkrumah or Amilcar Cabral were holding forth.

Hold up! Don't get the impression that other brilliant young, (and not so young), cadre have not – are not – contributing to this ideological struggle between Socialism and capitalism; there are, most notably, Jalil Muntaqim and some younger cadre who it would be best not to name here. Beyond that, I was thrilled to learn things about the author and his ideas that I knew nothing about. Mainly because he and I had corresponded once or twice over the last 3 or 4 years; the first time about collaborating on some art projects, but the "hot grease" that our two control units lockdowns be running us through sabotaged that; and the second time concerning an invitation to join the NABPP–PC being substituted by me writing a regular column for their *Right On!* newsletter, which was accepted by the author and the NABPP–PC Chief of Staff, Shaka Sankofa Zulu.

So *why* did I decline to join their fledgling NABPP–PC? First a little background. Prior to being asked to join the NABPP–PC, I was called to attend a surprise visit in our control unit visiting booths. There I met for the first time and spent a coupla hours with Tom Big Warrior, the head of the Native American Red Heart Warriors Society (RHWS). The visit was no small matter, due to the fact that I'm in a very out-of-the-way prison, and in a very repressive control unit, along with Mumia Abu Jamal and over 500 other men – around 150 of who are on death row. I later learned that Tom and our author are close comrades, and the RHWS and the NABPP–PC are allies in the struggle.

Tom's appearance is deceptive; and on first seeing him I was like, "Who's this big 'white' guy?" "What are they trying to pull now?" (Ironically, two weeks later a coupla "white" New York City detectives came to the prison to interrogate me about the killing of two New York cops in *1972.*) In our messed-up world, (and especially in my circumstances), a big *white* guy is usually bad news. While, in fact, Tom's roots are Anglo-Celtic-Native American, and after an introduction I realized I had previously read some of his writings; and although he had not been vetted, over the next hours he and I instantly clicked. We were jumping all over the place: politics, history, current events, human nature, racism, the Native American and New

Afrikan struggles and on and on–we were taking words out of each other's mouths! It turned out to be one of the most enjoyable and interesting conversations I'd had in a very long time. And afterwards, he and I began corresponding–although reading his handwriting must give the prison's censors nightmares–and he also began collaborating with people I also work closely with in the streets.

Thus the invitation to join the NABPP–PC came through Tom, along with the author's and the Chief of Staff's writings. And at first I was not in agreement with launching a prison version of the original BPP in the present repressive political atmosphere, but Tom provoked me to more closely examine the idea that even in this climate a new and more firmly (ideologically sound) grounded formation was needed. So I decided to at least put it to a test.

After further mailings and reviews of the NABPP–PC structural format, however, I was disappointed to learn that they had decided to adopt a *classical* form of Democratic Centralism (DC) to govern the group's internal operations. A *doctrinaire* departure from some of the more workable things proposed; and in light of my *later* readings of the author's ideas a baffling departure from the insights witnessed there, also. Especially in light of the fact that I already knew the author was also in a control unit, (and his later received manuscript removed *any* doubts about our constraints being similar), while due to my history of escapes, hostage taking, gun battles with the police and my original street charges, I suspected whatever he was under was probably double in my case…

Beyond that, for decades I've participated in any number of groups–both inside and outside–who attempted to also apply classical DC organizational principles to no avail. If anything, we've come to learn that if we don't wind up hamstringing the group, (which occurred even when there was much more prison openness, as well as broad support on the streets), due to our, (inside), lines of communications being straddled by the enemy, such classical forms simply do not work; leading to gross distortions of original intents, and the abuse of authority on the part of many cadre, which in turn leads to a lot of resources being expended in order to try to *make* an organization function; when instead more structural creativity could solve the problem.

Furthermore, despite Tom's overcoming my original objections, I knew from decades of intense struggle on many levels that we must have *a plan for winning and a plan for losing*; or contingency plans, especially in light of the fact that all indicators point to this government's plans to ramp-up its repression inside the prisons, in order to prevent their occupants from joining in the upsurge of world wide resistance to imperialism – like occurred during the 1960's and 1970's – a situation that a classical DC structure has even less chances of surviving under than our previous efforts.

So, following the old timers admonition " ... if you won't believe your own eyes ... " and my own experiences, I declined to join the party since I knew I could not adhere to its written DC disciplines, (nor could I see how others in my situation – *including the author* – accomplish such a feat). Thus, I offered my services in writing a column for their publication.

Even so, I'm still excited about the efforts the author and the fledgling party is making, because I can tell that they have the mental faculties to eventually solve the DC problem. And in the meantime, I'll continue to write the column and stay open to ways I can assist otherwise, and remain ready to join in if/when a more workable structure is developed.

Another critical aspect our author and the NABPP–PC must address concerns the absolute necessity of solving one of the problems the ABB, Atiba, and company never could, and that is a way to couch their Dialectical and Historical Materialist principles within a framework that takes into account that Afrikans (globally) need to grasp that Marxist-Leninist-Maoist ideas can and have been used to good effect by Afrikans in the past, and that – at bottom – to simply dismiss them as *Eurocentric* or foreign, underlines an ignorance of Afrikan history; since *dialectics* – contrary to popular conceptions – can first be witnessed in use amongst the *ancient Egyptians,* (whom the most rabid racist cannot justify as anything but *Black* – due to so many artifacts left by the latter), whom the early Greeks learned it from, passing it on to later Europeans, down to when Marx and company applied their minds to its further development. Simply because over 500 years of aggression, slavery, Arab and European *cultural imperialism*, colonialism, apartheid and under-development has left most people of Afrikan descent with low self-esteem. Frantz Fanon makes that clear in *Wretched of the Earth*. Plus, we can witness an example of it today in the Sudan, where a group of *self-hating* Afrikans is trying to annihilate another groups of Afrikans, because the latter are not *Arabs* (culturally).

An analysis of how Garvey was able to attract *millions* to join his banner, and the Afrikan Blood Brotherhood never had more then a few thousand, rests on Garvey's careful inclusion of mechanisms that constantly kept before the global Afrikans' eyes facts about the accomplishments of classical and contemporary Afrikans, coupled with a lot of public pageantry that allowed his followers to act out scripts that elevated their sense of self-worth in ways they learned that *their* ancestors had; and afterwards, that renewed enthusiasm

14

was used to further build the grassroots economic, social and political programs of the UNIA–ACL. Similar to groups such as Hezbollah – without its active militia since Garvey's Afrikan Legion was never active beyond the parade ground, and being used to disrupt other groups and secure the organization's property and leaders' physical safety.

Now Briggs and the ABB would laugh and call such actions buffoonery, but the ABB had no similar *mass line* methods of taking the (subconscious) ideas of these people and returning them in an elevated form conducive to moving them closer to achieving their goals. The ABB was in the same trap that Che criticized the Bolivian Communist Party for: they could produce cadre who knew Marxism/Leninism backwards and forwards, but they still couldn't field a machine gunner.

Then during the Black Liberation Movement of the 1960's/1970's these same two tendencies again came to the fore, and are best represented by the BPP and related groups, and those that came to be called Cultural Nationalist; with the BPP mirroring the ABB and the Cultural Nationalists a *truncated* UNIA–ACL, since the latter were generally *not* Global Pan-Afrikanist. Yet, since neither tendency ever developed much understanding about the earlier ideological questions and struggle, they both were (essentially) trying to *again* "invent electricity." And due to their rivalry compounded by intense government efforts to keep them at odds – they both became wedded to *dogmatic* views and concepts, which is mirrored in their literature and the ideological tendencies that follow their lead.

Alas, neither seem to realize that Garvey's approach was/is a model to address the deep seated *psychic scars* caused by the interruption and theft of the global Afrikans' culture and history; and the

ABB's championing of the utilization of DM and HM, coupled with the advancements in that arena introduced by Mao's *Mass Line and Party Line* approach, *synthesizes* the two tendencies. Therefore, our author and the NABPP-PC must guard against all of this. Since the truth is that imperialism is not just waging a war on terror, on the proletariat and captive nations; imperialism is at war with the entire universe! Such are the megalomaniacal forces we're contending with: a real live MATRIX. And although ever since I've joined our struggle, I've tried to keep my foot buried in their behinds – walking *between* the raindrops – the primary reason that a number of us 1960's vets are still alive, is because when we were captured the mass movement in the streets prevented our enemies from doing away with us altogether. Then the slump that our struggle has experienced for over 25 years added no urgent need to totally neutralize us. Therefore, I could be convicted of participating in an armed raid on a police station – resulting in the death and wounding of cops – spending a year and a half underground, being captured with machine guns and explosives, and no court would dare sentence me to death. Subsequently, giving me a chance to escape several times, and do damage to the war machine all along the way.

But there's no such fear on the part of our enemies now! They invade countries, kill, kidnap and torture people with impunity. In this country they execute people in the streets, let the old and infirm drown, kill through medical neglect, and operate *slaughterhouses* called death rows!

So make no mistake about it; they're gonna try to *murder* our author the first chance they get. If him and I were on the chopping block right now, they would jump over top of my old ass in order to get to him! They jumped over scores of other prisoners

16

to murder another NABPP–PC comrade (Hasan Shakur/Derrick Frazier) August 31st.

These are young lions ... they figure to wait me out ... So it's up to all of you to recognize how much we need him, and all of these *unmentioned* younger soldiers; comrades like him can raise us up. Put as much protection around him as you can. Our future depends on it!*

"Straight Ahead!"

October 6, 2006

— — — — —

* In response to Maroon's discussion of Democratic Centralism in the Foreword and as a part of a larger discussion taking place between Rashid and Maroon, Rashid wrote an essay titled "On the Roles and Characteristics of the Panther Vanguard Party and Mass Organizations" which can be read on page 351.

"IT SHOULD NEVER BE EASY FOR THEM TO DESTROY US. IF YOU START WITH MALCOLM X AND COUNT ALL OF THE BROTHERS WHO HAVE DIED OR BEEN CAPTURED SINCE, YOU WILL FIND THAT NOT EVEN ONE OF THEM WAS REALLY PREPARED FOR A FIGHT.... BUT EACH ONE THAT DIED PROFESSED TO KNOW THE NATURE OF OUR ENEMIES. [THE] ILLINOIS STATE ATTORNEY GENERAL SENT 15 PIGS TO RAID THE PANTHER HEAD-QUARTERS AND MURDER [FRED] HAMPTON AND [MARK] CLARK. DO YOU HAVE ANY IDEA WHAT WOULD HAVE HAPPENED TO THOSE 15 PIGS IF THEY HAD RUN INTO AS MANY VIET CONG AS THERE WERE PANTHERS IN THAT BUILDING. THE VC ARE ALL LITTLE PEOPLE WITH LESS GENERAL EDUCATION THAN WE HAVE. THE ARGUMENT THAT THEY HAVE BEEN

DOING IT LONGER HAS NO VALIDITY AT ALL, BECAUSE THEY WERE DOING IT JUST AS WELL WHEN THEY STARTED.... IT'S VERY CONTRADIC-TORY FOR A MAN TO TEACH ABOUT THE MURDER IN CORPORATE CAPI-TALISM, TO ISOLATE AND EXPOSE THE MURDERERS BEHIND IT, TO INSTRUCT THAT THESE MADMEN ARE COM-PLETELY WITHOUT STOPS, ARE

LICENTIOUS, TOTALLY DEPRAVED — AND THEN NOT MAKE ADEQUATE PREPARATIONS TO DEFEND HIMSELF FROM THE MADMAN'S ATTACK. EITHER THEY DON'T REALLY BELIEVE THEIR OWN SPIEL OR THEY HARBOR SOME SORT OF SUBCONSCIOUS DEATH WISH." G.J. 1970

GLJ

VC

T-07:
RASHID

Introduction

by Tom Big Warrior

That quantitative changes give rise to qualitative leaps is a basic principle of Historical and Dialectical Materialism. These pre-Party writings of Comrade Rashid demonstrate the quantitative changes that were taking place in his worldview and grasp of revolutionary theory and science leading up to the establishment of the New Afrikan Black Panther Party–Prison Chapter, and the leap he was making from lumpen gang-banger to proletarian revolutionary.

Like many comrades who come to the movement from the street, his initial orientation was towards a purely military viewpoint, and Che and his "foco theory" of guerrilla adventurism was only gradually being discarded at this point. But one can see the basic components of the revolutionary line of the New Afrikan Black Panthers taking shape. Rashid's basic humynism and "Panther Love" shines through brilliantly, along with his quick wit and raw intelligence. He absorbs complicated ideas and concepts and incorporates them at breakneck speed.

Where the Black Movement has for generations deadlocked over the struggle between assimilation (accommodation) vs. separation (running away), he almost effortlessly grasps that neither is the path to liberation. His revolutionary nationalism is a concrete expression of proletarian internationalism, a necessary step towards splitting the US proletariat from the grip of US imperialism.

For Comrade Rashid, the New Afrikan Nation's historic destiny is not to constitute itself territorially but to play the vanguard role among the gravediggers of capitalist imperialism. The merger of the struggle against racist oppression and the class struggle for socialist revolution and transformation predicted by Mao, (and given concrete expression by the original Black Panther Party), is firmly rooted in Rashid's consciousness.

The 1960's and 70's were a period of great revolutionary upsurge in the US and internationally, but a revolutionary situation did not exist in the US at that time, and Empire was winning the Cold War despite its humiliation in Vietnam. The Great Proletarian Revolution in People's China did not succeed in holding back the trend towards modern revisionism and capitalist restoration in China. The revolutionary vanguard internationally was insufficiently ideologically and politically equipped to keep moving forward and Imperialism still had great reserves to draw upon.

Empire is weaker now than it was back then. Victory in the Cold War brought on intensified globalization which has accelerated its decline. The principal contradiction in the world has shifted and is now internal to the empire between its desire and need to consolidate its global hegemony – its "New World Order" – and the chaos and anarchy it is unleashing by its unsuccessful attempts to do so. In just a few years, the US has gone from the #1 lender to the #1 debtor nation in the world. Its imprisoned population is a greater percentage of its total population than in any other country, and it keeps increasing.

A revolutionary situation is coming – not because of the actions of the Left and in spite of the Left's inaction and decline. Imperialism is at war with the world and with objective reality. It has no future to offer. History condemns it. It can only grow more dysfunctional and weaker. Imperialism is capitalism in decline – the final stage of capitalism. Revolution is the main trend in the world and nothing can change that.

The Amerikan razor-wire plantations of oppression hold many potential revolutionaries – Blacks. Indians, Chicanos, poor whites and Puerto Ricans. Comrade Rashid is one of them, and in a very real sense he is one with all of them. He is a true internationalist and intercommunalist.

The terminology of the past doesn't exactly fit the current situation. Huey Newton's theoretical conception of Intercommunalism, (which was not well received or grasped by the Left at the time) begs reexamination in light of the increased globalization. The Amerikan empire is not a classical nation state nor are the countries under its domination. Neocolonialism and a one-imperialist-superpower world have created new conditions.

The stated intention of the NABPP–PC to build the New Afrikan Black Panther Party wherever in the world Black people are concentrated and to build the White Panther Organization with it as an arm of the Party makes great sense, but that is in another volume of Comrade Rashid's writings soon to be published.

PART ONE

RASHID
'04

Rashid:
An Autobiography of
Revolutionary Development

I should begin by emphasizing that four traits are predominant in my character, traits that I believe are largely lacking within the Amerikan Left and Revolutionary Nationalist milieu, and are largely the cause of their strategic failures. These four traits are that I am an extremist, a tactical thinker, I have an uncompromising will, and I am willing to suffer and give my life for the people. And it is on account of these tendencies (and the results – although limited by my conditions – that I've been able to produce in my isolated struggles against oppressive institutions coupled with my present ideological and political development), that I believe enable me to offer some valid insight into effective methods of countering and ultimately defeating systems of oppression. Talking about abuse, merely telling people that they're being abused, won't check or stop the problem. Correcting oppression demands correct and organized mass struggle.

I've been imprisoned for sixteen years (since I was eighteen), the last twelve of which I've spent in solitary, confined almost always within specially constructed and modified cells, and often totally isolated from other prisoners. Although I was not exposed to his writings until just some three years ago, my actions against the pigs and their proxies have been motivated by the same drive that motivated George Jackson, viz., "I have always been inclined to get disturbed over organized injustice or terrorist practice against the innocents – wherever ... " And even though I was under illegitimate capitalist influences before and during much of my imprisonment, I've always been engaged in something of a running battle with the establishment.

The forces that combined to ensure this last lengthy incarceration were driven by my having earned the label while in society as a "cop killer," and personal revenge against me by some pig "victims" of my actions.

I was jailed twice in 1990; the first confinement being a brief one (I was acquitted), the second being upon the arrest from which I remain imprisoned. In order to give some insight into my present incarceration, the first 1990 arrest must be detailed and other background facts given. While I do not wish to glamorize my past antisocial activities, I must give some account of my past to allow an understanding of who I am today.

Like so many young Blacks, I was involved in the street level drug trade; only I took a different tack than most in my approach to "the game." I perceived myself as being a one-man army. Under various pretexts I would position myself on others' turf, first in a neutral role to study and take in what was going on, e.g., who the suppliers were, how much money came through the area in sales, pig activities, who amongst the sellers were about getting money and who were about gaining reputations as "gunslingers," the various weights and sizes of products being sold, etc. Upon gaining a good feel of the area, I'd move in and, using bribes and violence selectively, would basically take over. Those who sided with me had my complete loyalty. My methods led to many "wars" against rival groups, which I most often came out on top of. The opposition was all too visible, their hangouts, homes, and flashy cars being known and their patterns predictable. I, on the other hand, came and went unpredictably. I did no hanging out in clubs or otherwise, and had no known residence or method of travel. Observation, hit and evasion, was my mode of combat. When, because of these exchanges, an area became too "hot" for business, I'd move on to another area.

The last area that I frequented, I organized upon a more developed program. I didn't need to establish myself there, because my reputation was already known in the area. I suspected that my name was also known by the city pigs. So, I focused on driving the pigs and any competition out. Ironically, I was never really concerned with profits; I was more concerned with unity within the clique and developing community affinity.

Each weekend, Saturdays and Sundays, we'd organize community galas. Each weekend a different member of our clique would pay all expenses. We'd buy bushels of crabs, cases of beer, and pay the local "shot house" people to prepare all sorts of foods and beverages. Large, amplified speakers were set out on the curb, and everyone in the neighborhood ate and danced at no cost. This won us a lot of local affection within the complex and even with the complex manager. Violence within our group was strictly forbidden, as was flashing and randomly shooting off guns in the area. "Customers" were to be respected and no "sales" were to be made around children. Pig patrols were driven out, under gunfire. They only openly ventured into the area in convoys of six or more patrol cars, four pigs to each car. An isolated pig cruiser was apt to get holed. When they tried to set up watch posts in vacant apartments, the complex manager alerted us, with the result that the watchers got watched, and as soon as they left the post the apartment was raided and everything stolen or smashed.

The pigs finally took heart by building a containment fence (about twelve feet high) around the complex (we quickly opened holes around the fence); organizing neighborhood foot patrols by squads of pigs in plainclothes carrying rifles, shotguns and pistols in hand; and establishing a curfew in the area. If the pigs caught a young Black in the area after 9 PM without residential credentials, he was promptly arrested for trespassing. This is the context in which my first arrest in 1990 took place.

While sitting a block away from the complex one night, observing movements of the plainclothes pigs, a convoy of patrol cars converged on a brother I knew from the neighborhood, who was walking to his female friend's home. The plainclothes had apparently called in the convoy, which had obviously been on standby close by. Observing this brother surrounded by a hostile crowd of some twenty uniformed pigs, I (defying my instinct to stay put and observe) disarmed and approached the scene to see if I could defuse the situation.

Upon seeing me approach, a detachment of pigs broke off from the main group, stopped me some twenty feet short of the brother, and asked if I was his cousin, as he'd claimed upon seeing me approaching. He'd told the pigs, refuting their claims that he was trespassing, that I could verify his girlfriend's residence, and her home to be his destination. I acknowledged that we were related. I was asked my name, to which I replied, "Kevin Johnson." One white pig named Oink turned quickly to the brother and asked, "If this is your cousin, what's his name?" Not having heard what I said, the brother replied, "Rashid." All attention then immediately focused on me. Oink replied, "So, *you're* Rashid. We've been looking for you." He then recited a list of citywide and local incidents in which the name Rashid had come up as involved, including attacks on pigs.

I was promptly surrounded by the growing mass of uniforms with my back to a patrol car. Oink put in a radio call to a detective unit to determine if any warrants or indictments for my arrest were outstanding. There were none. Apparently, they had never been able to get an accurate identification on me. He then reached into the patrol car and came out with a Polaroid camera. As he prepared to snap pictures I began distorting my face. I crossed my eyes, protruded tongue, inflated jaws, flared nostrils, etc. Oink demanded that I straighten my face up. I informed him that I hadn't consented to a photo shoot, and until I did to be satisfied with what he got. Enraged, the pig forcefully pushed me back into the car. I rebounded, driving several jabs into his face. The other pigs converged, swinging flashlights, sticks, and radios. I drove through the mob leading the way with straight jabs, and just upon breaking out of the group of swinging pigs, I tripped and fell. I was promptly piled upon, handcuffed, and beaten further. Ironically, I wasn't beaten too badly – too many pigs. They were beating each other more than me. Experience has taught me something which may be of use to those resisting organized oppression: pigs don't tend to spontaneously beat a person who fights back as brutally as they do one who shows fear or passively accepts being attacked. Anyway, Oink arrested me on charges of disorderly conduct and resisting arrest. They forgot all about the brother, who'd walked a short distance away and watched the spectacle.

At court I declined an attorney and recited to the judge what had happened. He took it all in with barely concealed humor. He was especially humored about my making faces and my described reaction to Oink's pushing me. Oink was furious. When he turned to Oink asking if what I'd described were true, Oink replied, "Yeah, basically." The judge admonished Oink and told me that I was free to go. On the way out of the courthouse, Oink assured me that if he saw me in the complex again it would be him and me. My young pride never allowed me to refuse a challenge. I replied that I'd be there.

On June 4, 1990, I stood deliberately in front of the forbidden complex, in broad daylight and armed, talking to a sister who lived in the area. Suddenly, Oink pulled up at high speed, brakes screeching, and ran up onto the curb. He jumped out of his unmarked car with sidearm drawn – a .38 – yelling, "Rashid, I've got your ass now!" I darted around a building to get the sister out of the line of fire and pulled my own weapon – a .44 with a very long barrel. When Oink bent the corner, gunfire erupted. He dove headfirst behind a concrete porch. While I stood prone facing him, he remained crouched behind the porch shooting wildly in my direction. My gun empty, I ran through a nearby creek (ditching the gun in the process), sprinted through the complex, only to be tackled from behind (dizzy from blood loss) by about ten backup pigs. In the exchange with Oink a bullet had passed through my right deltoid muscle.

While I was lying handcuffed on the ground, with pig boots holding me in place, Oink caught up, .38 in one hand, my .44 in the other. He was hysterical, and obviously shaken but uninjured. He went into a frenzy, threatening to kill me, calling me every variety of "nigger" in the book, and pressing the barrel of the gun against my teeth. When he removed the gun, I told him that he should either do what he threatened or "shut the fuck up!" His response was to crack me across the head with the barrel of my .44, lacerating my scalp. What followed probably saved me from a vicious ass-kicking or worse. A brother came running out of a nearby apartment cursing the pigs for running around (chasing me) with guns drawn while his children played nearby. The pigs promptly swarmed and beat him bloody as his kids looked on.

While going through my pockets, the pigs observed blood running from my jacket sleeve. Upon a rough inspection, my shoulder injury was discovered. Regardless, the battered brother and I were dumped in a pig wagon and taken to headquarters. I was held in the parking lot with Oink and others running a stream of threats by me. Oink was obviously in a quandary to justify confronting me to begin with. He wasn't even on duty. He proposed that if I said nothing about his having shot me, he wouldn't charge me with any felonies – particularly for attempted capital murder of a pig. I gave no response. When finally taken to the hospital (Medical College of Virginia) some hours later, my shoulder and scalp were sutured and my arm placed in a sling. The cause of my laceration and puncture wounds being "unknown." I was charged with trespassing and merely pointing a firearm at Oink.

Upon entering the Richmond city jail this time I was compelled to take up an unfinished rival "war" where it had left off on the street. The opposition occupied an entire tier – some 120 cats – adjacent to my own. They were only prepared to jump me. I was, however, prepared to do a little more. I ditched the shoulder sling, procured some weapons, and the next day a standoff occurred. Me and five others against almost an entire rival tier. The pigs were apparently tipped off and swarmed the jail hallway before we'd revealed our weapons or the first blow was struck. I was packed off to another tier, only to sneak onto the rival tier (a dormitory) during the confusion of movement at mealtime several weeks later. A battle erupted as soon as the tier gate slammed shut. I ended up with a head laceration and about four of them suffered stab wounds before the pigs invaded the tier to break it up. Upon my release from solitary a few weeks later, a similar situation occurred. By then I was looked at as a 175 lb., 5'9" maniac, by both pigs and prisoners. The opposition offered a truce with amenities on the side. Upon agreement of some of my cohorts, the truce was accepted, but other conflicts persisted. Fights were frequent. I was stabbed in a couple incidents; in both of them my opponents were disarmed and butchered in return. It was finally accepted by all potential rivals that I was best left alone.

While jailed, an acquaintance of mine from the streets, Y, was arrested. He'd been a fugitive for some time, as foremost of Richmond's most wanted. Upon his capture he agreed to work with the pigs to get out of his own charges. Initially, he was placed on the tier with me, obviously to draw out information; however, I never discussed anything of substance with him, or anyone, especially since I'd observed that under conditions of confinement, he'd become a kitten. This was in total contrast to the vicious image he'd portrayed on the streets.

It was around the time of Y's capture that a flurry of indictments were issued charging one "Kevin Johnson" with among other things: murder, attempted murder, malicious wounding, etc. It was obvious that he was responsible although no one wanted to believe it. The incidents from which the charges stemmed were of particular interest to the city pigs. One involved a person having been shot by an alleged sniper, shooting from inside a project building. The pigs had responded by surrounding the entire block and calling in their own snipers, helicopters, and SWAT team. The pigs acknowledged seeing the shooter moving around in the apartment while it was under siege, yet when their SWAT teams raided it some ten hours later, they embarrassingly could find no one. Another incident involved the shooting of several people who were allegedly attacked because the shooter thought they were undercover pigs. I was further accused of shooting up several patrol cars with pigs inside them, shooting at pigs, etc.; however, no formal charges followed.

Guilty pleas were entered on the sniping charges to clear a cohort of involvement – he had a long suspended prison term over his head. Upon the testimony of Y, his girlfriend, and others (including Oink, who was instrumental in having the charges issued), convictions were entered on the other shootings, with sentences imposed of life plus. Y was returned to society, where he was allowed to carry out any acts he pleased, under complete pig immunity, as long as he aided them in entrapping, capturing, and convicting others. According to reliable sources, he'd become so bold that when the pigs converged on an area where he was present, he'd identify himself by name, state that he was armed, and then proceeded to finger everyone nearby him who possessed guns or narcotics and where the contraband was located. He was also involved in planting drugs in people's homes and then having the pigs raid them.

However, Y eventually destroyed his usefulness to the pigs by perjuring himself in a later trial. In that case (*Commonwealth of Virginia v. Shawn Marshall*), he testified to being present and witnessing three Black males shoot a pizza delivery man. When all other evidence at the trial completely contradicted his account, he admitted on the stand to lying for his own benefit. It was only then that Y was re-jailed on further charges and seriously prosecuted and convicted. I had the brief pleasure of getting a few passing licks off Y on the day that I was transferred to the prison system from jail. He'd been brought to the jail's transport area from his protective custody tier for court. I was in the area waiting for the DOC transport to pick me up. I saw him pass by en route to the area and hid behind a shower stall. When they brought him out, I managed to raise a few knots on his head – for lack of being able to locate any hard or sharp objects in the area – before the pigs swarmed in to pull me off him. I was locked in another holding area. As a juvenile, I'd avoided many upstate commitments by feigning the "nut role." I was very good at duping the "experts." Upon facing lengthy prison terms on the charges against "Kevin Johnson," I resorted to the same chicanery as an adult, to no ultimate avail. For a time I persisted in this role while in prison, which only prompted abuses from the pigs. The pigs have this instinctive tendency to openly abuse prisoners who are of unsound mind or of limited intelligence, since they believe that unintelligent persons are incapable of challenging their abuses, whether by direct action or by articulating complaints.

Because I accepted my lifestyle and all of its consequences, I was always reluctant to involve my family or others on the outside of prison in my conflicts with the pigs. I dealt with my own problems – directly. For a while I accepted some of the milder pig abuses with relatively minor responses. They'd tamper with my meals or refuse them altogether or become unnecessarily physical with me. My responses were to become counter physical. The situation intensified and ultimately led to my encounters with their goon squads on something like a thrice-weekly basis for months on end. Injuries occurred on both sides; in comparison mine were relatively minor. They were suffering broken bones, dislocated joints, and lacerations. Most of the goon squad encounters resulted in pigs taking injury leaves. The administrative costs of their mounting casualties (pigs taking sick leave with pay – feigned injuries were routine) outweighed the subjective benefits of seeking revenge. It became quite clear that terrorism did not work on me, except to provoke the very response the pigs wanted to suppress. They had no military option with me. So they pacified me in every way conceivable short of allowing me to walk free out of prison.

The pigs walked wide circles around me and instead targeted my less committed peers, which I found equally intolerable. My reactions quickly led them to also walk wide circles around my peers when I was around. When I left, it was a different matter altogether. As an indirect method of trying to neutralize me, the pigs routinely tried to proposition or instigate other prisoners into violent conflicts with me. These efforts usually failed, either because I'd target the instigating pig, mutual respect which existed between me and the other prisoners prevented it, (sometimes the prisoner would himself check the pig for attempting to provoke disunity), or I'd face the opponent down.

By 1993 I was on a cycle of being transferred on a weekly to monthly basis between prisons. The pigs being under the impression that I wouldn't be long enough in their presence to retaliate became determined to break me through increasingly severe methods. I, in turn, stepped up my own level of violence. I was being attacked with rottweilers and being bodily restrained to bare steel and concrete in the dead of winter with cell windows wide open for weeks at a time. I would break out of the restraints and destroy them on a daily basis. They'd fight me and strap me back down, often experimenting, trying to devise cramped and painful ways of putting the restraints on so that I couldn't get out again. I'd break out again. This went on until I had literally destroyed every set of restraining devices they had (which occurred in 1992 at the Buckingham prison, leading to my transfer), or until they'd give up.

I was starved, dehydrated and left naked in freezing cells for weeks to months in winter with windows open and the AC blowing cold air, etc. During latter 1992 to early 1993, I began fighting them so intensely (twice running the K–9's back out of the cell) that they simply would not fight me anymore no matter what the provocation.

During the middle of 1993, an attempt was made to intimidate me into submission by the pigs at the Powhatan prison bringing two K–9's in front of my cell and, with the dogs standing by, beating another prisoner in my plain view while he was handcuffed. My first response was to throw every item I could lay hands on at the pigs (the cells had bars instead of solid doors). This prompted them to move the dogs away and stop their attack. I then wrenched the metal sink/commode unit from the wall and flooded the tier. The pigs decided to leave as I was working on the sink/commode. Next, I fashioned a ten-inch rod from the commode into an ice pick. I sat that commode atop the bare bunk, sat on the commode, and awaited their return. For three days they tried to dehydrate me and negotiate me out of the cell; for three days I refused to be handcuffed. They still would not fight me.

For several months I'd been seeking a transfer to the relatively newly constructed Greensville prison, because the prison to which I was then assigned would not allow me in the general population. One of the prisoners with whom I'd been in a knife fight in the jail had me listed as an enemy. He was in the population. On the third day the negotiator came with the line that I was being transferred to Greensville where I'd been requesting to go. Expecting a ruse, I declined to be handcuffed. Another prisoner, for whom I then had some respect, reasoned that the pigs might not be lying, since they knew I could repeat the same and would not relent. He proposed that they might actually intend to transfer me. When the negotiator returned, I accepted the handcuffs and was promptly put on a van to Greensville.

What I was to encounter at Greensville defied anything that I'd expected. The pigs had a refined system and license for brutalizing prisoners. I was not to understand the magnitude of the situation until a few days after being there. The pigs had a tier of handpicked proxy prisoners, whom they used to violently suppress those who got out of line. The ringleader – I'll call him Pumpkin – was a career con with a reputation for butchering other prisoners. He had a trustee job (all trustees were similarly selected). Pumpkin was allowed by the pigs to keep weapons on his person. Part of the mental terror game was that while he was out cleaning (everyone knew he was a pig hit man and stayed armed), the pigs would bring others out around him in handcuffs (segregation prisoners must be handcuffed from behind when outside their cells, unless they have a trustee job, or are locked inside an exercise yard or shower stall). The she-pigs (guards and nurses) were the tools used to sic Pumpkin on others. He regarded and jealously guarded these she-pigs like actual mates, whereas all they did for him was bring him bubble gum, watch him masturbate in their presence and flirt with him.

The setup game usually went like this: one of their she-dogs would provoke an argument with the target (refuse him something he was due, etc.). She'd then report to Pumpkin that the target had "disrespected" her, or any of many other claims. Pumpkin would then come to the target's cell and start a hostile verbal exchange, send a challenge via third-party message, etc. Once the conflict was established, the pigs would move the target into the tier with Pumpkin and his cronies – the entire tier rode with him. The pigs would thoroughly search the target's property for weapons before moving him, to ensure that he had no means of defense. Once assigned to a cell on Pumpkin's tier, the target was fair game. If he was stouthearted, he'd stand his ground. The next day or so the pigs would put them on the exercise yard together, remove everyone's handcuffs except the target's (they'd put five to seven prisoners in each pen), and allow them to mob attack the still handcuffed target. Or if they wanted him butchered, he'd be unhandcuffed and left to contend unarmed against a knife-wielding Pumpkin.

Upon my arrival at Greensville's segregation unit, they immediately used a she-pig to draw me out. There was no cooling system in the unit, so cups of ice were dispensed several times a day. On my first night in the unit, one of the she-pigs came through with the ice, bypassing my cell, which led to harsh words when she ignored my queries as to why I'd been bypassed. She apparently went directly to Pumpkin and told him that I'd threatened her and him. I received a prompt third-party message from him that I'd have to live up to my threat. Knowing of no threat made, I asked to whom he was directing his message. The reply came back that it was clearly directed to me. At this point others on the tier explained what was going on with Pumpkin, the she-pigs, and the setups of unruly prisoners. I returned the message that I'd see to being assigned to his tier and that there was no need for further conversation. When I requested to be assigned to Pumpkin's tier the next day, the pigs declined. Apparently they'd never had a disruptive *request* to be housed on that tier. But they were predetermined to break me from the outset.

The next day a verbal exchange occurred between me and a unit pig, in response to his threatening another prisoner. The pig returned with a mob of guards under the pretext of conducting cell searches. They searched and trashed my belongings, returned me into the cell and closed the door. As I stood with my back to the door, waiting for them to remove the handcuffs, the pig yelled that I'd snatched the cuffs into the cell, pretending that he'd removed one cuff while the other was still attached to my other wrist. With riot shield already on hand, the door was reopened and I was rushed to the back of the cell and beaten at length, still handcuffed from behind. When they were done, my face literally looked like the elephant man's. From that point on, it was war. I immediately graduated from fighting pigs with empty hands to using weapons. After allowing several weeks for my injuries to heal, and for them to lower their guard, I proceeded to holing their bodies.

I reversed the terror game and ended with the entire unit (Pumpkin's tier being the one exception) riding with me against the pigs. An abuse of one was an abuse of all. Any pig that abused any prisoner was subjected to immediate attack. The pigs often brought me from the cells handcuffed while Pumpkin was working the floor. I'd walk past him, merely giving him a blank stare. He never made his move. He tried several times to send word to me, and to address me directly, contending that he hadn't sent me any message about me having to live up to any threat. He also denied allowing the pigs to use him to attack others. When I finally heard him out, I had to agree that I was not on his tier and thus had no personal knowledge of his actions or motives; the attacks he'd carried out against others he claimed were in response to their provoking him and not through anything involving the she-pigs. He expressed total respect for my position against the pigs. It boiled down to his word against every other prisoner's in the unit, and since I did not have personal knowledge – until later – of his working with the pigs, our conflict was dropped.

On account of our organized resistance to the pigs, their frequent attacks and abuses came to a total halt, and they attempted to pacify everyone on my tier. In segregation we are permitted only two telephone calls monthly; however, a telephone remained on our tier all day. Feces were no longer being found inside prisoners' meal trays (at that time protective custody inmates prepared the meal trays right in the unit. Each tray had the designated cell number written on it. The pigs would have these mostly informant and running scared types put all manner of foul substances into specified prisoners' trays.) Trustees would deliver tobacco products supplied by the pigs to dispense on the tier to those who were without cigarettes, etc.

Word got back to me that the cronies on Pumpkin's tier were making threats against me. A few days later I opened a hole in the fence of our tier's exercise yard and went around the building to their tier's exercise yard while they were outside. Without any comment, I set two knives on the ground and proceeded to work a hole in their fence. At which point several of the cronies began kicking the fence near my hands, so I couldn't keep a hold of it. They began yelling loudly to alert the pigs indirectly. They declined any ill will toward me. When the pigs came to the unit door and saw me outside the fence, they began yelling entreaties through the door for me to go back to my own tier's yard, which I finally did, since the cronies' continuing to kick the fence made it impossible for me to work a hole in it.

The pigs could never stop me from procuring weapons, even though they'd build special cells to house me in. I'd simply disassemble them and procure and hide more weapons. They'd search the cell anytime I came out, yet could find nothing.

On account of the systematic attacks on the pigs at the height of their abuses, the DOC's internal affairs office decided to get involved in investigating the years of prisoner complaints of brutality in the unit. In their efforts to neutralize our responses, the internal affairs unit ended up having a dozen pigs criminally prosecuted for brutality and using other prisoners to enter prisoners' cells and attack them – once allowing a prisoner to use riot gear. Two pigs were ultimately convicted. Pumpkin was also prosecuted and convicted for an incident where the pigs opened another prisoner's cell, allowing him to ambush him. The prisoner was stabbed multiple times. Pumpkin's trustee job was immediately terminated under the backlash of this incident. The incident occurred on the tier right above me. I listened to the entire situation from when one of the she-pigs instigated the conflict weeks before up to the final violent episode.

My response was to counter-ambush one of the pigs' other trustee hit men while he was out cleaning several days later. I was brought out for a legal phone call at which point – and to the escorting pig's sheer terror – I came out of the handcuffs, pulled out a concealed weapon, ran this crony of Pumpkin's down, and pushed holes through his neck and upper body. Once done with him, I walked up the tier (as the pigs retreated in the opposite direction) and back to my cell. When the cell door was quickly locked, I removed and flushed the cloth handle, washed the blade, broke the point of the blade off (wrapped it in a wad of toilet paper and flushed it also), and threw the remaining piece of benign metal outside of the cell. I then took the curtain down which I'd put up to prevent view of my activities. The pigs stood outside my cell, uncertain of what, if anything, to do. They ultimately did nothing and left. I sent a message to Pumpkin, reestablishing our conflict. Several weeks later I was transferred back to Mecklenburg prison, returning to the scene of past abuses. From the time of this last incident up until my transfer to Mecklenburg, the pigs' initiative was crushed; they were only more than solicitous of any and every prisoners' requests, and were fawningly attentive to everyone.

During my stay at Mecklenburg, one of the ranking pigs, who were instrumental in torturing me with the freezing strip cell treatment, was ambushed. On this occasion I'd been strapped to the bunk by the pigs. In order for a prisoner to receive meals and toilet breaks while strapped down, the pigs must come to his cell, remove the chains and straps and handcuff him. They will leave the cell, close the door, and remove the cuffs through a hatch in the door. However, during this 1994 episode, when the pigs came in to release me for a toilet break, the claim is that I'd gotten out of the restraints and was lying on the bunk under a blanket as though still strapped down. When the ranking pig and two others moved to lift the blanket, I allegedly rose up, with weapon in hand, and attacked. Two of them (the ranking pig included) received multiple stab wounds, and the third pig received a cracked jaw. This incident, in its obvious preplanning and execution, left the pigs in such a quandary that no retribution followed. Indeed, I was several days later transferred to Buckingham and quickly released into the general population. By this time it was realized that I was not insane at all, but calculating and determined. While prison administrators and those who proposed to "study" me from a distance put forward the fiction that I was inclined to "unprovoked" violence against the pigs, the pigs who dealt with me on a day-to-day basis knew, very clearly, that any violence from me was always in response to their own acts of violence or abuse of me or my peers. As long as the pigs remembered this, things went well, but there was always some lone pig with a cowboy complex who had to test his hand, and I'd answer it.

The majority of the pigs at Buckingham didn't want me in the population walking about. They therefore attempted several times through trumped-up reports to have me returned to segregation. On the last occasion that this was done, I was charged with being in an "unauthorized area" of the prison. The pigs waited until I'd locked into the cell at count time to come and lock me up in segregation. I refused to go peacefully. One pig threatened that if I didn't, I'd receive a severe "ass-whipping." In response I agreed to walk peacefully to segregation. When the pigs opened the cell door to escort me out, the threatening pig received a nose broken in two places. I've been in segregation ever since.

While in Buckingham's segregation unit, I observed a rookie pig slam a restrained prisoner's face into a steel door with no provocation. That same day I was accused of opening a gash in this pig's face with a razor blade.

A few days later the goon squad attacked another prisoner. This prisoner had a long gash in his arm with staples holding it closed. The nurses were to clean the wound and change the dressing twice daily. They refused to do so, and his arm became badly infected. The pigs refused to accept his emergency complaint seeking medical treatment. He finally broke a light in his cell to force some cooperation. The pigs' response was to send the goon squad to beat him down.

My response was to kick and shatter the glass in my cell door. A K–9 unit was called in to assist the goon squad with me. Meantime sarcastic negotiations were staged. I declined any conversation, which was what the pigs wanted, hoping for the opportunity to see me mutilated by the rottweiler. Several hours later all was ready. With the goon squad poised behind him, the dog handler, with oak stick in one hand and K–9 at his feet, demanded me to submit to being handcuffed. I declined. When he unleashed the dog and ordered the cell door opened to admit the animal, the handler was promptly snatched into the cell, the dog ran back out of the cell (clearing a path through the scattering pigs) and I came out on his heels flush into the crowd of pigs. (Some thirty or more pigs had gathered in the unit to watch the spectacle.) A battle ensued. I was swarmed by pigs and taken down in a flurry of punches. I was then transferred back to Powhatan and placed into a specially modified unit.

While in this unit I met another prisoner who had developed something of a reputation as a jailhouse lawyer and fighter of the pigs. Although many prisoners held him in high regard, I observed in him a predominant tendency to play prisoners against the pigs and vice versa, all to serve his own individual benefit. He only attacked and fought the pigs when they didn't cater to his ever-changing personal whims. This cat was one of the most crafty con artists and opportunists I was yet to meet. Crafty because he got results. I studied him and came to perceive through him that pigs fear the courts as much or more than they do direct action. Not because the courts will give any justice against them, but because the courts have the *power* to divest their wages. They fear what the courts *can* do, as opposed to what the courts actually *will* do. On this account, I saw that using the litigation process could be as tactically useful as direct action and with wider-reaching results. I also mistakenly believed that if one only learned how to navigate the courts correctly, litigation could produce continuous results in changing abusive conditions inside the prisons, as opposed to the mere temporary changes in pig conduct that my previous actions produced. Once I was packed off to another prison or unit, they'd simply return to abusing the prisoners as before. I would therefore learn to use both pen and sword.

From the end of 1994, I began studying Anglo-Amerikan law to the exclusion of all else. I studied each topic in the American Jurisprudence legal encyclopedia series, and read every law book I could lay my hands on from cover to cover. I had the entire tier getting the prison's attorney to copy articles from the various university law reviews. For years I'd strictly disciplined my mind and body through rigorous training and the conditions imposed on me by the pigs, to endure and absorb the most trying conditions. I learned the fundamentals of law in about eight months, and won the first suit I filed. I then studied all manner of books on trial tactics, influencing juries, etc. I entered the litigation process expecting that judges, when confronted with the law, would adhere to its letter. I couldn't have been more wrong. I appeared frequently in the courts – state and federal – for hearings and trials. Initially, I received routine compliments from judges – and grudgingly from defense attorneys – on my legal comprehension and ability. This all changed when I persisted in efforts to have the courts comply with the laws. I refused to accept the unwritten rule that certain issues are not to be challenged or exposed.

My efforts were calculated to bring the courts to bear on DOC officials at the highest levels, to force them to change the conditions under which we lived, and conform them to basic requirements of the written laws. The courts had other plans. The state courts were not willing to grant these sorts of relief, although the letter of the law required it. They attempted instead, numerous times, to grant my release from prison. I completely distrusted these offers. To gain this relief, I'd basically have to admit that I was not entitled to the other relief I sought. By no stretch of the imagination did I think that the courts would allow me to walk free from prison. So I adamantly pressed for the relief I'd requested (which the judges were unwilling to grant) and argued myself out of court each time.

When they refused the relief I demanded, I'd then turn my legal attacks against the judges, with the result of provoking their wrath. They then acted single-mindedly to shut me out of the courts. This process spanned from about 1995 through 2001. With the added psychological deterrent of litigation, my clashes with the pigs declined somewhat in frequency. They focused primarily on isolating me from others. Their efforts to perpetuate a discontinuity in our unity has been the pigs' only effective weapon against me. And they've admitted in a thousand ways that their greatest fear is ending up with many other prisoners on their hands who think and act as I do. Their isolating me was long a tactic that I could not devise an effective countermeasure against, that is, until after 2001, when I was first exposed to revolutionary theory and have since come to understand the role of ideology. Without a unifying ideology, there can be no unity of struggle. Ideology was something I'd never had, and thus something I could not share. The prisoners who'd united in struggle with me had done so *because of me*. Not because of a shared principle. Therefore, when I was no longer around, they lost the initiative to struggle on, and the pigs were free to resort to their old oppressive acts.

With the beginnings of my studies in revolutionary history and theory in 2001, litigation and my isolated clashes with the pigs paled in importance. My first exposure to revolutionary ideas came with my meeting Hanif Shabazz-Bey in 2001. Hanif is a political prisoner who is apparently well known within prison movement circles. Upon meeting we developed an instant affinity. He began sending me a variety of publications through which I was first exposed to the works of George Jackson.

I'd heard of George in passing and had been compared with him many times on account of my militancy. But somehow I'd never come across his writings, or any other progressive materials for that matter. My first reading of George was *Blood In My Eye*. Reading this book allowed me to see that the oppressive conditions within these prisons, indeed, the very existence of them could not be changed absent a fundamental change of the social economic conditions that created them. I had not been thinking in terms of abolishing prisons themselves (for me such an idea was not even conceivable). What I'd been trying to produce was nothing more than a reform in their internal conditions. I was instinctively opposed to the pigs because of their organized brutality and systematic oppression of disadvantaged and disempowered people. But I'd never questioned the inherently oppressive role of the pig in society, his function in preserving the interests and ruling power of the haves over the have-nots. For all this time I'd accepted the legitimacy of the established order.

If I agreed with George (and I did) that the order of capitalist society is illegitimate, then it was necessary to determine what order *is* legitimate, and *how* to get from here to there. I've always been a practical person, extremely so, and therefore I recognized, along with George, that merely talking about a better world, and criticizing the present one, will not produce the desired change. He'd summed it up quite clearly. Economics is the base of society, the rock of social power. Whatever class controls the economic arrangements controls the social order. The military (including police and prisons) and political institutions are the forces that preserve and protect that dominant class's controlling power over the society. It is therefore necessary to destroy those institutions in order to break that class's hold on society. And this can *only* be done by a revolutionary, mass-based, economic, political, cultural, *and* military struggle. Focusing on only one of these components will change nothing. Any valid struggle must incorporate all four of them. I suspected that a study of past revolutionary struggles and their ultimate failures would show that they did not succeed because one or more of these components was neglected or compromised. I had to study further.

I became engrossed in acquiring and studying all that George had studied and more, which included the classics and not-so-classics: Vladimir Lenin, Mao Tse-tung, Karl Marx, Frantz Fanon, Kwame Nkrumah, Che Guevara, Rosa Luxemburg, Harry Magdoff, Paul Sweezy, Albert Szymanski, bell hooks, Cornel West, Howard Zinn, Noam Chomsky, Edward Said, Vo Nguyen Giap, etc. I investigated the various revolutionary schools of thought – Communism, Anarchy, New Afrikan Nationalism, Feminism, and other left-leaning theories. I studied military thinkers and military history, sociology and history, political science, economic theories (left and right), revolutionary history, etc. and I am still studying, refining my views, and testing them in practice.

The more I studied, reflected, practiced, and drew insight from my own practical experiences, the more it all fell together, so clear and obvious. As my conceptualizations developed, I wrote a few essays, usually at others' requests, (my ideas were still forming, some I could not clearly articulate, so I adopted terms, thoughts, and ideas. But it was all quickly coming together.) I could see where the failures and successes had occurred in various anti-colonial, class, anti-racist, feminist, and anti-imperialist struggles. And I could see where the failure to apply the scientific Marxist approach to the study and practice of resisting oppressive conditions (Historical and Dialectical Materialism) resulted in failed idealist attempts to make the desired social changes.

In answer to those pessimistic about waging a successful revolutionary struggle here in the military stronghold of the global imperialist system, I found inspiration in one seemingly insignificant area of the Middle East, Gaza City. The Palestinians in Gaza, suffering under a brutal Israeli military occupation, have waged a heroic, successful, protracted struggle. They are living under the most primitive of conditions, with no economic infrastructure. (Open sewers, no garbage disposal, etc.) Gaza's economy is totally dependent upon day laborers and servants working in Israel proper. But under the organizing work of Hamas, their unrelenting resistance to Israeli forces is forcing the Israeli occupation and settlements out. The al-Qassam brigade (the clandestine military wing of Hamas) primarily focused its attacks on Israeli soldiers and settlers – the results of which can only be very limited. But did al-Qassam infiltrate and direct its efforts at Israel proper (at its economic base), and did Hamas's political leaders not entrust their ultimate political power to the corrupt and bootlicking Palestinian Authority and Yassir Arafat, and did the Palestinians join their struggle up with the Israeli working class, they would crush Zionist oppression at its root.[*]

Even with Hamas' political and military errors, Israel still proved to have *no military option* against Hamas; they can't infiltrate, neutralize, or contain al-Qassam. Yet Israel has much of the same military technology and hardware as the US – nukes and all. Hamas won the greatest loyalty and a secure base amongst the people of Gaza through establishing economic programs that served the people (e.g. building schools and hospitals, operating health clinics, food distribution centers, etc., all freely available to the people), through developing a reputation of scrupulous honesty (in contrast to the corrupt Palestinian Authority), and overall serving the interests of the people of Gaza.

Al-Qassam is fighting with next to no modern resources, in only a 144 square mile area, yet Israel (the region's most powerful military force) admits inability to contend with Hamas. The US is

— — — — —

[*] Of course, it should be kept in mind that the author was writing these words in 2004.

3.5 million square miles in area, with relatively limitless logistical resources.

I have long been responsive to the suffering of others, now more so than ever. I've come to recognize that a primary cause of peoples' suffering the world over is on account of forces that the Amerikan left and oppressed nationalities are in a position to contend with. But the leadership must overcome its fear, there must be reconciliation reached, despite different schools of thought. They must organize their forces and bring together their various educators and political workers and develop party and mass structure to coordinate the work of disparate and isolated activists and the people. The left must move forward with programs (economic, political, cultural, *and* military), which will displace those of the enemy. The establishment's prestige, its false sense of invulnerability, must be ripped away. Prestige must be vested in the masses themselves through mobilizing, organizing, and building a mass-based infrastructure within the oppressed sectors of the working class. We must work toward deconstructing the false concepts of racism, which neutralizes the capacity of the working class to struggle together. And it must prepare for war. Likewise, the oppressed nationalities must struggle for their own self-determination while linking their struggles up with that of the entire multi-ethnic working class to build a United Front Against Imperialism.

I still endure repression at the hands of the pigs, as do my peers. I still take a principled stand against this repression. But above all else, I am working on bringing my peers into a principled ideological and political consciousness that will give them discipline and a cause to struggle for, while simultaneously imparting to them the correct methods of mass based struggle. The pigs' response continues to be to isolate me. Their violence has proven futile. Even in this most totalitarian of environments, innovation and relentless commitment to an ideal has proven, to my satisfaction, that the oppressive institutions are not invulnerable. Fear is our greatest hindrance. Fear and half measures. They can isolate me, but they cannot isolate an ideal.

I have often defeated myself for lack of a broad vision. Because I had confined my efforts and ideas to this limited prison environment, I isolated myself from those on the outside. I had severed almost all outside contacts. I never expected to leave prison alive. However, I've come to realize that this relatively tiny prison environment, these concentrated islands of oppression (the conditions within which I daily witness driving my peers helplessly into insanity), are a small interrelated part of a much greater oppressive whole. We prisoners must be reached and we must reach out. We must be educated into an understanding of our victim status, made to understand the function that the prisons serve, the nature of government in stratified capitalist societies. At the same time a much larger and totally committed effort must be made on the outside to confront the enemy power structure. This has been my message to the outside.

Now that I've begun interacting with people on the outside, the pigs have acted decisively to frustrate and discourage those contacts to isolate me. Many contacts have been broken, on account of these obstructions. I've been hindered in many commitments. The impediments have perhaps left some to think me unreliable at best, or an opportunist, or worse. They clearly don't understand my situation inside here – and why should they? – I've never explained it.

I am perceptive if anything and understand that there have been many defections, betrayals, infiltrations, provocateurs, pig agents, opportunists, and cowards in the left and other revolutionary or progressive movements.

While others' opinions of me are unimportant to me in the personal sense, I recognize the need for unity, loyalty, trust, and total commitment if any real struggle is to be waged. It's by the designs of the enemy order that the masses and even revolutionary progressive leaders are divided by fear, suspicion, and distrust. It is for this reason alone that I have made the effort to offer some insight into myself. I refuse to be party to my enemy's divisive designs.

I *have* nothing and therefore nothing to lose. I have conditioned myself for every conceivable shock and strain – physically, mentally, and emotionally. I fear nothing. No threat or prospect of danger deters me; I've faced them all, continuously and by choice. I am willing to suffer with those who suffer, to die with those who die, and to struggle in the most extreme manner for their liberation. I've lived the past decade with no pleasures, no amenities, and no entertainment. I've conditioned myself for every extreme. This is the level of commitment that our struggle demands, and the level of commitment that I have, and those who share this commitment have my complete loyalty.

August 2004[*]

— — — — —

[*] By the date of publication of this book (2010), Rashid has been in prison for 20 years, the last 16 of which have been in solitary.

From Individual Struggle to Revolutionary Collectivism: Autobiography of an Outlaw

by Outlaw

In order to give concrete social meaning to the writings that follow, I felt that it was necessary to write a short autobiography that would explain the circumstances and conditions surrounding my development. Also I felt that "my story" is similar to the stories of so many others. Therefore, nothing is unique about me, because essentially it's "our story," and on the basis of this commonality, we can move to advance our common interests.

Poverty is the running theme of my life. My mother, a single parent, was committed to the ideal of the "Amerikan Dream." She believed that through hard work and persistence, anyone could lift themselves up out of their lowly condition. She was so committed to this ideal that she held multiple jobs to avoid going on welfare and she refused to live in the Black-inhabited ghettos, the "projects."

Being on the former and living in the latter carried a social stigma that was unbearable and unacceptable to her. It simply didn't fit in with her idea of what one was capable of accomplishing in Amerika. This industrious Black womyn possessed a profound sense of dignity. However, Amerikan capitalism with its peculiar indifference towards the needs of working-class people and Black/New Afrikans in particular, shattered the notions and beliefs my mother held, as constant financial difficulties literally left our family out on the streets.

In early 1989 the apartment we lived in caught on fire. There had been constant flooding in the basement due to a faulty sewage system. This time, the water reached such high levels that it made contact with an electrical outlet. One morning at around 3AM the basement exploded. My mother woke me and my siblings up and rushed us through the smoke-filled hallway to the safety of the street outside. We could only watch as the flames raged while our meager belongings remained inside the apartment. Besides wondering where we were going to live, the destruction of what I had considered a small fortune also ran through my mind. I had been collecting aluminum cans and storing them in big plastic trash bags in the basement, trying to save up a reasonable enough amount of money to be able to help my Moms out. I was ten at the time. I had already made up my mind at a very early age that I wasn't going to be a burden to my mother, that throughout my life I would strive to be a productive member of the family. The fire was the event that was to shape our lives for years to come.

Since the fire was due to no fault of our own, one would logically think that the government would have (and could have) provided our family with a habitable place to live, but no assistance was provided, so after the fire we moved around quite frequently. I was always the "new kid," whether it was on the block or in school. We once lived in an old folks home on Grace St. This retirement home was nothing like what one sees on TV. This was a retirement home for poor working-class people. There was no green yard with concrete walkways and ornate screened-in gazebos where the residents played bingo and enjoyed themselves. One didn't get that antiseptic modern feel that one gets upon entering upper-class institutions for the elderly. The tile floor was dingy and dirty with cigarette butts and ashes on the floors and tables. The staircase was wooden and worn and the handrail was white-brown. The only form of entertainment was a floor model TV that blasted at all hours of the day. The residents didn't have their own rooms with amenities like push buttons to alert the staff in case of emergency. They were crowded three and four to a room the size of an average bedroom. It was a very depressing place. The smell was sickening, and coupled with it was the sight of elderly folks that couldn't take care of themselves hygienically. I would have to sit at the table and eat with them, though I hardly ate. I would take two bites, or rather two spoonfuls, (they served soup all the time), look up, and instantly vomit. Mental patients stayed there, too. I was terrified of one elderly man who would rave, rant, and cuss spontaneously and without warning.

After leaving the elderly home we lived in motel after motel. Our family had to split up to ease the transportation burden on my Moms so she could focus on finding and maintaining employment. In 1990 we all moved into a first floor apartment at 505 East Grace Street. It felt good to finally have our family back together again. Grace St. was a "pivotal point" in my life. It's the heart of the city, populated by a mixture of social elements that combined to make up a very diverse whole. This had a lot of influence on my development.

There were Blacks/New Afrikans, whites, Vietnamese, Mexicans, gays, lesbians, prostitutes, panhandlers, college students (Virginia Commonwealth University - VCU - was right there), and I came into contact with all these elements. I used to frequent Monroe Park (right across from the famed Landmark Theatre), where I would kick it with the homeless people who lived there.

There was so much there in the way of human experience. I've always been outgoing, so I wouldn't hesitate to go and talk to anybody. The things I was seeing raised questions in my mind. I wanted to understand the world I was living in. I wanted to know why this family of four, two parents and two children, were living in the park and why this man who was blind was on the corner shaking a cup asking for change. Not to mention the fact that I identified with these people because of where I had been and what I was still going through. The fact wasn't lost on me that I could at any time end up in the same place these people were: in the streets. Side by side with the poverty and misery was the sight of the rich folks who frequented the prestigious hotel and the expensive lounges and clubs, jumping in and out of limousines that adorned the entrances of the "high society" establishments in the area. These contrasting images ignited my then naïve sense of class inequalities. Being poor, I was always the subject of jokes and taunts in school for my non-name brand clothing. In addition to being socially isolating, this affected my sense of self-worth.

It was around this time that I met Ricky, who became my closest friend. He lived upstairs in the apartment building next to mine. His situation was much like mine. We were the only two males in the same peer group living in the apartment complex. Well, besides Ricky's brother who stayed gone all the time. We instantly became accomplices as well as friends. It was when I went to the sixth grade at Binford Middle School that I began to engage consistently in criminal activities. I began skipping school and breaking into cars, stealing money, phones, and jewelry. Anything of value, I was taking it. We plundered the possessions of the white world at will. All those whites who commuted to the inner city from the suburbs and thought their property secure because it was wired with security alarms had to feel helpless upon discovering that their security systems had been repeatedly "breached."

I first got into trouble with the law when I was eleven years old. I got caught stealing junk food and boxes of gum, which I planned on hustling at school. The pigs came and took me home and then back to school where my Moms, out of the norm, picked me up, anxious to whip my black ass. During this time I kept being approached by a "pusher" who promised to put me on with something I could make some money with. I was scared of what my Moms would do if she found out that I was selling drugs. This was at the height of the "war on drugs" and I was under the influence of those anti-drug, "Just Say No" commercials being advertised. I repeatedly refused his offers. I thought selling drugs was "bad" when all the while I was still stealing and breaking into cars.

These were the contradictions governing my life, the contradiction between poverty and morality. Morality would have you obey the law, respect authority and so forth. But you may not be able to escape poverty without breaking the law, at least to some degree. We are told to seek legal means to meet our needs, but how are these needs to be met? The ruling powers tell us poor lower-class folks that we have an obligation, a social responsibility to society, to abide by the law, but they don't have any social responsibility to us to help us meet our needs. It's pure bourgeoisie class-based morality, a morality that serves the ruling class, not the masses of the oppressed.

My Moms kept my sister and me enrolled in some type of program, particularly in the summer, to keep us from being idle at home all day. I remember this one program called the SPARC (pronounced "spark") program. It was an acting program held in the basement of this half-a-block long cathedral on the corner of Monument and Lombardy. We were rehearsing to perform *Oliver*, a book turned play turned movie, by Charles Dickens, which was about these poor orphaned children in England who picked pockets for a living. There were only three Black/New Afrikans in this program: me, my sister, and another Black girl. Everybody else was white, including the counselors. This is one significant moment where I experienced racism. Predictably, a white guy was chosen to play Oliver, the main character, but I had the skills to act the part. I loved acting. Plus I got all the moves and lines memorized for the character Oliver. The white kid went on vacation and got badly sunburned, so he couldn't do the physical routines. So I thought, this is my chance to change the directors' minds and choose me to play Oliver. I rehearsed like we were live on stage (we were to perform at Dogwood Dell Amphitheater in a couple weeks), and everybody was impressed, praising me for my talents. A few white girls even got extra friendly with me, especially one older girl. I thought, "Yeah! I got the part! I'm Oliver." Well, as soon as the white guy who was originally chosen to play Oliver recovered from his sunburn, I was thrust into the background. Man I was mad. It was evident that I could outperform the white guy and that I deserved to be selected for the part, but I wasn't.

So I had this t-shirt that was donated by some white people. Ironically, the shirt read "FREE SOUTH AFRICA" in bold black letters on the front. Also on the front was also a picture of a white figure holding a rope that was around the neck of a much bigger black figure. And on the back of the shirt it read, "IT'S A BLACK THING. YOU WOULDN'T UNDERSTAND," also in bold black lettering. My Moms had told me repeatedly not to wear that shirt to the program 'cause she felt it would be offensive to the white people. Well, after the white people had let me know that I was not to play the role of Oliver no matter how talented I was, I became vindictive. I wore that shirt and slipped out of the house before my Moms could see my sister and me leave. With extra pep in my step, I walked to the program while my sister kept reminding me every other block or so that Moms told me not to wear that shirt. We got to the program and as soon as we entered all eyes were on me. It was a satisfying moment for me. Everyone was so nice and eager to talk to me, offering my sister and me rides home. I was just cheesing on the inside 'cause I knew that by my wearing that shirt I had tapped into the guilty consciences of these people who were cheating me out of an acting role, and more importantly, my freedom of expression and the opportunity to grow and develop artistically, all because of my race. Having worn that shirt I was resisting cultural domination (not to be confused with economic, military, and political domination). When I got home that evening and my Moms saw the shirt she got all over me but I didn't care 'cause I had done what I wanted to do. I told her I didn't have any other clean shirts.

In the summer of 1993 we moved back to North Side into a house, with the help of a privileged white family. It was a habitat house, but my Moms was glad to be in something that she would eventually get to call her own. She was to realize the "Amerikan dream" of home ownership, but at the price of our family's honor and dignity. The white family who helped us move into the house stopped by frequently to "check on us." We became well acquainted with their family too, but essentially it was a paternalistic relationship. Whenever they were coming over we had to tidy up the house and get freshened up ourselves in preparation for their arrival. My siblings and I were sternly advised to be on our best behavior. It was so artificial to be always smiling and yes siring and yes ma'aming. They inspected the house during their visits as if they were expecting our living arrangement to be in total disarray. It felt as if we were the study of some weird social experiment, always being observed and watched like they were secretly logging our behaviors and habits. They never ate or drank anything while visiting our residence, but we were frequently invited and actually did attend numerous dinners and lunches at their house.

Then reporters started coming to the house to interview my Moms about the trials and tribulations we faced. One interview was featured in the Richmond *Times Dispatch*. Others were in some magazines to promote a program (which I won't name) that touted my family as its first successful case. Pictures were taken of my family, but I avoided them 'cause I was ashamed and humiliated by having my poverty-ridden life on public display. Also my peers were commenting to me in the streets on how they saw my family in the newspaper and didn't know we had been through so much. Basically, I got a lot of unwanted attention. I knew some people in the neighborhood had formed unfavorable opinions about my family because of our social economic status, but that's the kind of society we live in. When you are poor you don't have any social respect or social worth because everything is defined in terms of money and how much of it you have. This is what capitalism does. It turns all values into commercial values, even the value of life itself. It was like because this family had money they could intervene in and influence the affairs of our family. We got all the charity case publicity while they got all the moral praise and honor for their efforts to uplift the poor. I won't downplay any sincerity on the part of this white family in truly wanting to help us out. The fact remains that these instances of private charity have no impact on the overall wretched conditions of the poor.

To add to this demeaning arrangement, my Moms, my sister and I would cater these social gatherings held by the white family's relatives. The only other Black/New Afrikan was the bartender. It was so reminiscent of the historical period of the Jim Crow era or when Blacks/New Afrikans were in chattel slavery. We were the socially invisible servants. I took coats, served drinks, and picked up trash, basically attending to the superficial wants of the guests, while my Moms prepared the food and set the table while my sister performed duties somewhere in between. While I won't deny the fact that my Moms was compensated for her catering services, I do not consider these traditionally oppressive and degrading roles to be a valid means of making a living. It was this type of experience that stimulated my interest in revolutionary class theory.

I was born in 1979, (the same year as the Iranian Revolution, the Nicaraguan revolution, and the liberation of Assata Shakur from prison), in Lynchburg, Virginia. However, by the time I was two years old, my Mom's search for job opportunities and for a chance to escape the monotonous and predestined channels of social development characteristic of small towns led her to pack up and move us to Richmond. We've been living there since then. I love Lynchburg, though. When I left home at 14 I lived there with my Pops for a brief period and I noticed a strong element of social cohesion there that was missing in Richmond. Plus almost everyone in the Black sector of Lynchburg is a relative of mine.

I used to think about death a lot at a very young age. I was heavily influenced by grown-ups who never missed a chance to talk about how Jesus was coming back to carry the believers off to heaven. But first Satan would rule the earth and people would have to choose between accepting the mark of the beast and facing sudden death. All I could envision was widespread fires and piles of corpses and suffering. One babysitter seemed to delight in telling my sister and me that the creaking noises in her house were caused by the footsteps of Jesus. I soon began to question the purpose of such things like working, going to school, homework, and even living: what was the use in spending my life laboring to achieve what was soon to be destroyed by Jesus upon his return?

After moving back to North Side, the white family that had aided us in moving into the house also made arrangements for my siblings and me to attend a private school, All Saints Catholic School. It was an all Black/New Afrikan school, amongst the students anyway. They were mostly from middle-class backgrounds. I was the new kid all over again, which is something I had grown accustomed to by then. But I guess because of my innocent facial expression and humble demeanor, I had always attracted unwanted (but prepared-for) conflict. I came to know the meaning of taking kindness for weakness all too well, as I've been the target of numerous schemes and cons by folks with predatory, capitalist-oriented objectives. I learned to make use of my "appearance" along with the knowledge of affluent white Amerikan etiquette I had gained while working at the white family's social gatherings. This also helped me to obtain and maintain employment in my later years. These skills were nothing but a means to an end for me. I've never accepted the idea of the superiority of white culture.

At age 15 I began stealing cars. Well, actually I was stealing cars before then. Fifteen is when I first got caught. One morning an accomplice and me were traveling in a stolen car, on our way to do another car theft. While sitting at a corner waiting to turn, a Richmond squad car swung around the corner in our direction. The pig inside grilled my accomplice and me. I was driving. I instinctively felt that the pig would make a U-turn and pursue us, as the car had just been stolen the day before in this same area. As I predicted, the pig pursued us and I floored it, cutting in and out of apartment parking lots through residential streets and finally speed-balled through a red light at 65 mph. By this time a second pig car had joined the chase. As I sped through the red light, there was a car in front of me, so I swerved to the right to avoid tail-ending that car, which also veered to the right, blocking my escape. So I pulled the steering wheel sharply to the left and avoided hitting that car only to run head on into another car in the oncoming lane. As a result of the collision, the doors on the car locked up, and I was struggling to jump out the window when the pig snatched me up at the back of my collar and delivered a mean blow to the back of my head with the butt of his gun. I was handcuffed and transported to Henrico Juvenile Detention Center, 'cause the chase ended up in Henrico. I stayed there for five months and had my 16th birthday in that place.

After that I was bent on concentrating on making some money. Stealing cars, which was really recreation, hadn't helped me in this regard. I also wanted to make things right with my Moms, so I got a job working at Pizza Hut. I managed to hold this job for almost a year, but it was another phase in a sequence of disappointments and frustrations. I was the youngest employee at Pizza Hut, and I was a quick learner. I breezed through duties traditionally assigned to new employees, duties like cleaning windows, washing dishes, and cleaning bathrooms, as I had already mastered those skills while assisting my Moms in cleaning rich white people's homes in affluent neighborhoods, like Short Pump, just outside of Richmond. I "moved up" to operating the cash register and waiting on tables quite efficiently. Management held this in-house capitalist competition among the wait staff to see who could acquire the most sales. Taken altogether, of course, this translated into higher productivity and profits for Pizza Hut. I remained in the number one position for weeks. Many of my older co-workers felt threatened by a bright energetic youthful worker like me. So in their efforts to curtail the effects of my above average performance, they always assigned me to monotonous duties like washing dishes. I was fully capable of managing the store and was always complimented by the head manager. I even accompanied one of my co-workers to his apartment to drink a few beers, which I interpreted as a sign of acceptance. After all that I only received a ten-cent raise on a five-dollar-an-hour wage.

I did manage to save up about $1,200, which my Moms advised me to use to enroll in a local community college. My brief stay in community college was abruptly halted when I dropped out because I was neither academically prepared for nor really focused on advancing in college. I was working full time, overtime actually, while attending community college, but I was frustrated by the lack of opportunity for social mobility. Because a car was totaled during the course of the high-speed chase, I was sued, so my credit was messed up and would remain so until I made a dent in the thousands of dollars of debt that I owed. I had never had a driver's license, but now the credit bureau effectively prevented me from getting one, which in turn prevented me from finding one of the better paying jobs which were all located outside of the city limits.

I had been selling weed, which got me close to $50 a day. This helped me keep some extra cash for cab fare to and from work and school. But then I was fired from Pizza Hut for insubordination; the shift manager had said he could handle things without me one night, so I left. I was essentially broke, having invested all my savings mainly in community college books and $100 calculators. I got further into the drug game selling crack and weed. However, in a last-ditch effort to find employment, as well as keep the peace at home with my Moms, I sought employment at a temp-agency located on East Main St. The temp agency provided low-paying day labor to non-skilled and some skilled people, mostly Black/New Afrikans, who were the city's vagabonds, addicts, alcoholics, and homeless. They were essentially that "reserve army of labor" that Marx describes in various writings. The temp agency paid only $30 a day, less than that after taxes, and considering that this social class of people didn't have personal bank accounts, their purchasing power was further reduced by having to cash their checks at convenience stores and check cashing joints that charge exorbitant fees for such transactions.

I myself was the victim of this money scheme one time. I worked at the temp agency for four consecutive days, the first at an industrial site doing light industrial work. The second day, I worked at a school that was being built, clearing debris and trash to make way for the electricians to come in and install electrical lines in the building. The third day I was assigned to an apartment complex out in Henrico, Newbridge apartments. I had to pick up trash and litter. This job wasn't as labor intensive as others. Matter of fact it was boring, but I had one moment of satisfaction. When combing through the small bushes in front of the apartment buildings, picking trash out of them, a dime sack of weed fell at my feet. I hurriedly picked it up and stuffed it in my back pocket where it remained until my lunch break when I was able to walk up to the local store and purchase some blunts. I walked back to the apartment complex and posted up on the back stairs of the building furthest from the main office and proceeded to stimulate my mind. Unlike Bill Clinton, I inhaled deeply. I was sick of this employment arrangement. I had no car, no money, and it was tough seeing others have what I didn't have even though I was working. I mean the social pressures to have the flyest ride, clothes, and financial mobility started to bear down on me. It's hard for a person to be without these socially valued possessions and feel like a whole complete human being.

The next day at this same job, I made up my mind that I was going to the game full time. Well, coincidentally, the apartment managers had informed me that my services were no longer needed at the complex, as they had no more work for me to do, so that would be my last day. I got off work and took the bus back to the temp agency to collect my check. That was the procedure. We workers come in at 5AM, receive a job assignment, sometimes they transport us to the jobs depending on the distance, and we come back later to collect our pay. Well, I walked into the temp-agency and gave the clerk, (a man), my name and told him I had completed my day job. He promptly began looking through some papers on his desk and aroused my suspicion when he obviously couldn't find what he was looking for. Then he looked up at me and said, "I'm sorry, but we have no record of your having worked today." He was referring to the timecard that we sign every morning. I started getting warm, but I remained calm and told him, "Look, I've been here for the past three days, not to mention the fact that you were the one who gave me these job assignments each day, including today." He pretended to act like he had no idea of what I was talking about, so I suggested he call the apartment manager at the complex I had worked at to verify my having worked. He shamefacedly declined to do so on the grounds that if I had worked, then he "would have the paperwork." By this time I was pissed and honestly ready to resort to a physical confrontation with this white guy who was knowingly cheating me out of my energy, money, and time. There were iron bars stretched horizontally across the front of the desk to form a barrier between the lobby and the office, I guess to protect people like this white guy from the unstable behavior of us social scum. Luckily for this guy, those bars were there, 'cause I was bent on going across that desk and whipping his ass. Out of anger and vengeance, plus being convinced that I wasn't going to receive my pay, I turned to my left and punched a hole in the wall, which was made of sheetrock, and proceeded to exit the building. As I was leaving, the white guy stood up out of his chair and hollered, "Hey, you'll pay for that," to which I replied, "F—k you, take it out of my check" and slammed the door. I wondered how many others had he done the same way, people probably in more desperate financial situations than me.

The drug game was not new to me, but there were certain dimensions of the drug game that were. When you're young and seeing the older dealers in the hood with money and cars it's automatically appealing. But these are only the superficial aspects of selling drugs. Paradoxically, selling drugs is like having a job. You gotta manage your money, stash some away for rainy days, and your "customer service" skills must be up to par in order to ensure the profitable disposal of your product. But in a more important way, like a job, selling drugs consumes so much of one's life. This especially applies to low-level dealers because they're pressed financially to sell and re-sell product in order to accumulate profits. This demands their constant presence on the "block." As a result, many of my peers have never left the "block," physically or mentally.

Frantz Fanon, in his classic work *The Wretched of the Earth*, described how a colonized people, (in this case the urban Amerikan colonies, otherwise referred to as the "hood," the "projects," and the "ghettos"), come to exist under a sort of "pecking order" where "the only law is that of the knife," brought on by competition for scarce resources that find their way into the resource-lacking colonies. Every drug sale is the object of relentless competition, and I vividly remember scrambling to "hustle" my product to prospective buyers with several of my equally-pressed peers right in step with me. To further illustrate this point, I myself got into a fist fight with a brother I've known since elementary school, 'cause he felt like I was trying to "cut his throat" on a sale, an apt phrase reflecting the reality of urban colonial existence, where committing such an act as "cutting someone's throat," (intercepting a drug sale), "is not a question of the negation of the property of others, nor the transgression of a law, nor lack of respect. These are attempts at murder."

This goes a long way toward explaining the fratricidal Black-on-Black crime and murderous gang wars that plague urban Amerika. Being diametrically opposed to senseless Black-on-Black crime, not proud of and downright uncomfortable with perpetuating the chemical addictions and hence destruction of Black/New Afrikan

lives, I stopped dealing. Through my intimate contact with affluent white Amerika, I took notice of the stark contrast between their
quality of life and ours. It was apparent that their leisure and luxury
came at our expense, (though I didn't know exactly how), so my
enjoying leisure and luxury by selling crack to pregnant Black/New
Afrikan wimyn and emasculated Black/New Afrikan men placed me
in an extremely uncomfortable role resembling that of affluent white
Amerika, and I couldn't accept that. I began to put my small arsenal
of arms to use for purposes other than strictly self-protection. The
business establishments became "sitting ducks" for my hit-and-run
tactics, that included striking during rush hour in order to ensure
my escape on foot while the pigs in their cars were effectively im-
mobilized and gridlocked by the swarms of concentrated traffic. I
would enter an establishment with one set of clothes on and one
block later into my escape be wearing a totally different outfit in order to avoid fitting any "descriptions."

Beginning to live the "good life," as that is defined in terms of
illegitimate capitalist values, I sought to move into my own place. I
located an apartment, but I was required to show proof of employment, so I conveniently landed a job at a Burger King in a shop-
ping center near the apartment. After having worked two weeks and
obtaining a check stub to show proof of employment, I called my
Mom's house to see if my sister and brother wanted some food from
Burger King. My sister answered the phone and immediately began
telling me that the pigs had come by the house looking for me. I
started retracing all my steps in my mind to try to locate and identify
any mistakes I may have made during my criminal activities. A week
later, I went looking for a fellow whom I'd known briefly, at his job.
I wasn't twenty-one years old yet, and he had a "connection" which

allowed him to obtain fake ID's – and I needed one. Upon approaching this fellow's workplace, I saw him standing outside. He was on his way to leave work, so I yelled his name. He turned and saw me, and for no apparent reason started running away from me. In this particular neighborhood this scene was abnormal, and it must have attracted the attention of someone, as the pigs arrived in what seemed like seconds to investigate what disturbance had occurred.

I was in foreign territory and had no escape route. I didn't want to go jump in the car that I was driving without a license, so I casually walked toward a fast-food joint, went in and tried to blend in with the patrons. Two pigs entered the fast-food joint and approached me while I was standing in line and asked could they talk to me outside. I calmly agreed displaying no sign of objection, as I didn't want to arouse the pigs' suspicion any further. Outside, standing next to the pigs' car, the pig asked me my name, and I countered by asking him was I under arrest. He replied, "No." He then asked did I have any weapons on me and asked could he search me. I agreed to the search, as I didn't have any weapons on me. He patted me down and found my ID with my real name on it, and handed it to his partner, who went to the car to run a check. The pig patting me down was taking all day to do it; obviously he was waiting for his partner to give him the results on the check. Then, with my back already to him, he grabs my arm and starts to handcuff me saying, "Now you're under arrest."

I was transported to the Henrico Jail, where I was held for several hours until the Richmond pigs came and picked me up. I was served warrants for robbery, shooting into an occupied vehicle, and two uses of a firearm. This was in 1999, two days before my twentieth birthday. At my trial, I was accused of robbing a store for

$5,000 and shooting at a witness while fleeing. The robbery victim testified on the stand that he could not identify me as the robber. Another witness testified that she saw my face for two to three seconds, however she was shown a photo lineup with my picture in it a few hours after the robbery, and she couldn't/didn't point me out as the robber then. But four weeks after my preliminary hearing, predictably, she identified me as the robber and shooter while I was on the defendant's chair – a totally suggestive identification. The detective assigned to the case testified at my trial that he had a conversation with a David Mosby, and with the information obtained from him, the detective got warrants for me. David Mosby didn't testify at the trial, (which was another violation of my rights, my right to face my accuser), but he wrote a lengthy statement which the detective skillfully quoted from, implicating me as the perpetrator. I found out later, after my sentencing, that in my pre-sentence report, David Mosby also told the pigs I had dropped a firearm, which upon hitting the pavement, discharged. This firearm "was recovered approximately 50 feet from where David Mosby was apprehended." The state never produced this firearm at my trial and as a matter of fact withheld this evidence by denying the existence of any such evidence in their response to my request for motion for discovery.

With the assistance of court-appointed counsel, I was railroaded into prison, where I've been for the past six and a half years. During my first few years in prison, I worked on my case doggedly, persistently foregoing the usual prison activities, trying to challenge the constitutionality of my convictions, as I had ample legal basis for my convictions to be overturned. I fought my case optimistically until my resources were drained from paying court filing fees, (imposed just for this purpose), and after denial after denial for not having what the courts considered to be a "substantial constitutional violation," the ruling handed down by the 4th Circuit Court of Appeals, I resentfully withdrew from pursuing relief from the courts. While in the hole (SHU) for assaulting another prisoner, who made verbal threats on my life, (threats to which I immediately responded with physical violence), I kept hearing George Jackson's name here and there along with exciting accounts of the August 7th Movement. This was Jonathan Jackson's, (George's younger brother), armed raid on the Marin County Courthouse in California in 1970.

However, no one I had run into actually had *Blood In My Eye* to let me read it. I did meet a self-proclaimed communist revolutionary, (who later proved to be a counter-revolutionary), who gave me some addresses to various book companies, one of which sold *Blood In My Eye*. I purchased the book and instantly related to George and Jonathan's world outlook as well as their militancy, intelligence, and commitment as being well worthy of emulation. Reading *Blood In My Eye*, I discovered that capitalist-private property relations are the source of class inequalities, which is the primary factor in my being a member of a class that bears all the burdens of society without enjoying its advantages. Under the influence of illegitimate-capitalist values, I was pursuing the alleviation of social-economic hardship through individual advancement. This is a wholly inadequate remedy to social problems because it doesn't challenge the fundamental injustice of class-exploitation and class-oppression, which are responsible for creating the socio-economic ills in the first place. Unaware of my class interest, I was perpetuating my own oppression by engaging in competitive capitalist practices that ensure the smooth functioning of the system as the exploiting minority profits in more ways than one off the division and disunity engendered by competition, so prevalent amongst the exploited. Look around: competition, euphemistically called "individuality," permeates and is systematically promoted to the masses of people while the corporate conglomerations and Fortune 500 are busy "merging and monopolizing."

Blood In My Eye inspired me. George's words resonated with me because of what I had been and am going through. Rallied to the cause of revolution, I enlisted. When a person desires change, whether personal or social, that directly implies that the person is willing to play an active role molding, shaping, and creating the type of change that s/he desires. Being emphatically displeased with this social, economic, and political order didn't automatically grant me the insight to know what type of change was objectively needed because I had no firm grasp of what was wrong with the present social, economic, and political order. Solely relying on outward appearances is insufficient, because only through intimate knowledge of the problem are we able to articulate clear solutions and erect safeguards against reverting back to ways of thinking and being that perpetuate the problem in subtle, disguised ways. Thus I began to seriously study the writings of revolutionary practitioners and theoreticians like Frantz Fanon, Karl Marx, Vladimir Lenin, Angela Davis, Frederick Engels, Bobby Seale, Noam Chomsky, and Che Guevara. I investigated the socioeconomic theories of socialism, communism, and capitalism. However, it was upon meeting Rashid, POW, revolutionary extraordinaire, my mentor, comrade, brother, ally, and friend, that my ideological, intellectual, and revolutionary moral development was accelerated. I had heard volumes about Rashid before actually meeting him. When I did meet him, he supplied me with the best of the knowledge, experience, and insight that he had acquired in the process of his revolutionary development.

To put people before profit, to value human life over and above objects and things, are revolutionary principles to which I am wholly devoted, as I am devoted to the struggle to revolutionize society on the basis of these principles. The illegitimate capitalist values that define human worth in terms of profit potential bear no influence on my consciousness, behavior, character, or on my social relations with others. I am the revolutionary free agent, committed to the struggle for liberation of the oppressed the world-over. Through the socioeconomic deprivations and hardships of hunger, homelessness, cold, continuous labor, self-medication, and overall means of survival that assist one in making it from one day to the next, I've been conditioned for the subsistence-level of existence associated with protracted struggle. This physical conditioning is reinforced by a mental and moral fortitude to endure and battle adversity, forged through my struggles with death, despair, confrontations with pigs, the emotional frustrations that poverty engenders, and the formidable repression that comes with being a victim of Amerikan colonialism.

Armed violence is inherent in protracted people's struggle, but the armed violence that has plagued my life and the lives of my peers, (for much less worthy causes), is no deterrent against my active participation in abolishing the suffering of humanity. I fully and willingly accept the responsibilities that come with placing my life at the service of The People. I endeavor to enlighten, uplift, and unite my peers into an organized revolutionary force, helping them to understand and eventually fulfill their role as the gravediggers of capitalism and makers of the new socialist society. Socialist revolution is the only road to happiness, security, and all 'round, unobstructed human development, free from the artificial social barriers constructed by the exploiting minority to dominate, exploit, and divide us. Amerikan capitalism has robbed me of all happiness, comfort, and any semblance of a meaningful existence. I have no qualms about the dismantling of a system that has demonstrated throughout its history an utter lack of respect for human life, within its own borders and across the globe. To the revolutionary cause and all those unconditionally committed to the liberation of the oppressed I pledge my loyalty.

LYNCHING
LEGALIZED

"Every day in Amerikkka the trek continues, a Black march to Death Row" Mumia Abu-Jamal

RASHID
7-27
'06

"The death penalty in Amerika has always operated as a legal instrument of racial terror. The death penalty evolved from, and assumed the psychological role of lynching. Lest we forget, every Black man lynched was supposedly 'guilty of a crime!'....There is not one legal or 'Constitutional' right Afrikan people have in Amerika that white folks don't have the veto over, or not subject to judicial review, including the right to life. A Black man's life is subject to termination by a cop or agent of the state at any given moment - without recourse to appeal."

Dhoruba bin Wahad

FIGHTING 2 LIVE

by Outlaw

Just when the sheet-like hail of police violence and brutality was
    being brought down
to cover my bullet-ridden body;
Just when the medical team of propagandists
had pronounced my body politic dead on the scene;
Just when the black hearse of exploitation pulled up
to transport my body off to a cold, lifeless, funeral home-like
    poverty;
Just when the judicial morticians had angled their gavel/scalpels
to cut the hole in my body from which to drain all the
    revolutionary blood out of me;
Just when the pallbearers of reaction
thought that my service to humynity was over;
Just when the grave digging racism had removed the last pile of dirt
    from the site of my predicted grave
in hopes of burying me six-feet deep in inhumynity;
My heart beat.
My blood raced to my brain.
My lungs expanded.
My nose and mouth sucked in air.
My eyes opened.
My consciousness was regained.
And when all those vultures standing around my body rushed to
    hurl me back into non-existence …
Like the scene at my emergence from the womb,
I fought like hell, defying the tomb.

PART TWO

Introduction

The following is a series of written exchanges between a young comrade, Outlaw, and myself. These exchanges occurred over a six month period in 2004, while we were housed in Virginia's Red Onion State (Supermax) Prison. Outlaw was housed during that time in what passes as the "general population" unit, while I was frequently rotated by the uniforms from cell to cell and back and forth between the prison's two "superseg" units (segregation within segregation). I am one of only two prisoners at the prison on this frequent move status. Our sealed letters were passed between us primarily by a lone "good cop" (whom we call the "taxi"). Our exchanges ended due to circumstances beyond our control.

...amerikan prisons and the activities which they prohibit are aimed at very distinctly defined sectors of the class- and race-sensitized society. The ultimate expression of law is not order - it's prisons. There are hundreds upon hundreds of prisons, and thousands upon thousands of laws, yet there is no social order, no social peace. The law and everything that interlocks with it was constructed for poor desperate people like me.
George Jackson

RASHID 7-27 '05

Turn the iron houses of oppression into schools of liberation

82

Defying the Tomb: Prison Letters of Rashid and Outlaw

1. To OUTLAW: I received your note. You asked about some "practical-tactical" literature. I'm sending you Sun Tzu's *Art of War* and George Jackson's *Blood In My Eye*.[*] I have other military works, but under the circumstances I'm not inclined to trust them to pig care, and besides, I'm not too optimistic about their safe return, with them routinely playing musical cells with me. You can keep all that I'm sending this round. Sun Tzu's is one work I study religiously, along with some other works (like Mao Tse-tung). *Blood In My Eye* – in the first letter – gives George's and his brother's views on applying Che Guevara's foco-military theory in an urban setting, and offers some critical analyses of the character and inherent inefficiencies of the empire's mechanized military forces.[†] I don't totally

---

[*] Sun Tzu was a Chinese general circa 500 BC.

[†] Foco theory centers on the idea of a small group of revolutionaries igniting a revolution, both creating uprising and the conditions that make it possible, rather than waiting until revolutionary conditions otherwise develop.

agree with him in all areas, but in general his proposals are relevant to his time, and are in some regards timeless ...

Were you ever able to study the military writings of Mao, you'd get a sense of Sun Tzu's military philosophy used in action and applied to more modern warfare. Mao is regarded as the foremost guerrilla theorist and strategist of modern times. He was the first to raise guerrilla warfare from a merely tactical level to a strategic level. Most modern works on guerrilla warfare borrow heavily from Mao and study of his battles and campaigns. His mastery of warfare grew out of his study of only the works of Sun Tzu and a couple of epic dramas on Chinese History, viz. *The Romance of Three Kingdoms* and *All Men are Brothers*. He had no exposure to the "classical" works on western warfare.

The Fred Hampton speeches[*] and my pamphlet were sent to you by W. He's in the cell you mentioned. I gave him those materials back when I was last in this unit. He was right above me. He'd mentioned you to me a few times back then – this is before you moved over there into population, and before LK told me about you. W and I talked on some things back then. He expressed that our discussions helped him put some ideas and thoughts he'd had into a more realistic and practical perspective.

You mentioned having "a lot of theoretical-oriented material." What sort do you have? What and whom exactly have you studied thus far?

— — — — —

[*] Fred Hampton joined the Black Panther Party at age 19 and quickly rose to the leadership of its Chicago chapter. He was murdered in his sleep by Chicago police and the FBI during a raid on his apartment on December 4, 1969.

By the way, LK mentioned that you were disturbed about my report on Mau Mau, and his pig conduct. I can understand. As I informed him, I have a fourteen-page letter from Mau Mau in which he admits sending the pigs to toss my cell, and attempts to rationalize his actions and (oddly) criticizes me for plotting to "assassinate" him (?!). The fella imagined that I was going to drill through the cell wall – he was next door to me – and murder him. Don't ask me … he just popped up with this idea out of the blue. While he comes across *sounding* rational and intelligent, he is either a delusional paranoiac, or a pig proxy. If you'd like, I'll send you his letter to read yourself. He's also proven to be a falsifier. He'd told me – back before all this happened – that he was close to a brother named SB, that SB was his "mentor." I've recently found out from SB himself that he doesn't know anything about Mau Mau. Never met him. So I'm inclined to believe that on no level can Mau Mau be trusted.

As far as you and I go (I'm accepting you on account of what I've *heard* about you), we maybe can dialogue productively on things toward both our development. I'm pretty well-studied in various areas, particularly on matters (relevant here) of politics, warfare, economics, history, as well as a little weaponry. The latter I see as valuable for our politicized peers since folks from our social sector generally can't even shoot a handgun straight, much less begin to envision using "real" combat weaponry.

Rashid

2.   To Rashid: I first want to express my categorical and undying opposition to any mode or degree of snitching. Since Mau Mau's cowardly acts engendered this occasion to address such, I felt it necessary to assure you of my position, and hopefully ensure that my actions will be judged by my actions alone. I did not know Mau Mau back in November '03 when I was in B-4 unit with him. He was talking some good shit that I had no reservations about supporting. After that I haven't run into him again. I've asked others about him to gain an understanding of who he really is and when I finally receive word, he turns out to be an agent. From what I hear about you, I have no reason to doubt what you're saying about Mau Mau. He was on some Russian nihilist shit, which he said would make me just as paranoid as him – the reverse role of suspecting someone else while all the time he's suspect. I will assuredly definitely keep him in mind.

Now I know it was W. I didn't know before, 'cause the speeches and pamphlet just came out of the blue. No note, just the materials. Hopefully your knowledge and experience will supplant my development and inexperience regarding W. At the time we were together (me and W) I was essentially a neophyte and was not yet capable of expounding revolutionary theory in its practical day-to-day form. I'm still not there yet. All I felt I could do at that time with W is share the literature I was getting with him, in hopes we could've developed together, and since knowledge is perceptual (I mean I couldn't *make* him read and try to grasp these principles). Hopefully you can help him develop some initiative and willpower to want to know and understand the true terms on which he and all of us exist.

As far as materials, I possess 1. *Capital Vol. 1* (Marx), 2. *Wretched of the Earth* (Fanon), 3. *Seize the Time* (Seale), 4. *Dialectical Materialism*, 5. *Historical Materialism*, 6. *Selected Works* (Marx and Engels). I have other papers, like Nechayev's *Revolutionary Catechism*. I also have some outdoor and hunting literature. I'm familiarizing myself with outdoor survival skills, weaponry, and where can be applied their features and usefulness under certain conditions. Just like you said, most of us can't even shoot a gun straight, while these civilian militias and NRA members are dangerously proficient.

Overall, my knowledge is fragmented. I don't feel that cohesiveness that is necessary. Another thing is I'm not able in this environment to put certain theories into practice, and to be perfectly honest, I'm like, really the only one over here concerned with such. People have expressed that I "don't have to be serious all the time" or lame shit like "you gotta have fun sometimes," or people are just wrapped up in escapism and seeking some kind of entertainment. Everybody seems to be like that, but my frame of mind won't let me not blame myself. I held and still assume the role of political agitator at this time, however stealthily – that little voice reverberating in someone's ear urging them to enlist in the People's Army. You up on Dead Prez?

I've had to regroup too, because I've been told I'm too overbearing, the same almost like George saying he was brow-beating people into accepting, or at least acknowledging, the validity of tactics. What all do you feel will be conducive to my development in furthering the movement? Don't hesitate to enlighten me. I understand and deeply respect your commitment (exemplary, I must say). It's just people's minds like yours that are lacking; that element is missing. A lot of qualities are missing; new standards need to be set. Right now it's cool if you're ignorant, self-destructive, and basically a coward fighting and victimizing the next victim. Holla at me.

Outlaw

3.   To Outlaw: Your position on Mau Mau is well taken. Your merit will be determined by your actions alone. So you've had the opportunity to note his extreme paranoia? Cowardice as I see it. You'll likely find over time that many personalities who profess commitment to revolutionary ideals will turn out to have one foot in the revolutionary camp and the other one in the enemy's. In order to assess true comrades and allies versus actual and potential enemies, it's necessary to examine their class background, viz., their relations (objective and subjective) to the social mode of production.

You might note that Marx perceived the lumpen (our class) to be an unreliable and reactionary class (although many stout and sincere revolutionaries may be found within it). This is due to the values we've internalized from our roles of functioning outside of and many times against the laboring classes. Ours are the values of illegitimate capitalism, and deep down our tendencies – if we don't strive against them unceasingly – will be to fall back into the unprincipled and predatory tendencies of anti-working class and anti-social behaviors and values. In process of mobilizing the social forces for revolution in China, Mao first systematically analyzed each of the Chinese social classes, their relations to the productive forces, and their inherent class tendencies – pro- and counter-revolutionary – and thereby determined who were allies and enemies of the Chinese revolution. He recognized that those classes whose own class interests would be benefited by changes developed along the revolutionary road would support revolution only up to the point that the struggle served and furthered their class interests, e.g. the national bourgeoisie would support China's anti-imperialist national liberation struggle so to defeat imperialist domination, and in its place rise to the top as the national ruling class. The national bourgeoisie opposed being subordinated to outside imperialist countries and their Chinese Comprador bourgeoisie puppets. So he accurately perceived that the national bourgeoisie will support the revolution up to the point that it serves to defeat imperialist and comprador rule; however, the national bourgeoisie will jump ship, and indeed struggle desperately against the revolution (even to the extent of going over to the imperialist camp) at the point when the revolution seeks to effectively put the working masses in power as the new ruling class instead of them. This is in fact what happened throughout the Third World during the various national liberation struggles that swept the globe from the 1950's through 1970's, and is why most of them became only nominally independent yet remained still economically owned, exploited, and dominated by the West.

So one must first recognize the tendencies of certain classes when assessing how far they will go in support of revolution or even in other mundane affairs which threaten their class standing. It must first be remembered that we are products of the very society we wish to change, and have internalized many of the negative values of that society. So we must make a realistic assessment of how totally we're committed to committing "class suicide" (i.e. destroying those subjective anti-working class values which the society has instilled in us), in order to determine our subjective (mental, moral) commitment and revolutionary loyalty.

Much of this might explain Sergei Nechayev's views in his *Revolutionary Catechism* that the genuine revolutionary's attitude towards the society and its members must be undeviatingly pessimistic, destructive, and suspicious. Hence reactionary nihilism. While I certainly understand the basis of Nechayev's pessimism, I, like George, do not agree with this approach. Revolution should be love-inspired – and that love is based in and for the people. In fact, Nechayev's approach runs counter to what is necessary to politically organize a people and mobilize and field a People's Army. This is why a deep and thorough grounding in correct ideology is fundamental for developing revolutionary commitment and loyalty to a democratic socialist class struggle. The revolutionary leadership must thoroughly understand the classes in the society and the class objectives of people's war; otherwise, even were we able to mobilize a fighting force, it would end in losing its revolutionary purpose and ultimately develop what Mao called the "mercenary mentality" and "warlordism," viz. pursuing violence for its own sake instead of to wrest political and economic control out of the hands of a wealthy minority and turning that power over to the broad masses.

The leaders of China's revolution won the revolutionary war in 1949 because they practiced the opposite of nihilism. They fielded and organized such a stout and effective fighting force as the Red Army by winning over the enemy's forces, not by treating them with suspicion and antagonism. The Red Army educated and treated the captured enemy soldiers so well that many of those prisoners who returned to the enemy camp would in turn surrender to the Reds by the battalions, bringing with them entire convoys of weapons vehicles, and supplies. It was on this basis that Mao states in 1936, "We have a claim on the output of the arsenals of London as well as of Hanyan, and what is more, it is to be delivered to us by the enemy's own transport corps. This is the sober truth, not a joke." This was sobering to no one more than the US elites in 1949 when the Red Army marched victoriously into Peking armed exclusively with modern US weaponry and even US-manufactured uniforms, after

90

Amerika had spent billions financing, backing, training, arming, transporting, and supporting Chiang Kai-Shek's national (turned comprador) bourgeoisie Kuomintang army.

Furthermore as George and his brother Jonathan observed, the loyalty of the revolutionary must be judged by their actions, their commitment determined by their continued performance under fire. As for the less conscious, the beginnings of their loyalty may be won by causing them to see and feel the material benefits and need of revolutionary change. Fred Hampton and George emphasized this. This work is the role served by the political cadre, namely providing for the material needs of the people (as the Black Panther Party did with its community survival programs), which the enemy state cannot and will not provide. This is the how-to of building a secure mass base from and within which a People's Army can effectively operate, and from which the movement may draw workers and soldiers.

You have some good theoretical literature on hand. Some of them contradict each other in some respects of revolutionary class analysis, e.g. Fanon (like Mao and the Comintern), promotes the lumpen and peasantry as the main revolutionary forces (because the most alienated and numerous) as opposed to Marx and Engels (and post-Lenin Russia) who focus on the urban proletariat. This is understandable since these thinkers experienced capitalism and imperialism at different stages of development and experience and study of different social conditions.

You seem to have a clear and organized mind, quite capable of comprehending, measuring, and in turn articulating sensory input. From this distance I can't account for your practice just now.

As for warfare, it is as much a discipline requiring intensive study (and practice) – having principles as intricate and variable as any others of the social sciences. So you'd want to give as thorough a study to military history, theory, and practice as you would to social-economic-political theories, etc. On all accounts you're on the right track.

Actually, having investigated the class character of the right-wing militias, survivalists, and military hobbyists you mentioned, I see potential allies in them. Some of them (not speaking of the racist elements, of course) were in empathy with our Black liberation struggles in the 1960's and 70's. They have a serious beef with imperialist monopoly capitalism, but their analysis and understanding of its class nature is confused by muddleheaded conspiracy theories and Christian fundamentalism. They desire a return to bourgeois democracy of decentralized "free market" capitalism (laissez-faire), that decadent form of unregulated capitalistic competition that resulted in the Great Depression and nearly destroyed capitalist domination in the early 1900's. Capitalism has no good forms. But as to these marginal groups, my enemy's enemy is my tactical ally.

Yes, I'm familiar with Dead Prez. As to your work as political agitator, I've heard about your persistent and relentless approach – nothing wrong with a little zeal (smile). But we must remember that persuasion is an art, and we must be sensitive to the character and conditioning of the people we seek to influence. We must be able to relate to them and speak their language in a convincing and non-alienating manner. But ultimately it's our example that makes the most profound impression. As Huey Newton observed, Black folk in Amerika are not a reading people; they tend to learn more readily by example and participation. Fred Hampton emphasized this in those speeches of his you have.

Rashid

4.   To Rashid: For the sake of understanding and revolutionary development, what do you define as practice, outside of study and political agitation, in this prison setting? I have yet to formulate a palpable concept to be applied in my attempts to proselytize individuals. I have noted some recurrent factors that have proven to bottleneck any progress toward revolutionary ideology, the subjective factor being at the focal point of this discussion. For one I concur fully with your analysis and conclusions regarding the domination of "illegitimate capitalist values" and their subsequent ill effects on members of our social class. For Blacks, we have a veritable counter-defense and reference with which to denounce those essentially European "illegitimate capitalist values," namely African history.

This is no attempt to "fight fire with fire," but just a presentation of facts in the form of African customs and traditions. To my understanding and study of African history, terms, ideas, and practices, like honor, loyalty, mutual cooperation, respect for nature, safety and security of the whole village, really altruistic activity is, or at least was, the norm, and most distinguished the characteristics of African peoples according to explorer/imperialists like Cecil Rhodes and David Livingstone. In fact, these same explorers were allowed, and greeted warmly by African peoples owing to the innate benevolence of the African people themselves. I'm not discounting the trinkets that these explorers/imperialists used to manipulate certain Africans; I'm more so relying on the noted custom by Africans and Indians of accommodating and treating guests/travelers as one of the family.

Since most of us Blacks can or at least try to relate with peoples of the African motherland, in my view and I'm sure others', special attention should be given to these elements, along with the organization of those societies to point out the socialist-oriented nature of them and their people. Do you feel like this is an effective approach?

Furthermore, this, I think would be very helpful in establishing some self-worth amongst Blacks and not commodity value. Have you read Fanon's conclusion in *Wretched of the Earth*? Well, in that conclusion he calls on Africans and people of the earth in general to "not follow Europe," "If we want to turn Africa into a new Europe and America into a new Europe, then let us leave the destiny of our countries to Europeans. They will know how to do it better than the most gifted amongst us."

I don't believe in blind faith, e.g. cultural nationalism to the point of hypnosis with such. But Fanon's conclusion of denouncing Europe and essentially exalting Africa in instances where he points out that criticism, communal self-criticism, as he describes it, is an African institution. However, this is something abhorred by Blacks (especially younger ones) today. We detest criticism, feel offended, and react. I understand the causes of this effect (years of emasculation, ignominy, etc.). However, we fail to perceive the real attacks on our manhood inherent in the capitalist system. I've had many discussions with people who will discuss and attempt to understand, but I send a book to 'em and welcome open discussion on the book, any texts, for clarification, and I don't hear no more about it. Or I've had someone tell me "we can't do nothing but talk about the revolution." Well, shit, what would you prefer to talk about, a freak book, what you had on the street, tapes? Essentially frivolous shit. Of course this is interpreted as an aspersion of some sort and draws no intelligent feedback, only aggravation or rationalization. So how or where does the practice come in?

I've heard about your particular form of practice. However, like Seale states in *Seize the Time*, brothers related to "only the gun" and neglected all political consciousness/awareness, and that's something I've taken into deep consideration. Also the mutual relation of both. I've been in a quandary over this subject. I ran into a few people like N (white dude), Lil' Willie, et al., who have expressed their admiration of your, I'll say, initiative. However, when I probed into their level of political awareness/consciousness, they were totally lacking, and at times reticent. In my present position as political agitator, I'm constantly concerned with developing and improving method, and it's on this premise that I seek your input/knowledge/ experience. You as well as George have expressed disagreement with Nechayev's extremism on particular points. But don't you think this extremism is a necessary element? This is the same extremism that motivates suicide bombers and militants in general to make the ultimate sacrifice for the common good; that same sacrifice that this generation has failed to grasp. Or do you think that extremism will surface in the process of liberation? Though I think it to be a prerequisite. Enlighten me.

I've read the letter to your comrade; sorry to say, at this time I haven't accumulated enough perceptual knowledge to make that leap to conceptual knowledge, thereby allowing me to offer any meaningful input. I'm familiar with certain points, only because George, in *Blood In My Eye,* stated things similar.

You will have to teach me the art of persuasion. I've never been effective in persuasion except by force or the threat of force, sometimes acknowledgement on someone else's behalf, but rarely. Somehow after reading your letters I feel like I'm talking to George Jackson himself; honestly it's almost surreal. Dead Prez asked on they video/song "Are you ready to get your hands dirty my nigga?" My reply: Hell yeah! (A reference to their new song, "Hell Yeah.")

I received another pack of texts; do you need them back? There was no note indicating such. There's a note from S enclosed.

Outlaw

CAPITAL

ALL DOING TIME

"At the end of this massive collective struggle, we will uncover our new man, the unpredictable culmination of the revolutionary process. He will be better equipped to wage the real struggle, the permanent struggle after the revolution - the one for new relationships between men." G.J.

" AS FOR LOVE OF MANKIND, THERE HAS BEEN NO
SUCH ALL-EMBRACING LOVE SINCE THE HUMAN RACE
WAS DIVIDED INTO CLASSES. THE RULING CLASSES
HAVE PREACHED UNIVERSAL LOVE, AS DID TOLSTOY.
BUT NO ONE HAS EVER BEEN ABLE TO PRACTICE IT
BECAUSE IT CANNOT BE ATTAINED
IN A CLASS SOCIETY. "

DREAMERS
ARISE

RASHID
7-   7'02

5.   To Outlaw: You asked my definition of "revolutionary practice" within the prison setting, beyond study and agitation. Well, there are several further aspects to practice, a principal one being committed struggle with one's own revolutionary development and growth. This entails a conscious struggle to totally destroy the values which this society continuously instills and reinforces in its members. Our struggle in this regard runs completely against the current of the hostile individualist, nihilist, cynical, cutthroat economics, which produce these same values in and between the people in their political, cultural, and social relations. When we understand that, as Amilcar Cabral recognized,* "the basis of culture is economics" (i.e. how we interact with and relate to one another in our efforts to survive determines what types of social relationships we develop) we then realize at what material level our practice must be focused. In other words, we must change how we interact with one another economically (practicing to be cooperative, instead of competitive and domineering with each other) in order to begin the necessary process of revolutionizing our own values.

This conditioning with the wrong values and the need for conscious reconditioning provides the source and answer to your two quandaries: 1) your question related to the benevolence of historic Afrikan societies, which we Blacks today seem to retain no traces of, while we presume to look for some mental and emotional consolation (against our present colonized conditions) in the fact that we descended from these same rich and noble societies, and 2) how to

— — — — —

* Amilcar Cabral was the Marxist leader of the PAIGC & the national liberation movement in Guinea-Bissau. In January 1973, just months before the victory of the national liberation struggle, Cabral was assassinated with the help of Portuguese agents operating within the PAIGC.

relate to our peers in such a way that they become receptive to and not alienated against and insulted by political education.

On your first issue, it is indeed true that many of our ancestral African cultures were rich in communistic values, which stems from the material nature of their economies, the nature of which promoted values of loyalty, community, and trust. However, the values instilled by today's dominant capitalist economics are those of competition, avarice, and deceit, they having evolved from the domineering paternalistic tribal economies that existed in Western Europe, principally amongst the Germanic (Teutonic) peoples. The latter developed warlike dispositions due to the poverty of their environment, an economy based on hunting and which exalted the role of the predatory hunting man, and a relatively low cultural development, this prompting them to expand beyond their native region and resort to plunder, brutal conquest, and service as mercenary soldiers in other European armies as their economic norm. A principal early victim of these "barbaric hordes" were Slavs (from which the term "slave" derives) – the Slavs being amongst the first peoples systematically colonized, overrun, and "enslaved" by these Nordics. In fact, this historic ethnic animosity between the westerners and eastern Europeans and the historic military "superiority" of the westerners was the condition that the German Nazis played up to mobilize the Germans under national socialist trappings against the other imperialist powers during early last century (WWII). On account of the constant cycle of Nordic attempts to conquer other ethnic Europeans and resistance thereto, warfare became the common trend of European society with entire ethnic groups decimated and empires rising and falling overnight. There was not a day since the BCE that a bloody war was not raging in Europe.

When the Western Europeans began exploring outside of

Europe in the fifteenth century, they were compelled to do so by searches for vast stores of gold and natural wealth, with which to sustain their empires, but principally to pay the mercenary armies that the competing principalities of the time had to hire for their protection and expansion. European monarchs dared not arm large sectors of the populations they plundered under feudalism, and were thus dependent upon "professional" armies that sold their services to the highest bidder, hence the need for vast stores of gold and natural wealth, with which to hire the best armies and increase their own stores of wealth.

Obviously because most of the peoples encountered by these warlike Europeans had not evolved warlike skills, tendencies, and callous disregard for human life on a par with them, the Europeans found relatively easy prey amongst the dispersed tribal peoples they encountered in many of the resource-rich, tropical climates inhabited by people of color, which they discovered, and referred to – then and now – as "paradise." The peoples in these climes had not developed the Europeans' tendencies to be possessive, covetous, or any of the other vices that came with poverty, because in these tropical climates basic necessities were right at hand. However, many of the civilizations, which the Europeans encountered – as in West Africa – were well organized, with formidable militaries and civil systems not easily penetrated by European domination. Becoming dependent upon the abundant wealth and labor of these colored peoples the Europeans – unable to conquer so vast a number and territory of people with force alone – had to invent a sense of material and psychological dependence of those people on trade with them. This they did with their cheap, manufactured trinkets, alcohol (vast quantities of rum produced from the sugarcane harvested by Indian and Afrikan slaves in the Caribbean Islands), and the self-serving, deceitful claim of religious and moral duty to "civilize" the less technologically dependent and advanced peoples. This became the doctrine of the "white man's burden" and whites' "manifest destiny" to "civilize" (i.e. Europeanize) people of color: making all others perceive themselves as innately inferior to white civilization, culture, politics, and religion, and prompting the natives to envy and desire European-style civilization and values. With this program the method of Europeans exploiting the wealth of the colored world went from military domination to cultural domination, from pure plunder to colonialism, and the permanent program of Europeans molding the world in their image with a culture based upon the hostile competitive economics of capitalist trade (from mercantile to laissez faire, to modern monopoly capitalism), and racial/religious/political supremacist indoctrination and oppression. These are the values that have till today been systematically and brutally drilled and instilled in us by our historic Euro-Amerikan oppressors, and it's the tendency of the oppressed to develop the characteristics of their oppressors. It's on these bases that Fanon recognized the need of the colonized Third World people struggling for national socialist independence to not look to Europe as a model for their future social development.

Mao promoted the same principles as Fanon in this regard, which was at the root of the Sino-Soviet conflict. Mao refused to allow the USSR to dictate the course and current of the Chinese revolution, so Khrushchev and his followers reneged on their promise to aid China's industrial development and agricultural modernization, leaving China to suffer massive droughts, floods, and consequent famines without the means in place to provide for the people's needs – costing millions of Chinese lives, losses which Amerika's propaganda machine blamed Mao for.* This is when the Chinese Communist Party closed China off from the west and the USSR, and categorically aligned China to support unconditionally the anti-colonial struggles throughout the Third World, as against both western and Soviet Union domination. In fact, Mao offered Blacks here in Amerika whatever assistance we required to resist our colonization and oppression here. In something of a contest to win Third World influence, the USSR then provided military and marginal technical aid to the Third World independence struggles.

Your second issue obviously connects with the first, being rooted in the fact of our having adopted the values of our historic oppressors. We've been conditioned to interpret criticism as an attack – one who has no desire to change their wrongs doesn't desire

— — — — —

* There was actually no "Great Famine" resulting in tens of millions of Chinese deaths. This story was actually first concocted by the CIA-funded *China Quarterly* journal. It has also been revealed by William Hinton, a noted authority on China's revolutionary years who spent a number of years living, teaching and documenting on the ground developments in China during that time, that no evidence of such a famine exists. That not only did people living during that period in the regions allegedly affected not remember serious starvation much less tens of millions dying, but none of the calamitous events and large social upheavals that attend major famines occurred in China during the claimed famine period. The only "evidence" found of the claimed famine were unsubstantiated census figures and records composed 20 to 30 years after-the-fact when Mao's capitalist rivals came to power after his death and began reversing and maneuvering to discredit China's socialist gains. See: William Hinton, *Through A Glass Darkly: U.S. Views of the Chinese Revolution* (NY: Monthly Review Press, 2006), pp. 241-42.

to have their wrongs exposed. Our enemies have always feared having truth spoken to or against them, because of the tendency to expose the true character of its arrangement to the displeasure of the misled and miseducated masses; while on the other hand, in order to promote the farce of democracy, the established powers must leave the masses with some semblance of available avenues of complaint, thus the courts, legislatures, and dominant media set the very limited framework and orientation within which public criticism of the existing powers may be made. On account of these conditioned perceptions of criticism's being a weapon, and the simultaneous evasions of genuine criticism, we've come to interpret criticism of ourselves as the equivalent of a physical attack (fighting words), therefore, the knee-jerk defensive reactions of people when criticized.

As an example of how deep these tendencies to avoid criticism run, I was engaged with a brother I've previously mentioned in some written exchanges on political issues. The brother is keen in his political-economic analyses, but tends to write essays in very complex language that the common person, unfamiliar with the particular terminologies of certain schools of thought, would catch a migraine trying to understand. I pointed this out to him, and my observation that George tended to do the same thing in *Blood In My Eye*, with the result that most from our class who've read him (as I've observed) comprehend nothing he's building on and become attracted mostly to his mind and militancy (to him as an individual, instead of the principles he stood for), without understanding the basis of either. Lacking comprehension or ideology, they end in becoming deformed imitations of George, with ego as their sole driving force for "struggle," and pursue reactionary, failed violence which serves only to impede rather than advance the real struggle.

The brother's reaction to my criticism was obviously defensive (evasion and retreat), since he abruptly terminated our exchange from his end. And this is a "conscious" brother. (I'm speaking of SB).

Other forms of practice include taking principled stands, sometimes backed by force (when circumstances are favorable, of course) to resist conditions created and perpetuated by the opposition, e.g. racism, suppressing informants, retaliatory counter-violence, etc. I agree with you on the average Black's tendency to glamorize violence while evading political education and discipline, which, like all else is – once again – a product of our conditioning in a society which romanticizes violence and indeed depends upon it for preservation of its economic domination of the world's and its domestic labor forces. We've been, however, so conditioned to perceiving the power structure as militarily invulnerable, that we're fascinated by anyone (particularly those from our own social sectors) who'd dare test the system with arms. All else to them is the same empty talk that has pervaded our history of oppression while changing nothing. We've seen no benefits won by words, but feel at least some temporary vindication for centuries of emasculation in individual acts of daring, sensational – although failed – violence, with the result that failed violence (as with any failed tactic) serves to generate pessimism and the sense of facing an unconquerable foe. Therefore we glamorize those we call "crazy niggas" who in spite of "knowingly" facing "unwinnable odds," defiantly test the pigs with blows or arms. It's not that we Black men don't recognize that the capitalist system is the real attack on our manhood, it's that as a group we choose the relative comfort and safety of evading acknowledging this openly, because – as George observed of his father – it would mean identifying the enemy that's attacking us and being forced to either fight back or admit our cowardice.

You mentioned several of our peers as speaking admirably of my "practice" – what we might call "spectacular violence" against the pigs and their proxies, yet finding those same folks upon investigation to be lacking political consciousness. Fact is, one of those you mentioned is a pig proxy. I've experienced too many times folks using my name to give themselves "credibility" with others (name-dropping). The other fella you mentioned, N, I never really got to know. We were in the unit together only briefly. He'd overheard me on the exercise yard talking politics with others and later sent me a note stating that he'd heard others speak favorably of me. He expressed interest in studying the issues he'd overheard me discussing. I sent him some materials and invited his feedback. Only days later we ended up fighting the pigs (N included) behind their attacking a brother while he was manacled. I haven't seen N since, except in passing.

So, the two you mentioned, for reasons stated, I'd not been in a position, or on terms with to get deeply immersed in political agitation. Now there are others whom I have, whom hopefully you will run across somewhere. Then there are others, like LK for example, who have resisted progressive commitment for reasons of unwillingness to make certain sacrifices. LK is also highly individualistic and has shown something of a complex against feeling to be following anyone else, no matter how correct their position. So, while he will passionately resist the establishment on all levels, he's not been receptive to the necessary Unitarian discipline of burying his own ego. He recently admitted to me that he often agreed with me on many things, but resisted me and those ideals, because he didn't want to admit to my being correct and therefore seem to be following me. He's recently begun to accept and practice self-criticism.

I can't emphasize enough to you here the indispensable

requirement of proselytizing amongst everyone, everywhere, in all that we do, which is why I strive to keep materials on hand to dispense. But the pigs are determined to disrupt such efforts, especially in that they feel I'm organizing and mobilizing our peers objectively and subjectively against them. I also must be highly selective of those whom I invest efforts into. Many are simply not of the mindset or character to adopt Unitarian values at this stage, then there are those who are simply pig agents, agent provocateurs, control freaks, egomaniacs/megalomaniacs, hermaphrorebels (part-time rebel, part-time rat), etc. I've had extensive experience with all kinds, and one must be able to recognize and weed them out. The peculiar conditions within Virginia's prisons allows for all types of twisted egos to promote themselves as principled and committed. Some even fight the pigs and perform in other areas which cause the less experienced to look up to them with respect and admiration. In all regards, while I'm not always successful in influencing our peers politically (many are limited mentally because of complexes created by our historical conditioning and will actually refuse to advance their minds beyond trivialities and sensational entertainment), but I can often reach them in terms of promoting the need and benefits of unity and struggle. Problem is, they are receptive only as long as I remain in their immediate environment; once I'm gone they regress back to their former complacency. The pigs know this, which is why they keep me on the move. I remain involved in so much, especially with outside commitments, rendered forever precarious with these pigs frequently tampering with and vanishing my mail. I don't have time to waste on those who are obviously less-than-committed or prone to vacillating as their whims take them. I have to at least see some potential for commitment before I would invest my limited time in protracted efforts to win them over. This is not to say that my judgments of people's characters and motives have always been accurate, but I feel that I've been proven correct more often than not.

As to Nechayev, perhaps you misunderstand in what area I disagree with his *Catechism*. I do not denounce extremism; in fact I am myself quite an extremist. What I reject is his position that the revolutionary should alienate himself against the masses of people. The revolutionary's duty is foremost a political one, and there is inherent in this the function of winning over the masses as allies, not perceiving, relating to, and treating them as the enemy. As George, Che, and most other revolutionaries of note observed, people's revolution is inspired by love for the people. Without mass support, there can be no mass movement; indeed our struggle is nothing if not mass-oriented. Isolated from and against the people, we become warlords – no better than the enemy.

As for the "how-to" of persuading folks, George exemplifies methods of skilled persuasion and indirect criticism in his *Soledad Brother* letters, especially in those to his parents. He'd use easily recognizable dysfunctional situations and social relationships, and cleverly analogue them to situations and relationships of our own oppression and exploitation to expose the foul nature and motives underlying our conditions. He in the process educates and persuades, through indirect rather than direct criticism, recognizing that the latter would be perceived (as you've experienced in you own efforts) as an insult and attack.

An easy example is one I've sometimes used to challenge my more religiously reactionary relatives' claims that world problems must be resolved with faith and prayer (escapism, shirking responsibility). Instead of criticizing prayer and religious faith and thus almost certainly provoking them to reject anything else I might say, I simply ask if faith and prayer are their heartfelt solutions to changing physical conditions, why then do they work to acquire necessities? If faith and prayer are all that is needed, they should simply pray that each meal, shelter, baby's needs etc., be provided and go on about their merry way trusting in the divine. When they acknowledge the need to activate blood, muscle, and brain to acquire the means to meet these needs, I then ask why they suppose they have a right to sit by idly and wait on prayer and faith to produce those changes needed to correct a dysfunctional social order. That if everyone sat back waiting for someone else to put shelter over their neighbors' heads, we'd all be out in the cold. Likewise, because everyone else is looking to someone else to produce a proper social arrangement, we're all left to suffer.

You're not the first to compare me to George; however, and without presuming to be modest, I find myself wanting in many respects in comparison with him. I hold his example in the highest esteem. At the same time I find errors in some of his approaches and views, which I strive to correct in myself. Above all, I'm struggling forward.

Rashid

> *A brief note was sent to Outlaw in which I asked if he'd ever read* The Prince *by Niccolo Machiavelli* – that it gave some insight into people's psyches and methods of persuasion, although for unsavory reasons. I also sent him some reading materials.*

— — — — —

* Machiavelli has been called the creator of modern political science; he is considered the originator of the idea of a political pragmatism that says, "the end justifies the means." His 1513 book, *The Prince*, is a rumination on the acquisition and uses of power.

6.   To RASHID: Yes, I've read *The Prince*. I have a few quotes in my possession now. Books and authors like *The Prince* and Machiavelli have, for me, provided insight into the character of men and the means with which to manipulate that character. This is what I've observed to be the most recurrent theme in these types of writings. The last book I read in the same category was *The Social Contract* by Jean-Jacques Rousseau.* That's in the library up here. There's another book someone else told me to get called *Letter from a Stoic* by Seneca† (also in the library here). Lately I've shunned those types of materials because of the trickery and deception involved, and this behavior is contrary to the type of society/world I aspire to help create. However, there are some good thoughts in that kind of literature; this brother just sent me a quote from *Letters from a Stoic* – "Rehearse death! To say this is to tell a person to rehearse his freedom, a person who has learned how to die has unlearned how to be a slave. He is above, or at any rate beyond the reach of

— — — — —

* Rousseau was an 18th Century political philosopher whose ideas had a great impact on the French Revolution; *Discourse on the Origin of Inequality* (1755), maintained that every variety of injustice found in human society is an artificial result of the control exercised by defective political and intellectual influences over the healthy natural impulses of otherwise noble savages. The alternative he proposes in *On the Social Contract* (1762) is a civil society voluntarily formed by its citizens and wholly governed by reference to the general will expressed in their unanimous consent to authority.

† Lucius Annaeus Seneca served as a tutor to the young Nero, and when the boy became Roman Emperor in 54 AD he retained Seneca as his advisor.

all political power. What are prisons, wardens, and bars to him? He has an open door. There is but one chain holding us, and that is our love of life. There is no need to cast this love out altogether, but it does need to be lessened somewhat, so that in the event of circumstances ever demanding this, nothing may stand in the way of our being prepared to do at once what we must do at some time or other."

See, shit like that, that way of thinking, has also been expressed by Sun Tzu, Che, the Palestinians! It manifested itself first on the African continent, of course.

I was surprised to see a review of *The Forty-Eight Laws of Power*** in the *OFF!* magazine. My opinion is we're in harmony on the reviewers' opinions. I've seen the Forty-Eight Laws and run across dudes who hold them in high esteem; however, I know that UNITY is a power, but there's no mention of that in the forty-eight. It promotes distrust and baseless suspicion, all in the name of wealth, and we're already at each other's necks over bullshit, so I have a disliking for that way of thinking generally, though I agree with and might even adopt certain points, such as the above in particular.

Making copies of these books is something I need to start doing. I have only hand-written copies of some books. This is something you will have to share with me on getting done: it's harder up here so I've been saving and holding back on buying certain books until I get somewhere where it's a little more breathing room and I can disseminate the literature where it's needed (amongst us). I have not met any people of our kind at any other prisons (here in Virginia) at all; everybody I know that has even entertained these

— — — — —

* By Robert Green, Viking, A Joost Eiffers Production, 1998.

thoughts is up here (in Virginia's supermax prisons). So, it's like Fred Hampton said, we up on the hill when we need to be down in the valley amongst the masses.

Whatever you can send me is needed considering the tasks I'm shouldered with. All those 5%er "ciphers" and crap games I used to be involved in being counterproductive, I plan to be right back in them being productive. I've realized I'm trying to change people's minds, but it's hard – hard! Bringing me to my point on my cellmate S. I challenge his way of thinking, non-antagonistically, but I challenge it. He lacks discipline. I don't watch TV. I treat myself as if I'm still in the hole to some degree. I intentionally abstain from turning my TV on as much as possible. I read. I welcome open discussion.

Just like when you asked to read *Seize the Time* (Bobby Seale), S wasn't finished with it, so we took turns reading aloud the last two hundred-plus pages. I'd drill him on his vocabulary going over words and their meanings, applications, etc, all these exercises to stimulate and further his development. This is what I did myself. But I've been moderate with him really, exploiting his interests or points of interest to clarify things, relate it to him, but there's no willpower on his part to continue on this path. He doesn't have that love of knowledge yet. He lacks that extremism, that do-or-die. He likes the daytime dramas and any other entertainment, self-indulgence, or hedonism, as it's called. This revolutionary ideology appeals to him, but it hasn't become real to him. I haven't alienated him in any manner, but he has books on mysticism, esoteric, occult shit, three (**3**) bibles(!), one Qu'ran. He's soul-searching, trying to escape through escapism and his soul, so this is what I'm dealing with. I have attacked that way of thinking from all angles. It's like now only time will reveal the fruitlessness of his thinking and behavior. He's a good dude, but he's got to start seeing this shit for what it is. He says he does, but I beg to differ.

See, I'm looking at it from how I would be in his shoes too (time-wise); there's no way I could ever be complacent or fooled or anything less than vigilantly looking for my practical-tactical way out. Like George said, there are only two types of men that come out of these places, the broken and the rebels. I'm a rebel to the core. A lot of the cats are broken, whether they admit it or not. They don't even entertain the thought of freedom. So I'm trying to get into their minds, 'cause they're (we're) not thinking correctly and if that isn't it, it must be cowardice. Honestly, I don't think it will become real until traumatic events take place in people's lives, until they are able to say, "Damn, did you see that?" or, "Did you hear about this?" "I know him." They're (we're) still in awe. I'm up against a power, a juggernaut. This is no time to be weak, especially mentally. The enemy is training; we're dancing, singing, laughing. Think about all the people that died at clubs and parties and dances. Dead Prez. Them's my NIGGAZ! Them niggaz is saying what nobody else is saying in the rap game. They whole tape is revolutionary. Not half-and-half or one fourth. The whole shit.

But I envision the prison yard to be the training camp, mentally and physically; it's some soldierz here. Niggaz got to seize the time, though. You are a talented individual (no ego-stroking intended); I seen all the drawings and treatises; I'm like, damn! Holla at me! I thought you was gone.

Outlaw

7.   To OUTLAW: Nah, they haven't moved me again – yet. I'm with you on the works of political chicanery – I've studied them more so for perspective on the origins and development of the organized fascistic versus communist schools of thought. These works provide invaluable insight into understanding political deception and the subjective (mental and emotional) factor that allows the common people to fall victim to them.

As for our peers' seeming lack of receptiveness to the revolutionary ideal – as expressed by George, Sun Tzu and many practical thinkers, people respond positively to such when they've been placed into positions of seeing a chance of success. Sun Tzu emphasizes that the leader (military commander) is the ultimate architect of his army's morale. If he leads them into battles and campaigns, which they can and do win, they will have a high morale and confidence in the struggle; if he leads them into repeated losses, their initiative will flag and fail. Sun Tzu recognized that an army's morale, indeed, its success in battle, turns on the commander's skill. Likewise, Mao and George recognized that when revolution fails, when the struggle is defeated, it's the fault of the vanguard, i.e. the political and military leadership.

This has been our problem – African descendants here in Amerika. We've had umpteen leaders, but none – as George observed – knew how nor were prepared to fight. So each time the enemy establishment moved in with guns and infiltration schemes to smash these leading elements, the result was to reinforce in the masses' minds the belief that we can't win – loss of morale, pessimism. This is the faithlessness you see in our peers. They've been conditioned to feel we can't win, so they just flow with the current and avoid confronting the reality of our conditions. You mentioned the apparent need to shock our peers into recognizing the need to resist. George prescribed much the same – using the enemy's repression as a catalyst for provoking mass resistance. He proposed this – as did Che – as a tactic, viz., the military vanguard's attacking the enemy and provoking it to bring repression down on the masses. You can learn quite a bit by watching the footage on the Iraqi occupational war. TV can have its uses.

Let me illustrate something for you. Back in 1993 at Greensville [prison], the pigs were out of control. When I showed up, they were literally beating people down at will – breaking bones and such – putting shit (literally) in meal trays, and they had a clique of inmate lackeys (clowns with reps for butchering folks) whom they were using to intimidate and attack dudes they disliked. Back then I was deemed a violent psychopath by the pigs, based upon my reacting in kind to their own violence and abuse ... members of a victim class ain't supposed to fight back. Anyway, I set it off on them. Started hitting them up; came out of the cuffs and butchered one of their trustee hitmen. I told everyone in the unit to inform me if any pig mistreated them; when they did I retaliated. I ended with everyone from known rats to ass-kissing pig sycophants pulling with me against the pigs. It broke the whole situation up. Shit got so hectic for them that the internal affairs unit stepped in to try and neutralize the situation by prosecuting numerous pigs. They were terrified by the united and counter-violent responses that were spinning out of their control and therefore came with the cop-out measure of "doing their job," by using the system to pretend to correct itself. I mention this because, by example and participation I was able to mobilize the most uncommitted sections of our body to take up violent resistance and turned even the pigs' own allies against them.

The cops would bring boxes of cigarettes onto our tier to distribute, give us the telephone all day, extra meal trays, etc, trying to proposition me to contain the cats in the unit. People react when they see that resistance is possible, and their morale and desire to participate in resistance reach unforeseen heights when they see the supposedly invulnerable pigs vacillating and trying to cop-out. As the old cliché goes, terrorism works only as long as the victims believe it can continue indefinitely, i.e. only as long as they feel powerless to stop it. I didn't come at those cats with politics or ideology. I gave them an example of organized resistance – the rest followed.

You mentioned my art – I enclose some copies you can have.

Rashid

8.   To RASHID: Look, I agree with your tactics used at Greensville; it couldn't have been carried out more effectively, especially with the effects of "bloodshed." However, the conditions (objective) have changed dramatically. I mean, specifically Red Onion and Wallens Ridge [supermax] prisons, 85% laws didn't exist back then. And these places and laws have a deep psychological and physical impact on our peers today. For one thing they can't get past the veneer of privileges/incentives/pacifiers to see the benefits of organized, conscious activity. Two, the effects of separation/individualism are so deeply ingrained in our peers' minds that it's not "cool" to help the next man, or espouse his cause, knowing he's being fucked over, and they resist the notion that it could happen to them by conforming and ignoring the threat. My own case in point, or take another

example: last week a brother was in the chow hall and the sergeant was rushing them all, him in particular, to "hurry up and eat" one of those so-called double portion trays they serve on the weekends.* The dude expressed that he wasn't being allowed enough time to eat, so the cops locked him up.

Now, the rest of the prisoners afterwards "blamed the victim," the dude who was locked up. They said he knew better (picture that, he knew better), and he was stupid for having not just done what the cops said. So it's now perceived that those who stand up are fools; however, the real fools came back to the pod, 'cause the pigs have been rushing everybody. Then for some reason, dudes have foresight into the consequences of their activity, and they see in that activity and consequence, futile, fruitless, senseless results. So that tells me we need to escalate our activity in the area of establishing our own "prestige," our own "shock and awe." But my attention has been on external assistance. This is future-focused of course, and I'm being practical – national liberation, "pardons" of prisoners won't be realized within the confines of the gulags at this present time of our low morale. Individual acts aren't a remedy. Like someone expressed in the *OFF!* magazine: *are you people on the street that scared?*

In here one of Malcolm X's statements is applicable. He was saying, when everyone is passive (the majority), then the one who stands up looks like a problem or irrational, and his actions are deemed to be just that, 'cause everybody else is saying nothing. That's the situation we're in. My primary targets for enlistment have been the

— — — — —

* In Virginia's supermaxes, prisoners receive only two meals on weekends and holidays, with portions increased to supposedly equal the normal three daily meals

short-timers. They have the chance to implement things in the area of result-oriented actions. I feel frustrated by my own self being neutralized, but in the pursuit of raising consciousness I keep that influence ever-present and if I see the time to seize the time, it's seized.

A lot of my adverse feelings are toward us – I blame us for our failure to act, to unite, to learn, to grow. We have problems, character deficiencies, mental glitches that amount to observationism, not thinking long-term about our futures. I use history to validate my points. My uncles, father, big cousins' generation, hustled, pimped, robbed, in and out of prison, street lifestyle, street mentality. They did what we (my generation) are doing. However, these people are older now, with no security; they're crackheads, stuck in youth, doing life. In other words they failed in their attempts to live underground, or outside of society, which is the path so many of us have taken and continue to take. In the process, our children are neglected, deprived of father figures, and the children grow up to suffer like their predecessors, and the cycle continues. Their children go through the same things, like me and my peers, the majority got kids, but they're in here, or dead, or living the street life, so their children are out there in the world missing that father figure, being influenced and drawn towards the glitz and glamour of the streets, and it's all false values and definitions of what a man is. This is a cycle.

My mother used to say, and every parent from our social sector has said it, "I don't want my child to go through what I went through." However, the reality is we have. We are going through the same things, because the circumstances that produced us, conditioned us, have not changed. You are already aware, but the majority, our peers, are sadly not. Individual accomplishments and achievements in the business world won't affect the masses, but we don't understand this yet. Like you were saying about the occasional "crazy nigga" doing shit to avenge injustice even though he knows that failure is imminent, his actions are destined for failure. Well, the same concept to a degree applies to the "street game." People tell us beforehand "ain't nobody retired from the game." Failure is implicit in that statement; however, we jump straight in the game because of the short-term pleasure, and we are desperate due to our socio-economic status. So could it possibly be that the occasional "crazy niggas" is not crazy at all; it's the majority of us that's crazy.

I have some notes from the *Revolutionary Party* (Worker's) by James Cannon,[*] and in those notes he says that "the party is not to be a refuge for sad and poor souls," and I agree. I'm not a psychiatrist, or counselor; in some instances I might be, but I have an intolerance for grown men being and acting as anything less than grown men. I'm not here to hold nobody's hand and console them – I say that 'cause of our culture (sub-?) of being gangsta, thuggish, the "tough guy" and the omnipresent "real nigga." I mean, all just said we should be more than ready to face **this reality**. A rare quote from 2-Pac: "Now if we wanna live the thug life and the gangsta life and all of that, okay, so stop being cowards and let's have a revolution. But we don't wanna do that, dudes just wanna live a character. They wanna be cartoons, but if they really wanted to do something, if they was that tough alright, let's start our own country, let's start a revolution, let's get out of here, let's do something."

— — — — —

* James Patrick Cannon (1890–1974) was an Amerikan Communist and Trotskyist leader. Cannon was the founding leader of the Socialist Workers Party.

I appreciate the art, 4-sho! Art imitates life, and your drawings are a correct reflection of what has been done and what needs to still be done.

Do you understand *Dialectical-Historical Materialism* in its entirety? I myself have read it (them) a few times, but I've failed to grasp its practical application in certain areas. These papers* helped elucidate some laws, but I'm still lacking. I agree with the New Afrikan point about focusing on our own internal flaws; I adamantly agree. Malcolm did it. George did it. 2-Pac did it. Garvey did it. We are our own worst enemy right now.

On the Iraq war, they don't show the actual combat – they might flash militants training, but they offer very little insight on military tactics and strategy. The results of casualties expose the tactics and strategies used by militants, and George's assessment and theory of urban warfare has proven correct. The ten-to-one ratio seems right. The U$ has managed to dominate 'cause of their dominant technology, but ground-wise, they have proven most vulnerable. The militants have also the requisites 1) continuous supply of arms, 2) friendly border sanctuaries, and 3) popular support. The last one accentuating George's view of them not knowing who's who.

Outlaw

— — — — —

* *Vita Wa Watu* – a New Afrikan theoretic journal published by Spear and Shield of Chicago, IL.

9.   To Outlaw: This isn't a full reply to your last missive. It's running late, and I wanted to get the enclosed items over before the taxi pulls a late-day vanishing act. I disagree with your conclusions concerning conditions (subjective) amongst us in the present place/time. I don't disagree on our pervasive mindset, but I do disagree that we are beyond mobilizing. I need give you but a brief reference. Recall that N and other cats fought the pigs with me (six total) last year. Most of them were total noncommittal types (in the sense of attacking the pigs). Again it only requires the skill of being able to **properly** appeal to people to mobilize them to resist. There's hope. The cycle can be broken. Yes, I understand the evolutionary and polar concepts behind dialectic materialism. Will elaborate later – want of time, or will perhaps send you more clearly expressed analyses of the concepts. If one understands the principles of warfare, much can be gleaned from the small amount of war footage offered on TV/radio. What's happening in Iraq militarily is a textbook case of what George expounded.

Rashid

My next letter to Outlaw was discussing an informant in my unit having sent the pigs to shake me down and their confiscating various items from me during the search.

10.   To RASHID: The whole situation is puzzling. The whole prison system has been and is permeated with rat-informants. Everything you described about that rat I would have recognized off top who it was without the slightest mention of his name. And as for W, I thought maybe he'd learned something from bitter experience. As George said, his and our peers' character deficiencies and overall self-assigned ignorance only reinforce and buttress my conviction in "shock therapy" as a means to liberation. Where are the she-comrades? Have you established any bonds in that area? I'll return this last book you lent[*] on Friday. I need to know where I can get this book. Elaborate on productive and nonproductive sectors of society. This book is detailed; I like how it provides detailed analyses of capitalism's economic institutions and functions in the whole capitalist society, something I wasn't and haven't been able to identify and elaborate on. Give me some concrete examples of productive and nonproductive classes.

Outlaw

------

[*]   *The Political Economy of Capitalism.*

11.   To Outlaw: I wouldn't say that this system's infestation with vermin (rats and moles) is puzzling – in fact, it's quite understandable. In one of your recent letters, you addressed the subjective conditions that make it seem improbable that our peers could be mobilized against the pigs – it's those very conditions and their demoralizing effects that prompt cats to side with them.

Yes, I know a few conscious wimyn. Not all are ideologically advanced, but they're for the most part progressive/ing. I'm speaking of those with whom I correspond.

As for your inquiry on productive versus nonproductive sectors of society: producers are those who perform socially necessary labor, i.e. those whose labor involves extracting, developing, and organizing basic necessities: food, clothing, shelter, and also those inside-the-factory setups who assemble material objects for social consumption. Essentially, they are the manual laborers, the proletariat and peasants. Nonproductive workers are those who perform in the service trades: for example, banking, education, administrative, insurance, secretarial, hotels, entertainment, government, etc. Basically, this category is those referred to as paper-pushers; they do not provide socially necessary labor that relates directly to social needs. These are the petty bourgeois, or middle class.

As for the class that owns the means of production (capital – that is, land, factories, machinery, equipment, etc.), and force the masses to sell their productive and nonproductive labor to them for a wage, while itself doing no work, this is the bourgeoisie. And the lumpenproletariat – that would be our class: consists of the beggars, hustlers, pimps, drug dealers, addicts, street thieves, essentially the "dregs of society." This class tends to overlap with the proletariat since many within it drift in and out of wage labor, and are concentrated around or within enclaves of the urban centers. This is a basic categorization of the classes in relation to social production: bourgeois, proletariat, petty bourgeois, peasant, lumpen. Of course, the bourgeois are nonproducers also.

I have no idea where you might find this book. As you might have noted, it was published in the former Soviet Union. A comrade got it for me. I had it photocopied just so I could make more copies to circulate relatively conveniently, but I have now to deal with this idiot counselor who won't copy anything. At some point, however, I should be able to get you a copy made. I was just able to exchange some books from my stored property. I got a couple with you in mind. One is *Contemporary Capitalism and Marxist Economics*, which gives a study of relatively modern Western European capitalist economics under Marx's political economic theory. Another is *The Essential Works of Lenin*, which contains several of Lenin's "most important" essays, one of which I recall you saying you have, viz., "What is to be Done?" Another is a biography of Mao and some others. Which do you prefer to read first?

Rashid

12.   To RASHID: Send me *Contemporary Capitalism and Marxist Economics*. Answer this: how do I simplify the process of exploitation, explain it in layman's terms, and relate it to modern times? I have presented the division between necessary and surplus labor; however, I was more so centered around the competition between individual enterprises and how that contributes to reduction in personnel. I haven't been able to fully grasp the process of exploitation; it's still abstract to me. I can't relate to it now.

Outlaw

13.   To OUTLAW: As for an explanation of capitalism's exploitative character in layman's terms, George gives a good one in *Soledad Brother* – see his letter of April 17, 1970. He relates modern capitalist exploitation to the exploitation of chattel slavery. In the past chattel slave system, the enslaver profits from the free labor of the slaves through their working land owned and controlled by the "owner." In order to keep the slaves in good working order so they could continue to produce for the "owner," he had to provide them with the necessities of survival and personal maintenance, namely food, clothing, shelter, medical care, and recreation/entertainment (the latter serving a placatory and diversionary purpose). Essentially, because of his/her forced ties to the land and whims of the "owner" for survival, and kept in check by slave patrols manned by poor whites (the plantation system's police), the slave had no real freedom of movement. In a near-identical context, the capitalist today requires the labor of the worker to produce or serve in his production and

service industries in order to turn his profits. But instead of directly providing for the maintenance needs of the worker, the capitalist pays the worker a wage, with which the worker must purchase his own subsistence needs and entertainment. The wage doesn't compensate the worker for the actual value of the goods and services his labor produces (the "boss" keeps that as "profits"), but only enough in wages to temporarily provide for basic needs to keep the worker functional and dependent on continued service to the capitalist boss for the continuing wage. Like the chattel slave the wage worker (wage slave) is tied by dependency (on her wage) to the capitalist's enterprise. The modern specialized police/administrative system operates to keep the system running smoothly and the workers from expropriating the "owners."

If the wage slave refuses to work, s/he, unlike the chattel slave, is free … to starve, to suffer exposure to the elements, and to go without meaningful medical care. If the chattel slave refused to work, s/he might be brutalized a bit, but would still be provided for, if for no other purpose than to keep fit for resale to some other "owner." For the capitalist there is always a large pool of surplus workers to choose from to replace present workers, and because the wage slave is not his own "property," like the chattel slave was to the "owner" of his day, the capitalist does not care whether the wage slave is fit or not, as long as the work is done; if the worker becomes stubborn or unable to perform, s/he's replaced with another.

Like any slave, the modern wage worker must tie his/her whole personal life to – indeed, s/he must completely organize his/her life around – the job. S/he has no freedom, not even to spend quality time with his/her own family. There is no "freedom" or means to travel freely, to enjoy life. Only the capitalist (bourgeoisie) enjoys this luxury, and at the expense of the workers. No matter what the wage slave's **"standard of living"** may be in theory, his/her actual **"quality of life"** is empty of meaning. The owners of the economy understand this, which is why there is such a vast entertainment infrastructure aimed at appeasing and diverting the working classes from a life empty of any quality and meaning whatsoever. The entertainment thus functions to romanticize the capitalist class's values and lifestyle and to recreate a life that capitalism robs its working classes of – "bread and circuses." And because the capitalists are unwilling and unable to provide employment for all of the working masses lest they lose all profits, the capitalist system itself produces the criminal and lumpen class that is forced to live outside the system, to survive and cope by "illegitimate" means. Hope this will answer your question.

Rashid

14.   To RASHID: This book is real good. I particularly like the chapter on applying Marxist theory, how it defines, identifies specific functions of capitalistic enterprises, the state intervention, the international scene; that's the insight for me. I never considered certain activities to be nonproductive. I thought all "created value." These the type of books that help me get past the phenomenon and discover the essence, to speak in materialist terms. I wanted another book along the same lines, but Mao I wouldn't mind checking out ...

I thought the taxi was going your way. They deferred the trip for right now.

Send me some Lenin this time. In retrospect I realize that I've been mostly concerned with ideology in the strict sense of ideas. I need something that's gonna help me apply that ideology, or maybe I just need to keep studying regardless of what. I enjoyed that catalogue, 4-real.

Out of what you've been sending me between the New Afrikan People's Organization, MIM [Maoist International Movement], and the other organization [African People's Socialist Party], which do you subscribe to? The purpose of that question is to get your opinion on nationalism. This is like a double-edged sword. I like each of the above's ideology and program for different reasons, but I favor New Afrikan more.

What is your take on 5%er ideology and Dead Prez's ideology? They've fused the 5% with revolutionary theory. "Resurrecting the true and living back to power, devils getting devoured, niggaz heard the god holla." I'm waiting on they two joints called "Revolutionary but Gangsta" and "Get Free or Die Trying." They are only on CD, but some place says they can get it on cassette.* I stayed up all night to finish this book; however, I still didn't finish until about 9:00 AM. I had to learn and read at the same time, but I love the challenge. Alright bro.

Outlaw

——— ——— ——— ——— ———

* Virginia supermaxes do not allow prisoners CD players, only cassette players.

15.   To OUTLAW: As for Dead Prez and their consolidation of the 5% with revolutionary socialist theory, it's a step in the right direction, but as an end in itself (viz., 5% socialism), it sounds little different than Hitler's Germanic National Socialism – simply another variety of fascism. I'm not partial to this Black superior/white inferior thing. I've often had to bring many 5%ers to second-guess their school of thought as counterproductive and having no practical relation to the real world. I'll leave it at that without going into a more in-depth critique of the 5% ideology, unless you invite it, of course. But if Dead Prez is setting something of a groundwork for evolving the young brothers toward revolutionary nationalist ideology, then that's clearly progressive and I embrace it. But if the object is to bring about a struggle based on 5%er ideology, I'm not interested and it won't go far anyway. Produce only a race war at best; we'd be clearly at a tactical, strategic, and logistical disadvantage in any such fight, and the capitalists would turn it to their own benefit.

Rashid

16.   To RASHID: I admire your insight and eloquence; therefore, I'm going to invite that dreaded critique of the 5%, if it doesn't bother you or take away from your time. We're still being productive; I think it's healthy if you will, that we renounce the 5% ideology, being that you and I recognize the whole concept as inane and impractical. Considering the fact that a large percentage of our peers subscribe to the 5% and are neutralized or reactionary/racist as a result, and therefore alien to revolutionary theory and practice, in

that state of mind they can only be a detriment to themselves and us (the People's Army and New Afrika). Actually you can help me go at that ideology from an effective angle without me being my erstwhile alienating self. I've always focused on the twelve jewels and the content of that. Particularly Freedom, Justice, and Equality, and point out to an individual that we possess neither of those three things, and that making a declaration that we're gods and earths is not going to change that fact and win us Freedom, Justice, and Equality. Then I end up, due to an external impetus, going into a tirade about the "white man" having full and free reign over the quality of all our lives and destinies. Then I've had these egomaniacs (certain ones) tell me how the prison lets them get their newsletters with the 5% emblem, that they're recognized as an official organization, blah, blah, blah. It's a fetish, if you ask me, at worst, or a failed attempt to identify ourselves independently of Euro-Amerika, at best. Plus there are other contradictions inherent in their ideology (though it's not really an ideology in the conventional sense). There's no responsibility, no purpose, no direction.

My theory is, to use one of their most beloved references, that the Egyptians seeing that they were able to rise above their animal instincts, giving them domain over the land (as expressed through the meaning behind the Sphinx) as men, they then referred to themselves as gods. And it was Alexander the Great who recognized that he himself was a man and possessed the same abilities as those who referred to themselves as gods. He therefore proceeded to assert his "manhood" by invading Egypt and seized the throne as one of the "gods" who ruled over Egypt. I think the term god itself was a matter of status and rank in those ancient times. Then I point out how the Egyptians were proficient at math and science and government, reflecting their profound knowledge of the world around them; 'cause individuals, 5% and the like, have this tendency to mystify shit and gawk at all this esoteric shit. That goes back to the function of government and how government from day one [beginning with priestcraft] became a means to manipulate and exploit the masses. 5%ers don't want to grasp it.

But when we jump on everything else or things that have no long-term benefits to our future security, I mean it's like we're suffering from an extreme case of myopia. It's my fault for real. I gotta get better at presentation and practical application of revolutionary ideology, but still an individual got to be willing, damn, at least willing to open they mind and stop letting the TV and magazines and other trivial things and people think for us. I'm very pessimistic/conscious. I put these two together because I see the dire situation. I see our plight, that's what I'm concerned with (to explain the former) and I'll do whatever is necessary, by any means necessary to change that (to explain the latter). You know, I used to be reluctant, very reluctant, to use the word *revolution*. I didn't feel I was worthy to be identified with such, and our peers generally don't know the true meaning of revolution and what it entails. But now that I've developed to a degree, I think I should use it and put it in its proper context to clarify things and give cats exposure to it. Some familiarity because I somewhat believe "niggaz fear what they don't understand."

Oh yeah. Overall Dead Prez is progressive. I say that because they are trying to mobilize us on all fronts – 5%, gangs, women – and they are socialists fighting for the self-determination of all Afrikans.

Have you ever read the I-Ching?* Dead Prez always refers to it, and I bought this pocket-sized book, but it did nothing for me. It doesn't provide any meaningful insights. It's a fortune book, or an oracle, but it does emphasize practical knowledge. Yes, but I look forward to your discourse on the 5% ideology. Not just to renounce it but I was thinking about it being in the area of "reductio ad absurdum." I see what you were saying about a person's class background and the class distinctions overall. I've learned and am still learning a lot since I've come into contact with you – I salute you!

Something else ... I have an immediate problem. Our peer, my cell partner, all day he watches TV, sleeps, eats. It's pathetic to me. The TV, his is out right now, and he can use mine, except my concern is the TV is propaganda, a brainwashing machine, and I feel like 'cause it's my TV I'm guilty for his continuous state of stagnation. I don't want to seem hostile or alienating, but I will be that way if I see that's likely the only way someone will take what I'm saying seriously. I'm fighting against ignorance as well, and it's like dude will listen and agree, yet at the same time he could have just as well ignored everything I said, 'cause the daytime drama is coming on, and he's making no attempt to educate himself. It's like he's just deadweight; he's just rotting and I could be tacitly agreeing with his self-destruction by allowing him to use my TV. It's not like I would

— — — — —

* The I-Ching is the oldest of the Chinese classic texts. A Symbol system designed to identify order in what seem like chance events, it describes a system of ancient cosmology and philosophy that is at the heart of Chinese cultural beliefs. The philosophy centers on the ideas of *the dynamic balance of opposites, the evolution of events as a process,* and *acceptance of the inevitability of change.*

turn the TV around and watch it myself – I won't cut it on at all! This is a pressing issue for me, 'cause I know I will encounter these types numerous times within the time I have left, and I don't feel like I'm being dogmatic or impatient – maybe impatient.

Outlaw

17.   To OUTLAW: Quick reply to a few previous issues … About my choice between the politics of New Afrika, MIM, etc., I'm more favorable to New Afrika. The politics of the Left Wing are sound, but lack the necessary component – thinkers and organizers to practically enforce the territorial demands and sovereignty, which would obviously call for a protracted struggle. We Blacks in Amerika are among the few remaining colonized people (along with the Palestinians, Basque, Irish, and a few others) whose struggles have not won us some territory and political sovereignty. True, most of those Third World movements that did win territory and "independence" from direct European and Amerikan colonization and domination ended up becoming imperialist lackeys and simply converted the newly "liberated" nations into neo-colonies still ruled by the same forces but only with token native faces at the head of the government instead of white faces. But we Blacks in Amerika never cleared that first hurdle of acquiring our own territory. In most respects New Afrikan People's Organization chairman Chokwe Lumumba and I see eye-to-eye. NAPO's mass work could improve, though.

As for MIM, given the times, their sort of agitation and methods seems impotent. This mere proselytizing in a vacuum is a long-proven failed tactic in pursuit of winning mass support or at least neutrality for the extremes of struggle. They analyze the Black Panther Party's destruction without an understanding of the BPP's failure being in its not mobilizing an armed mass base and using counterintelligence measures against enemy disruption. They see in the BPP's destruction an indication that no independent Black revolutionary political party can ever hope to operate aboveground in the US at all, which is not true to my thinking. Yeah, MIM has some good analyses – like most petty-bourgeoisie radicals (I'm almost positive they're middle-class intellectuals), but no clear functional solutions, nationalist or otherwise. They have no social service programs through which to materially reach the broad masses, showing them the need for struggle and giving them something to fight for. In effect, they do little more than pass pamphlets and conduct a lot of critical dialogue (mere verbal agitation) railing against capitalism, imperialism, gender oppression, etc., yet doing nothing by way of getting their hands dirty with mass-based projects (organizing the people around their needs and meeting those needs.)

MIM then distorts George's military theory as one promoting armed struggle without a mass-based political movement; criticizing his theory as all military and no politics. [I do agree that following the successful revolution that used Che Guevara's foco theory in Cuba, the foco approach of small guerrilla units operating without a mass base and liberated areas has proven catastrophic in other places.] But George, who promoted a variant of urban-based focos, emphasized that a principal purpose of revolutionary armed struggle is to not only destroy the enemy's forces, but to protect the political work and workers, and that armed struggle must take place within the matrix of a mass-based movement – that politics takes primacy.

In reality, MIM promotes this idea of a bloodless revolution, taking this "let's wait" line; "if we organize for a fight, people will only get killed." Well, that's what happens in wars, especially in revolutionary wars. Mao didn't talk procrastination. In fact, he stated that "a revolution does not march in a straight line; it wanders where it can, retreats before superior forces, advances whenever it has room to advance, and is possessed of enormous patience." Revolution to Mao was nothing short of war where the movement assumes the offensive not employing the Fabianist* method of sitting about passively criticizing the enemy. "A revolution or a revolutionary war is on the offensive, yet it has its defense and retreat. To defend in order to attack, to retreat in order to advance, to take a flanking position in order to take a frontal position, and to follow a corkscrew path in order to go directly to the objective … " This all implies constantly maneuvering to create advantageous conditions for taking the offensive. As he emphasized, "passivity is fatal to us; our goal is to make the enemy passive."

When Mao and Zhu Deh set out at the head of the Red Army in its 1927 ascent into the mountains to establish their first base area, after suffering catastrophic losses at the hands of the Kuomintang, their forces consisted of a few thousand half-starved, lice-ridden men and wimyn, who bore not even a remote resemblance to a

— — — — —

* Founded in 1884 by Beatrice and Sydney Webb, George Bernard Shaw and H.G. Wells as a group promoting non-Marxist evolutionary socialism, the Fabian Society constitutes a faction within the British Labour Party.

fighting force. They were armed with more farming tools than firearms. Yet they went on to succeed in a revolutionary war, then in little more than two decades later took power in the largest nation on the planet. And only a year after taking power, China fought the day's most advanced and powerful militaries (the United States and United Nations) to a truce in Korea. The conditions that MIM says are necessary – i.e. US military overextension, etc. – are present right now, yet they're still just talking. They don't seem to be working to build a broad-based mass movement. Mao emphasized that a movement does not wait passively for the enemy to become weak and helpless, it must **make** the enemy that way itself, the revolutionary workers must always keep the initiative. A lot of what MIM seems to claim grows out of Maoist philosophy appears contrary to his tactical prescriptions. Again, I tend to agree that applying Che's foco theory in a vacuum, without a political movement based within the masses, is a flawed approach to revolutionary struggle, but George did not promote that.

Take what Hamas has accomplished in Gaza against the Israeli occupation there. Their guerrilla underground (al-Qassam Brigade) has stopped Israel's settlement activities in their tracks, and has both the US and Israel talking seriously about pulling out of Gaza altogether, or trying to bring Hamas to the negotiating table by recognizing it as a "legitimate" political party instead of stigmatizing it as being an "illegitimate" "terrorist organization." (Never mind that as part of the strategy of driving Palestinian people off the illegally occupied land that the racist Zionists are daily stealing from them, Palestinian children are officially deemed legitimate military targets.) They can't control or neutralize Hamas, and Israel has much the same military technology and hardware as Amerika. I've done some study of Hamas, its methods of recruitment, its organization and compartmentalization of guerrilla cells, its system of logistics, and especially its aboveground political work, which has won it broad appeal and support across the masses of Palestinians in Gaza, such as setting up and operating free health clinics, schools, clothing and food services, youth recreational facilities, etc. As for their guerrillas, the militants' identities are so well concealed that even their own families don't know of their membership in al-Qassam unless/until they're killed, at which point Hamas conducts a gala funeral for the martyr and provides monetary stipends to the family. The children emulate Hamas, many wearing homemade green Hamas banners. They've won such a broad consensus of mass support that now that Israel's begun openly targeting Hamas' political leadership with assassinations, the people shield them, taking them into their homes to protect them – frustrating Israel's ability to easily locate and target the leaders. Gaza is only 144 square miles in area; the US is 4 million square miles.

Time is running tight for me. I'll finish this off and respond to your query on Dead Prez and the merging of the 5% with revolutionary socialism at a later date. Plus my fingers are a bit sore, dig? …

Rashid

18.   To Outlaw: I'm sending you seven new pieces of literature you can have. I was able to run into one of the counselors today whom I could get to copy some publications for me. Enclosed are:

1. *The Roots of the New Afrikan Independence Movement,* by NAPO Chairman Chokwe Lumumba.
2. *The Political Thought of Comrade George Jackson,* by Eric Mann
3. *Message to the Black Movement*
4. *The Political Economy of Capitalism*
5. *Revolution in Central America,* by Daniel Fogel (this is the best study and analysis I've read on the revolutionary struggles in Central America during the 1950's through the 80's. It stops just short of the period when the US openly invaded Central America [Nicaragua] and when the Contra scandal was in full bloom in efforts to crush the struggles there).
6. *On the Black Liberation Army,* by Jalil Muntaqim
7. Another copy of *Blood In My Eye*

I've been tied up in some extensive writing and got sidelined from completing my reply to your last letter. I should get back to you today or tomorrow.

See, I can come through sometimes too, bro!

Rashid

19.   To RASHID: You sho' nuff came through. I got all seven pieces of literature. This is a very brief kite. I lost track of time, somewhat. I'll be at you tomorrow. I agree wit' you on your points in the kite. The Lenin is enclosed.

Outlaw

20.   To Rashid: There's a piece in that last lengthy letter I sent detailing interpersonal issues concerning me and my cellmate, and us Black men in general. I'm not saying that this problem is solved, but through me "initiating" open discussion, questioning his way of thinking, and a few other things, I've discovered a few things about us, and how to go about organizing us. I presented that to you because I respect and admire your organizational skills, judgment, and character, so it's only natural for me to look to you for solutions to some things. Since then, he's shown more interest than previously. I know I ran the risk of alienating him and possibly others. It's like in the statement made by the ignominious Ron Karenga, that we must challenge each other to take a principled stand in matters concerning us, our communities, our liberation, our welfare, and I see the truth in that statement, despite who it's coming from. And the context in which he put that statement and others wasn't far from a call for mobilization. I find it ironic that Karenga would be making such statements, considering his betrayal of the movement in the 1960's and 70's. Those statements are in a library book up here called the *Reference Library of Black America*. I believe it's Volume One, at the Million Man March – I attended that march. I'm agitating.

I'm sitting here reading *The Roots of the New Afrikan Independence Movement*, and I definitely wasn't aware of the major disagreements between the New Afrikan Independence Movement and Omali Yeshitela, chairman of the African People's Socialist Party (UHURU Movement). Yeshitela appears on Dead Prez's "Let's Get Free," as you probably already know. I never had, still don't have, any program of Dead Prez or of their affiliates outlining their goals, objectives, etc. But from what I'm getting from this essay by Chokwe Lumumba, the APSP advocates a multiracial socialist revolution and they want us all to "return to Afrika." I don't agree with this at all, for one I agree with Chokwe that we need land, our own territory on this continent. For me personally I am suspicious of any great migration back to Afrika which involves all members and descendants of the Afrikan race and heritage being concentrated in one place, rendering us vulnerable to one devastating attack and possible extermination, especially considering the fact that the Afrikan continent and all its various governments do not have an efficient defense system to counter or deflect any attacks on the inhabitants of the continent. So I feel for that purpose we should be spread out to some degree to "hold things in check" on all continents that we do inhabit until we are readily able to defend ourselves. Secondly, like you stated, in previous moments of our liberation efforts we did not win or establish any land in the empire as our own which has been an impediment to our growth, security, and welfare (politically, socially, economically, and culturally).* And as much blood, sweat, and tears as we've shed and invested in this land, we have justifiable claims and connections to this land. But my first point is essentially a strategic one. But I don't see a real major difference between Chokwe's and Omali's outlooks. They're both scientific; they both want liberation for all Afrikans and all oppressed; they're both anti-imperialist, anti-racist. I mean, there is overwhelmingly significant common ground to disregard the differences and just work together directly and indirectly in their respective areas – we all want the same things!

All these so-called intellectuals – I'm challenging them. I'm also learning how to talk about phenomenon of the capitalist system

— — — — —

* And I would add, our self-identity —*Rashid*.

and express dissatisfaction without saying "revolution," especially where that word is not needed. I think this is good because revolution is too big for some of us to grasp, and it's better to point out specific characteristics and effects of the capitalist system, 'cause they seem to be easier to grasp. I'm conscious of it because of the feedback I've gotten in certain conversations in my attempts to proselytize individuals. They're relating at least to some extent. Don't forget to send me some Mao and any other literature you believe will be integral to my revolutionary development. I passed off your essay "What's Left of the Left?"* to one person so far. He noticed right off the seriousness of the content and remarked on your "militancy," though not the word used, that was the roundabout expression. Dudes is dissatisfied; they/we just ain't organized. I salute you!

Outlaw

21.   To OUTLAW: Finally, a moment to return to our previous discussions and your questions. I should first deal with the 5% question. Well, there was no actual question from you on this topic; you asked me to propose a critical approach to the 5% school of thought that would be receptive to 5% adherents without alienating them, and to give my renunciation of their thinking as ineffective for winning us freedom. The former is a somewhat difficult request, since it's generally one's manner of approach to criticism, as opposed to the actual criticisms made, that determines people's responses. Keep

— — — — —

* See page 289.

in mind that people like to laugh. One must also be understanding and sensitive to the emotional and psychological compulsions that lead our kind here in the US to adopt and embrace impotent theories like those taught by the 5%, in order to know how to deconstruct such doctrinal systems without offending their followers. We have been historically conditioned to react and respond emotionally and not logically to things we feel threaten our beliefs and desires, so it's unreasonable to expect intelligent responses to logical criticism. Furthermore, many who adhere to such schools as the 5% and Nation of Islam don't really believe in the principles taught by these schools, many simply join because of the innate human instinct to seek security in numbers (longing for community), which is why they just as easily fall into street gangs. Anyway, these systems must be deconstructed (and replaced where able) from the root.

Our progenitors suffered centuries of emasculation, degradation, humiliation, and classification as less than human. Our response has often been to cling to doctrines (predominantly religiously oriented), which confirm our humanity and promised us redemption (usually in some other world). Consequently we were never able to marshal the essentials needed to successfully resist our oppression in **this** world. We were trained and conditioned to search for redemption, consolation, and rescue in religion and superstition. Therefore we failed to comprehend and apply that sort of secular materialism that Martin Robison Delaney pointed out. "That which is Spiritual can only be accomplished through the medium of the Spiritual law; that which is Moral, through the medium of the Moral law; and that which is Physical, through the medium of the Physical law ... Does a person want a spiritual blessing, he must apply through the medium of the Spiritual law – pray for it in order to obtain it. If they desire to do a moral good, they must apply through the medium of the Moral law – exercise their sense and feeling of right and justice, in order to effect it. Do they want to attain a Physical end, they can only do so through the medium of the physical law – go to work with muscles, hands, limbs, might and strength, and this, and nothing else, will attain it." While he neglects the guiding factor of intellect in all this, the point is still made – to change physical conditions compels physical actions, not passive resort to faith and prayer and other appeals to the "divine." Frederick Douglass, a devout Christian, who educated himself, escaped slavery, and went on to become a leading voice in the anti-slavery struggle, made the point perfectly when he said: "I prayed for freedom twenty years, but received no answer until I prayed with my legs."

In addition to keeping us academically ignorant (stagnating the development and use of our creative rational faculties), the enslavers and their hirelings (as the imperialist power structure does today) always projected themselves as invulnerable to any successful physical challenge by us. And when we did dare to defy the odds (with total lack of coordinated unity and attention to strategy, tactics, and logistics), we were conditioned to believe (with some justification) that their reflex violence, their revenge, would be so brutal and widespread that the resulting suffering which our resistance provoked wasn't worth the effort. Therefore – failure leading to pessimism – any idea of waging a successful struggle for mass freedom was neutralized. Those who did fight back really had no long-range vision (no ideology) of any certain benefits to be gained from struggle, and the omnipresent slave patrols manned by poor whites kept the Blacks from getting together in any large numbers except during religious get-togethers (which were monitored and penetrated by informants). So the armed rebellions – although frequent – were mostly small and acts of desperation and frustration. Had there been a unified idea **what** to do with freedom and that it would offer real gains, there would definitely have been a more single-minded and determined struggle. I can give two examples as proof of this point. The first being our role in the civil war (1861–1865). During that war southern Blacks in the confederate states were given concrete bases to struggle in all-out war against slavery (namely, the US falsely promised them both freedom and the right to take possession of the land taken from the confederates – forty acres and a mule for every Black family if they joined the Union Army against the confederates.) With these promises, Black folk fled the plantations in droves to help fight with the Union Army. We were the decisive force that defeated the confederacy. But instead of honoring the promise of freedom and land, presidents Johnson and Garfield restored the land back to the confederate owners, the "freemen" were driven off the promised land by the Union Army and the same basic system of slavery was reinstituted under sharecropping, debt tenancy, peonage status, etc. The second example would be Haiti. There the enslaved Blacks, inspired by the revolutionary struggles and gains of the Jacobins in France, rose up in the most powerful slave revolt in history (1791) against the French colonial empire and defeated not only the local white slaveowners, but successive military invasions by Spain, Britain, and then France under orders of Napoleon (one of Europe's most acclaimed military leaders), who suffered his first Waterloo at the hands of Black people's war of 1802–1803 that won Haitian independence. The Maroons and Seminoles would be perhaps one of the only exceptions to our general lack of organized strategic and tactical initiative during slavery, but they were ultimately co-opted and defeated or dispossessed. Therefore, without a clear, unified vision of what we stand to gain from struggle, our most enduring mode of resisting perpetual degradation took the form of emotional and religion constructs, usually to find or reclaim our human worth. It must also be remembered that many of the Afrikan societies and cultures that our forebears came from (village societies) were deeply superstitious ones. In fact, holding on to many of those irrational beliefs and tendencies was seen as a form of rebellion against white domination, as our retaining essential features of Afrikanness.

Anyway, as you're aware, the 5% came out of the teaching of the NOI.* The NOI itself was but another of our many psycho-emotional and metaphysical responses to centuries of being dehumanized, and accounted as the inferior. The approach this time was to reverse the roles, raising Blacks to the superior status and reducing our historical white oppressor to the inferior. But this is as far as it went. There was not intent to do more than what cultural nationalists do in general, viz., refer to and imitate the features of cultures and societies of Afrika's past in attempts to reclaim our lost dignity, identity, human value, and respectability, except the NOI proposes not to refer to Afrika, but to prove that we are equally able to excel at the "white man's" capitalism. To create a humane and dignified bourgeois Black capitalism, but one without any contiguous land base. A curious anti-political eclectic mix of certain features of Black capitalism, cultural nationalism, and an eccentric Islam. The NOI was always anti-political (refused under Elijah Muhammad to become involved

— — — — —

* The Nation of Islam, also known as the Black Muslims.

in the civil rights or revolutionary Black nationalist movements of the day), which is one of the reasons Malcolm X became disillusioned with the NOI – in fact, he was silenced by Elijah, ostensibly because of making political statements about the assassination of John F. Kennedy at a New York rally.

The NOI was also anti-military, another element that estranged Malcolm. In fact, it was Malcolm who developed the Fruit of Islam to be a militant arm of the NOI. However, the FOI are used only as bodyguards and security guards (unarmed) of NOI elites, property and Black entertainers. While they've never had problems with taking militant postures against other powerless Black folk, when NOI leaders are confronted with the need to confront the continued abuses of Blacks by the imperialist power structure in similar fashion, the reply is to revert to the old slaves' position of turning our eyes heavenward – that "Almighty God Allah" will judge and deal with them. In criticism of the NOI and his own inactive role in the struggle while a member, Malcolm stated during February 1965, a few days before his assassination, that "We were in a political vacuum, we were actually alienated, cut off from all types of activity with even the world we were fighting against. We became a sort of a religious-political hybrid, all to ourselves, not involved in anything but just standing on the sidelines condemning everything. But in no position to correct anything because we couldn't take action."

The excommunicated Clarence 13X took the same anti-political, anti-military, pro-capitalist cultural nationalist mindset into his 5% school that he learned from the NOI. All still shrouded in theology – instead of the Black race being perceived as ordained by God to be a superior life form above whites as in the NOI, in the 5% school, the Black man became God himself, and the white man the devil. The claim to a "national" identity by the NOI and 5%ers has always been idealistic and subjective. They have no concrete plan, or idea of how or what to mobilize, towards achieving an objective and self-sustaining nation. In fact, they don't even know what the essentials (political, military, economic, cultural, and identity) of a nation are (especially in the case of the 5%, although I'm positive that Farrakhan knows these things, though his followers may not), therefore, any concept of revolutionary nationalist struggle for the followers of these schools of thought is meaningless, just as it was for our enslaved forebears. We obviously can't forge a united and determined struggle if we have no concrete idea what it is we're struggling to achieve. If we have no strategic objective, how is it possible to formulate tactical methods of getting there? This is why the concept of struggle and revolution is abstract and unreal to our people – they have no idea what the material features of these things are. To them, it's just another metaphysical concept that we've never seen but hope will one day bless us with a better life.

Again, the NOI promotes this bourgeois Black entrepreneurial capitalism as the goal of our struggle. This entrepreneurial thing is tied into, serves, and will remain subservient to the enemy central-ized corporate capitalist system, and will serve to enrich only a tiny upper elite while the masses are exploited of their labor and remain poor. The typical capitalist class conflict. You can see the same class structure within the NOI. Black entrepreneurial capitalism can't possibly break ranks with the imperialist capitalist market struc-ture, and even were it possible, there would only be the same un-checked competition between various enterprises that will prompt the frequent cycles of economic recessions and depressions (the un-avoidable capitalist "business cycle") as occurred here in the 18th through early 20th centuries and ended with the Great Depression of the 1930's which finally destroyed all confidence of the big capitalists in the "free market" (laissez faire) system of unregulated competition. These crises were what compelled the capitalists to agree to allowing state regulation of competition and demands on the state to subsidize the private corporate sector with public funds (Keynesian controls),* producing the consolidation of the fascist process – that is combining big business and the jingoist, militarist state. All of the big capitalist countries did this to survive the Great Depression – Amerika, Germany, Italy, Japan, etc. ... George gives a good analysis of this process in the section of *Blood In My Eye* under the heading "Classes at War – Mobilization and Contra-Mobilization." The Keynesian system of controls applied here are purely exploitative, as John Maynard Keynes admitted in the

— — — — —

* An economic idea based on the ideas of 20th century British economist John Maynard Keynes. Keynesian economics promotes a mixed economy, where both the state and private sectors play an important role. Keynesian economics differs markedly from laissez-faire economics (economic theory based on the belief that markets and the private sector operate well on their own without state intervention).

In Keynes' theory, macroeconomic trends can overwhelm the micro-level between individuals. Instead of the economic process being based on continuous improvement in potential output, as most classical economists had believed from the late 1700's on, Keynes asserted the importance of aggregate demand for goods as the driving factor of the economy, especially in periods of downturn. From this he argued that government policies could be used to promote demand at a *macro* level, to fight high unemployment and deflation of the sort seen during the 1930's.

foreword to the German edition of his treatise "General Theory" on September 7, 1936:

> The theory of aggregate production, which is the point of the following book, nevertheless can be much easier adapted to the conditions of a totalitarian state than the theory of production and distribution of a given production put forth under conditions of free competition ...

This is why in essence the NOI and 5% are illogical types, having little to no familiarity with factors that affect social conditions and the state of the world here or abroad. They in fact serve the interests of empire, diverting a large sector of our people from organizing toward achieving genuine liberation (Farrakhan even wants to disarm Black folk, rendering us totally defenseless against enemy attack!) This all is why although the NOI is presented as controversial and oppositional to/by empire, Farrakhan is still breathing today and able to move about openly. He shares the elitist bourgeois class interests of the imperialists. If he dared break with capitalism and used his influence to mobilize his followers to pursue real independence (struggle for reparations in the form of fertile land, sovereignty rights, collective land and capital ownership, full equality of all power and rights for wimyn, arming the masses for resistance, and developing liberated areas), he'd be driven underground, or he'd be dead the next day of a brain aneurysm or some other modern method of covert assassination. But we've got to come together, all tendencies within our body. We must be willing and able to accept criticism and correct our errors.

Rashid

22.   To Rashid: I know you use the word "missive," but the last one you sent was more of a missile! I couldn't resist sharing that with the 5%ers that are over here, and the response was, "That's some deep shit," and one even went so far as to copy the missive down. Your insight is phenomenal, coupled with your mastery of elocution. I read your other essay as well, and once again, how can I disagree? On what grounds? It would be illogical, inane. Do you think anyone at that conference will take heed to your call to put theories into practice? You are correct that there is an excess of "armchair revolutionaries." I was attempting, at this stage of development, to assess whether conditions are ripe for protracted struggle. I mean things can be "manufactured," of course, but the empire has enemies (external). Our history under empire's control is plagued with the same scenario: external enemy = call for help = token awards = going nowhere (prolonging self-determination). The problems still exist with our tacit consent. Anyway, you're already aware of all this; it's just so many people are in a position to actuate things, and who are aware, but are doing nothing. I don't know how to explain it, plus I don't want to waste your time with my rambling on.

There's some dude over here named E from Petersburg, says he knows you real well, speaks highly of you, but he's preoccupied with ignorance. He's still under that hustler, slick nigga state of mind. You know I'm agitating and he always agrees, but yet, like with S, he could've just not heard anything I said, 'cause he jumps right back into counter-productivity. So now it's coming to where I'm putting people's minds into a corner – I'm challenging them to think, to be intelligent. It's all there in the responses – emotional, irrational, illogical, illegitimate capitalist values. Rashid, I sincerely wish there was more I could be contributing at this point, but you know education is indispensable, and from my assessments (estimates, actually) it seems practical for me to do what I'm doing. But out of the desire to do more and also unable to do what I want and therefore what I am doing I aim to be "professional" about it. I just need some reassurance that my efforts are revolutionary. Like I expressed before, I didn't and still don't feel worthy to be identified with such, though I strive to be worthy. Maybe, you know it's like what George was saying about that "obligatory duty that is ours once we become aware." I want to fulfill that duty.

Outlaw

23.   To OUTLAW: I have your last letter responding to my position of the 5% – which was by no means an exhaustive critique. I've just been overwhelmed with writings and requests for materials from outside folks. I'm still overwhelmed at this very moment. Before going any further, I'll give my answer first to your question (your uncertainty) about whether your efforts are revolutionary. In my opinion, certainly. But you know I was thinking – we need to get some organizing work going on within the prisoner body. I'll elaborate further elsewhere. I'm thinking that much of your labors (agitation) have seemed in vain, since there's no **organized** alternative to offer these brothers that can compensate for their loss of "belonging" to something, a community of purpose.

The taxi just came in ...

Rashid

24.   To RASHID: What you proposed in the way of organizing our peers is exactly the way it's supposed to be; however, the way it is, dudes ain't committed. I had plans to circulate these politics thoroughly. Dudes' mindstate is real to me now, 'cause I'm first-handedly experiencing this shit now. At this point I'm seeing I must be very selective and possibly gentle with a generation of thugs and killaz. I see what Jalil Muntaqim was saying about undermining our people's psychological dependency on empire. I had experienced dudes over here repeatedly expressing how much opportunity there was, how many rights and freedoms we have, and how successful we have the "opportunity" to be, but yet none of these people are the beneficiaries of any of the opportunities or rights. So it seems to me that they are thoroughly and wholly under the spell of empire's "dream," and totally disregarding the roots of that dream, the people behind it, their motivations, their plans. I sit here in front of the TV, thoroughly pissed. Watching the schemes implemented by empire to undermine and divert our movement, with tokens and "dark faces in high places" – it's been intensified here lately due to external forces.

Then I see the misguided, misdirected actions of activists and their civil disobedience to protest atrocities like genocide, slavery, rape, murder over in Sudan. Waiting on empire to sincerely and adamantly correct the wrongs of the Sudanese government. Another manifestation of that psychological dependency again. You're right; all my efforts do seem in vain trying to raise the awareness of our peers. I got your auto-bio and request for critique. I have none. I see all your actions towards the empire's agents as natural response, and I'm wondering why these killaz running around here with double-life don't possess the same courage and wit as yourself, or at least strive to follow your example. If I see anything doubtful or that I am just not knowledgeable about I will bring it to your attention.

That *Revolution in Central America* is the shit! M-1 of Dead Prez was on Rap City week before last. One thing that caught my attention is he gave out a shout out to niggaz in the street hustling and I understand they have revolutionary potential, but to shout them out is like justifying their destructive activities. I don't know how to balance that. So far, I've only come up with that niggaz' needs are legitimate and healthy, but the means they're using to meet those needs are destructive and unhealthy, individually and collectively.

On that publication you're considering composing–I don't mind the outside criticism; it's conductive to growth and development. I'm sure you're using pseudonyms, right?

Outlaw

25.   To Outlaw: I just got word from the taxi that a package you sent was taken by the "higher ups." Something was apt to go awry sooner or later. What all had you sent–or returned? I presume that a letter was included. If a kite **was** enclosed, what was said? I suppose the Mao biography was also included? Holla and let me know what all was there–otherwise let me know your position on the message I sent earlier.

Of course, the upper brass know about the taxi's activities; they use him tactically–good cop thing. But depending upon the content of that package, they may have second thoughts about his working around me.* They being reactionaries, I expect some reaction.

Rashid

26. To RASHID: You're not going to believe this here. Upon the taxi giving me your kite this morning, I simultaneously gave him a package for you containing Mao's biography and the other documents you'd sent. Well, the building sergeants came into the pod and the office where the taxi said he'd temporarily placed the package. Well, the sergeants "took" the materials and either threw them away or who knows what, so now they are lost and nowhere to be found. The sergeants have been in this building all day. I don't know how I could replace those items. The documents I believe can be obtained. The Mao, you said that Mao is hard to come by. I assume the taxi was putting delivering the package off until he had reason to be at your cell (serving meals), which has been the norm. Other people's packs got torn off as well. Let me know something.

Outlaw

— — — — —

* Passing items between the segregation and population units, which is formally forbidden for guards to do. Guards do this for different motives and incentives, including pacifying "unruly" prisoners. It is also not uncommon that a prisoner will trade his rec time in exchange for getting a letter, book, or other item passed to another prisoner. This is appealing to guards who don't want to put in the effort involved in transporting a prisoner to the outside rec cages.

27.   To Outlaw: Just got your note about the loss – I'd already just given the taxi one for you on the matter. How can you replace the loss? I don't think you have any attachment to those sergeants, so I don't think it's **you** who owes anything. The pigs took the materials, not you. We both know that's the risk we run in using any uniform as a go-between. Calculated risk. No big deal. Some losses must be risked or accepted in order to win other gains – the object is to maneuver to gain more than we lose. I think what we've gained through our exchanges far outweighs that lost material. We're clearly ahead.

Rashid

28.   To Rashid: Nothing exactly incriminating was said, just a statement "one can expect no mercy from the state," and a question about the difference between guerrilla and mobile war. Oh, I did mention how guys out here were commenting on your "going through walls" and your noted pursuit of "avenging injustice" with the pigs. That's it. That's the most inflammatory content, if you can consider it such. And yes, Mao was unfortunately included. I don't suppose anything was in there they don't already have a good idea about. Yes, shit happens. I agree – the taxi is state-owned. I guess the contents of that package would "expose" more about you; I can't say I'm exactly exempt. Time will tell. Whether declared or concealed irreconcilable differences remain between us and the forces of reaction.

My desire to replace the loss was probably misguided, but **I just want results**. I'm tired of playing "away games." Our powerlessness in result-oriented action or our lack of ability to produce real changes is highly frustrating! Plus I don't like seeing you in that position, not being able to properly defend yourself and knowing you share the same situation as George did – anyone who passed the civil service examination could liquidate you/us today with complete immunity. So when I say something like that, it's just me. I've always been sensitive to the next person's needs and situation, especially someone like you. I know 1001 homeboys who are killaz, but they hold no weight when compared to you. They crack under pressure. You have proven your resilience and tenacity time and time again. You are the *True Soldier*,[*] and that's what I respect, and I aspire to be the same. No ego stroking intended at all. I had several questions about Mao in the other kites; I'll repeat them here: 1. What is the essential difference between strategy and tactics? 2. Why is a war of attrition to be avoided? And does this in any way contradict Mao's saying that "we must concern ourselves with the spoils of war" since the spoils are the enemy's? 3. Why did Mao find it necessary to develop capitalism or protect large landholders? Why didn't he just build socialism? Why was foreign capital necessary to build such? Taxi is here.

Outlaw

— — — — —

* See page 320.

29.   To Outlaw: On possibly publishing our exchanges – a pseudonym can be used to shield your own identity – as for myself, I expect that the opposition has acquired something of an idea of who I am and what my views/values are. I'm already exposed in this regard. So as George stated of himself, I can say what I please without fear of self-exposure … "they can only kill me once." To return to your previous questions:

The difference between strategy and tactics is essentially the difference between end and means. Strategy is the objective; tactics are the methods employed to achieve the objective. For example, in the game of chess, the strategy (the objective) is to corner and checkmate the opponent's King. The various combinations of moves of all pieces toward capturing the King are the tactics (the methods). To put it in a more systematic context, take warfare; military operations divide into three components: strategy, tactics, and logistics. **Tactics** relates to battlefield operations, methods of employing weapons in combat. **Logistics** deals with procuring soldiers and supplying them with sufficient food, clothing, shelter, weapons. **Strategy** incorporates tactics and logistics to determine and accomplish the objectives of the war. Generally in military operations there are three aspects to the concept of strategy: 1. Grand strategy, which deals with relating the political objective with one's military ability, to determine how to pursue the war to accomplish the desired political objective. 2. Strategy proper, which deals with mobilizing and moving fighting forces, and 3. Grand tactics, or lower strategy, which deals with maneuvering the fighting forces in preparation for and execution of battles.

When Mao spoke of avoiding a "war of attrition," he meant that in revolutionary war, the object is not merely to fight the enemy to wear him down, but to totally annihilate him. When the revolutionary army pits its forces against the enemy's, the purpose is to destroy that force. As Mao stated:

> A battle in which the enemy is routed is not basically decisive in a contest with a foe of great strength. A battle of annihilation on the other hand, produces a great and immediate impact on any enemy. Injuring all of a man's fingers is not as effective as chopping off one, and routing ten enemy divisions is not as effective as annihilating one of them.

There's nothing contradictory between a war of annihilation and emphasis on seizing spoils. In any battle the gains must outweigh the losses, otherwise the battle is perceived as a lost one. Mao adhered to Sun Tzu's prescription that an army must live off of the enemy – recruit soldiers from enemy ranks, acquire material and supplies from enemy resources. One can certainly live off the enemy in process of annihilating him. Nothing contradictory between avoiding a war of attrition and emphasizing spoils.

The CCP found it necessary to temporarily preserve aspects of capitalism in China to encourage foreign trade and investment of the capital needed to facilitate agrarian reform, that is, the mechanization, development, and consequent increase of agricultural production. So to displace the slow and decadent semi-feudal mode of production. This would therefore advance the living standards of the miserably poor Chinese masses and develop the peasantry into a more disciplined and organized labor force. The metropolitan capitalist countries had the advanced capital and technologies (developed industries and sciences) needed to increase China's capacity for production, so the CCP needed to encourage investment and purchases from the centers of capital in order to acquire their advanced capital, technologies, etc. Other reasons included the CCP's concern to build as broad an alliance as possible across the various Chinese classes in the resistance to the Japanese invasion. This meant not alienating patriotic landlords and gentry by expropriating their holdings and giving them to the poor peasants.

As for the I-Ching, it is one of the five Confucian classics. It is in fact an oracular divination system. The actual maxims that underlie the sixty-four hexagrams (i.e. those series of mixed broken and unbroken lines – six of which in each hexagram) give some acute analyses of human and cosmological nature; however, the system is used in casting oracles via yarrow stalks to invoke answers to various problems (the yarrow stick casting would produce one or a combination of the hexagrams as the answer to whatever question was asked of the oracle). The Chinese used the I-Ching for answers in all areas of life, including warfare. So instead of giving an objective analysis to conditions relevant to military operations, the Chinese military commanders of old would base battlefield decisions on casting oracles. This is that superstitious approach to war that Sun Tzu ridiculed and revolutionized in his *Ping Fa* (Art of War). Likewise, it was the elitist and superstitious Confucianism and idolatry that Mao and the CCP despised and adamantly worked to purge from the Chinese psyche and society – replacing superstitious idealism with dialectic materialism. We Black folk here in Amerika have a similar attachment to and heritage of superstitious and metaphysical assbackwardness. Instead of making informed decisions, we prefer to rely on metaphysical invocations and passive reliance in this faith in the unseen. Despite that, the unseen leaves us to suffer, starve, be brutalized and live in perpetual enslavement to those who use their brains to acquire their ends. Guess the unseen figures we'll wake up sooner or later, or else go extinct on bending knees. Here I must quote Emiliano Zapata: "I'd rather die on my feet than live on my knees." But hell, we ain't living; we dying off. The hexagram that appears on the cover of Dead Prez's album *Let's Get Free* is the I-Ching hexagram that represents "The Army." We need one.

I agree that there should be a reconciliation of differences between the NAPO and the APSP, and while it appears that Chokwe has attempted this, Omali seems resistant. I could be wrong, but this does appear to be the case, thus keeping our people divided along purely tactical lines, since I presume the objective of both movements to be total elimination of all forms of exploitation, whether by white or Black.

Humyns have an innate tendency to seek approval and acceptance from their peers, especially those they've come to admire and respect. Playing to these tendencies can be very useful in our education efforts. I've sometimes had to trick our peers into progressive activities by just such maneuvers. You've got to experiment with different approaches – become intimately familiar with the humyn psyche. I've mentioned the tendency of people to pursue acceptance because this tendency can be consciously used to draw them into the struggle. I've had cats who're adamant about study, growth, making principled commitments, etc., become very motivated after the fact of being given the silent treatment. Of course, this particular approach isn't universal, but all people have some – what you might call – tendency that can be appealed to draw them into principled commitments. You just have to know how to find and appeal to them. A lot of this is what the art of persuasion entails, and are the tendencies appealed to in the weekly block parties as an example that people can be mobilized to support, or at least be neutral toward, most any cause – even something as counterproductive as an open-air neighborhood drug market – if they're given a sense of objective benefit, security, and community. Perhaps this can help you in resolving the obstacles you keep encountering in trying to politicize our peers.

I knew you'd enjoy Fogel's *Revolution in Central America.*[*] I'm working on getting his other work, *Africa in Struggle: National Struggle and Proletarian Revolution.*[†] Fogel has some solid analyses on Third World revolutionary struggles and presents them from an excellent, accurate, and honest materialist perspective.

On your question about the difference between guerrilla warfare and Mao's concept of mobile warfare: by now, I'm certain you understand guerrilla warfare to be that mode of combat using surprise attacks applied by an irregular fighting force operating in small groups and in territory occupied by a regular and superior enemy force. Of course, guerrilla warfare has an inherently mobile character, since a ragtag guerrilla force can't go head-to-head with an established regular army in positional battles. Mao's concept of mobile warfare implies a war where the revolutionary forces operate without fixed battle lines. Meaning that the revolutionary army and the base areas in which it operates remains in continued motion, never remaining in fixed positions. Hence the revolutionary army operates upon the same principles of fluidity as a guerrilla army.

— — — — —

* Daniel Fogel, Ism Press, 1984.
† Ism Press, 2nd Edition, 1986.

The Chinese Red Army's "battle lines" were in constant motion and determined by the size of the base area, which was constantly expanding to embrace more and more territory and people. When the base area could no longer expand in a certain direction because checked by superior enemy forces, it would retreat, but continue expanding in other directions. Obviously base area expansion – in whatever direction – was determined by the Red Army's ability to defeat or avoid enemy forces in the given direction(s) of expansion. The Kuomintang's efforts to defeat the Reds was by encircling and trying to gradually contain and occupy the Red bases with separate divisions. One of Mao's methods of defeating these forces was by drawing isolated divisions deep inside the base area and then concentrating a superior number of Reds against and annihilating the isolated enemy division. They'd accomplish this, for example, by having a Red detachment or guerrillas attack the chosen division and then retreat into the base area to a designated place where a superior number of Reds would be waiting in full force. This was the principle embodied in his slogan "lure enemy deep penetration," and "terminus of withdrawal." His slogan that the "first engagement" is decisive in battle is what he applied by having the Reds initiate the provocative attack and then run away, luring the enemy to pursue the withdrawing force, rushing headlong and disorderly into an ambush which was set up deep in Red-controlled territory at the "terminus of withdrawal." Hope this answers all your questions.

Rashid

30.   To RASHID: I keep your kites; they are like reference notes for me; I read over them from time to time. Any literature pertaining to psychology, human nature, or biology that you can share or refer me to – do so. I see what you're saying about having material benefits available so people will "feel" the sense of community. It's just that I am not in a position to provide those things. I was considering something over here like a "People's Storebox" where there's no interest, just return what you borrowed; you know, it's a step in promoting some different economic and social relations.

Your auto-bio was well above average; it's hard to say I'm not stroking your ego and still move in that direction. I mean, it's not even that; it's just about putting things in perspective; however, it's impossible to overlook or disregard your talents and qualities.

Please don't perceive my concerns about using pseudonyms as paranoia, like our old buddy Mau Mau. I logically assume the opposition will know thoroughly about me as well. I just don't want the fire to be put out before it gets going by some trumped-up conspiracy scheme – "it's predictable as nightfall." I favor the concept of "public clandestinity."*

I copied other works by you down. I plan on typing and copying these papers for rife dissemination throughout the prison population, you know, at the same time undermine the other weak-ass

— — — — —

* By now (at the time these letters were published), prison authorities are fully aware of who Outlaw is and have responded through such methods as cutting off his visits with loved ones, preventing him from making calls to them, and outright threatening his safety. Their repression of Rashid, that began long before this writing, continues along similar lines but employs more extreme measures as well.

pseudo-ideologies. That's why I don't have any critique of your "approach to practice," in the area of organizing our peers politically; it's exactly what I had in mind – your insight clarified a few things for me. I agree with your theory about it spilling over into the streets. A lot of things that are fashionable started in prison.

Man is animal. I've heard this and believe it. Consciousness and instinct. I've seen analogies between the two to justify capitalism and all its social phenomena. How do you see this? I myself believe laws were established to define the line between man's instinct and consciousness, and, of course, regulate the former, but I want your input on the matter. If man is animal, then consciousness is somewhat a destructive element, 'cause man consciously distorts the natural ecological balance. George spoke on it, but not to my satisfaction, or maybe I'm missing something.

Revolution in Central America spoke about homosexuality as "sexual liberation," do you concur with this view? The concept in that context is new to me. I personally don't have a problem with gays and lesbians as human beings. Though I don't approve of homosexuality, I don't think they should be persecuted for their preference. I wonder what chemical imbalance produces a gay or a lesbian. Have you ever entertained this idea?

Look, I ran into this dude who gave me a paper about secret societies in general, the Skull and Bones in particular, and the plans to be implemented were exactly like the ten demands in the *Communist Manifesto*, abolishment of private property, graduated income tax, etc., all with the intentions to return the world to reliance on reason. I'm suspicious, of course, 'cause I know socialism can be manipulated as pointed out in *The Occult Technology of*

*Power.** I wonder if the modern efforts to implement Globalization were connected in any way with Skull and Bones' plans. Do you know what Globalization is, what result it would have? I can only see it as an international global alliance and consolidation of power for the capitalist elite, keeping the masses in perpetual slavery.

Oh yeah, I was surprised to find out that you were exposed to George in 2001. I was sure you were for years involved with revolutionary politics – like ten years at least. Your auto-bio left me wanting to know what your upbringing was like, what conditions produced such a paragon of a Black man and revolutionary. I can understand the role that admiration and respect play in organizing people, but as for me, I'm probably respected, but admired, I truly doubt. I've always been an outcast, and what I represent is not desirable or popular, so it's like at this point in time, my "lone wolf" rep is being reinforced, so to speak.

Strategy and tactics I got now. In Nechayev's *Catechism* he stated something like, in the event a comrade is in trouble and the issue arises whether to save him/her or not, the decision should not be based on sympathy but on the impact on the expenditure of the army. What is your take on this? I have many more inquiries in the way of application of strategy and tactics to objective reality – they'll be here and there.

Outlaw

— — — — —

* A conspiracy theory classic, purported to be written by the son of a monopoly capitalist.

"Black Wimyn are equal to their men in the repression they suffer. They w
their men's equals within the slave community; and they resisted slavery
a passion equal to their men's. The punishment inflicted on   the Wimyn
exceeded in intensity the punishment suffered by their   men, for
Wimyn were not only whipped and mutilated, they were   also rap
Rape was a weapon of domination and oppression,   whose
covert goal was to extinguish the slave Womyn's will   to
resist and in process to demoralize their men. The   is
of sexual abuse has been all but glossed over in the
traditional literature   on slavery."   Ay

Ella Baker

Panther Love to New Afrikan Warrior Wimyn!

RASHID
7-27
'06

The Black Womyn has in the past few hundred years been the only force holding us together and holding us up. She has absorbed the biggest part of the many shocks and strains of existence under a slave order. The men can think of nothing more effective than dealing drugs, pimping, gambling, or petty theft. I've heard men brag about being pimps of Black Wimyn and taking money from Black Wimyn on relief. Things like this I find odious, disgusting — these Black men have proven themselves to be utterly detestable and repulsive in the past. Before I would succumb to such subterfuge I would scratch my living from the ground on hands and knees, or die in a hail of bullets! My hat goes off to every one of you, you have my profoundest respect."

George L. Jackson

31.   To OUTLAW: On the homosexual question: I believe the tendency itself to be primarily a subjective one, that is, principally in the mind. I don't suppose it to stem from any "chemical imbalances," at least not in the majority of cases. Given the patriarchal context of Amerika, I suppose that homosexuality can be perceived as "sexual liberation." I have no qualms with gays/lesbians one way or the other. [In fact, we should see them as likely allies, since they're not enemies of the people and are perhaps the most persecuted of all social groups. Huey Newton came to also recognize this.] I regret to say that I have, numerous times in my younger days here on the inside, raised a few knots on several gay cats' heads, on account of their refusing to accept that I personally have no sexual attraction to men. A related curiosity I've long had concerns why Amerikan wimyn tend to feel a need to duplicate the western "masculine" distortion in order to be assertive, whereas 3rd World wimyn [and the Black sistas of my generation in general] can maintain complete and undistorted feminine qualities and still be quite assertive and even vicious when necessary.

The Skull and Bones thing obviously is an order promoting a one-world capitalist (global) economy, with a tiny group of men controlling and "owning" it. To maintain and protect such a system there is need for a globally consolidated political-military superstructure. Hence, your one-world government. As US elite have admitted, the term "globalism" is merely a euphemism for Amerikan global military, economic, political, and cultural domination. This would be the consolidation of fascism on a worldwide scale – the US is aiming to achieve what Hitler only dreamed of. So no matter how noble the rhetoric promoted by the Skull and Bones order sounds (many male Yale graduates are members of this exclusivist group – George W. Bush and John Kerry are members), any arrangement allowing a small group of people to monopolize world power is invariably corrupt. The mass-oriented rhetoric is only so much propaganda to confuse the masses, making the globalists' true fascistic agenda seem to be the objective of socialists, and the true socialist agenda to be their own. Globalism and fascist capitalist imperialism are synonymous.

I suppose that I might one day write my full auto-bio.

I agree with Nechayev 100% on the point you referred to him on, although I completely oppose any tendencies towards betrayal. Point is, we should not compromise the overall struggle for individuals, sacrifices for individuals must be balanced by their value to the struggle. In all battles, the gains must exceed the losses.

As for my methods of relating to people, they've mostly developed from experience (trial and error) and in-depth self-study. Very little was acquired from academic studies, although I have done some investigations into various schools of psychology; however, I have no such texts on hand. I've simply come to recognize that three general tendencies underlie most, if not all, human actions – all of them subjective, but having grown out of objective necessity (community-oriented social survival), they being a search for acceptance, safety, and control. One can basically identify people's true motives – despite their stated intentions and projected images – by merely relating their actions to these basic impulses. Take for example cats who are obsessed with using violence to get their way. I have yet to meet any truly vicious, black-hearted, savage types. Most who appear to be, develop or use this approach out of seeking acceptance, safety, and control. And nine times out of ten, they are themselves very intimidated by superior violence. They use on others the very thing they fear themselves. Notice that most violent types tend to respect other violent types; predators give each other wide berth unless they are forced into a contest with another predator to protect their own prestige (that is, the sense of protecting an established sense of acceptance, safety, and control), thus driving them to challenge someone they actually fear. This is why a soldier or a pig who'd be terrified if left to fight alone, may become over-zealously violent when he has his peers by his side or watching him. "A coward is brave when surrounded by friends, but terrified when surrounded by enemies."

I can feel the "People's Storebox" idea, but along with the program should be the requirement of political education. Those who are "permitted" to participate should be allowed to do so as a sort of reward for political study. Or along with participation should be an incentive to push them to study and then return with the ability to elaborate on what they've studied. Sure, man is an animal, but a social animal. The incentive of community itself (group acceptance, safety, and control) is all the control factor people need to conform their conduct to a pro-social ideal. Humyns respond to positive reinforcement. People naturally conform their conduct to that which the group rewards with positive feedback (acceptance, which equals safety [in numbers] which equals control). Laws are artificial creations used to keep oppressed masses of people "in their place," so as not to resist an artificially stratified social arrangement imposed by a minority elite from above. Laws came about with the development of state-level societies (states are inherently stratified; rich/poor, ruler/ruled, etc.) If you investigate pre-state band and village societies, you'll see there were and are no laws, since there is no established, specialized domestic police force to enforce them.

People's actions are governed by their sense of need to adhere to the communal will. People become destructive when the sense of community is undermined. The goal of communism is to return people to a social stage where the sense of community replaces that of competition and coercion that exists under capitalism.

But let me return to the issue of appealing to people's impulses. I've studied people and their reactions. I've done things – which to an observer might seem rather odd – to gauge and confirm or disprove my predictions about their reactions and motives. By testing my predictions with action, patterns develop and correlate. One can thereby learn individual and group strengths and weaknesses, what they find threatening and what comforting. Emotional reactions are hard to feign. And one can generally detect when another is masking or creating their reactions – emotions tell all. Understand that people (whether individuals or groups) react with negative emotions to things they feel threaten their senses of acceptance, safety, and control. They react with positive emotions to those things that reinforce or promote these needs. And people are only totally indifferent to those things that they do not see as affecting these one way or the other. Now this is not to see people in a cynical light, since inherent in the needs for acceptance, safety, and control are affection, sympathy, empathy, love, and other emotional attachments. So, people whose communal instincts remain more or less intact are able to feel as powerfully a perceived threat or benefit to someone else's needs as they would for their own. So by accurately reading and interpreting a person's reaction to certain stimuli, you can discover what their true underlying values are – even if they don't know what those values are themself.

But the predominant impulse of all these three is the individual and social need for control, control over and concerning one's life and environment. Ask yourself what one condition makes any person respond negatively – if you think on it, you'll probably answer that it always involves the inability to exert a desired control over someone or some situation. Nothing irritates these pigs more than the inability to control a prisoner, or a parent more than a rebellious child, or a tyrant more than an unruly population, etc. – always a loss of control. In fact, the basis of government is what? – control. Whether self-government by the masses or one imposed by a small elite, it's universal. And once you know what a person's desires for control are, you can use phenomena to control them. In his *Art of War* Niccolo Machiavelli promoted that the best way to catch your enemy at a disadvantage and throw him off guard is to do voluntarily what he desires to have you do by force. Think on that.

Well, it's getting late, and I want to give this to the taxi when next he rolls through. I'll finish up later. I anticipated you'd be surprised to find that I'd only been studying revolutionary ideas for two and a half years – I learn quickly.

Rashid

Outlaw next sent me a letter from another prisoner in his unit with whom he'd been engaged in various political discussions. Outlaw had this brother (T) write to me to get my perspective on T's positions on some of the issues they'd been discussing. T's letter to me was lost; however, my reply I feel makes apparent the issues he'd raised in his letter.

32.   To T: Your expressed lack of faith in people and your belief that revolution will not create a broad and genuine change of corrupt society is reasonable **only** if your **assumption** that people are corrupt by nature is true. I don't agree with your basic assumption that people are foul by nature, so I obviously don't share your pessimism towards revolution. Now, my view of humyn nature is not based on assumptions or merely what I see in this immediate environment alone, but on my study and understanding of history, economics, culture, and **actual** patterns of humyn behavior. Elites or those who aspired to elitism were the **creators** of the claim that people are inherently corrupt so to justify their claim that the masses needed to be ruled over by them.

The earlier elites (priests and monarchs) claimed that they were ordained or inspired by God to rule over the masses or that they were descendants from god(s), and therefore, because of their claimed connections to the divine, they had qualities, intelligence, and powers that were greater than those of the common people. When these tricksters effectively convinced people to see them as the "rightful" rulers, they then educated (indoctrinated) the masses into the common belief that without them as the rulers, the societies would go to shambles and chaos would prevail. So people became less and less dependent on themselves and ended in transferring power of social control and control of the doctrinal systems over to these self-claimed rightful rulers. Needless to say, these rulers plundered the people and with specialized military and police forces, repressed and terrorized them so to preserve holds on power, with the obvious result of provoking slave and peasant insurrections. These revolts gave rise to the doctrine of republicanism, which is that the masses of common working people (the producers of the society) had a right to be heard by the kings and priest class by "representatives" of their own class (the role of lawyers and counsel grew out of this doctrine) – the kings and ruling religious elites did not permit peasants and slaves to obtain an audience with them, but lived in hidden splendor inside ostentatious and fortified palaces and cathedrals, etc., which were built by the backbreaking labor and wealth produced by the slaves and peasants. Obviously the "representatives" of the people had their own power agendas, which were inconsistent with the interests of the laboring masses, and developed into their own desire to seize power. So, becoming yet another class who aspired to rule in place of the monarchs and priest class, these bourgeoisie elements, agitated amongst the masses for the overthrow of the old ruling system with the result of wars being waged (with the common people as the cannon fodder) to unseat royal and priestly class rule and replace them with "republican" forms of government that now put wealthy bourgeoisie elites in the saddle – this is the wave of republican nationalism that swept Europe beginning in the 18th century, and was in fact the basis of the Amerikan revolution that produced these united states. Now with these republican governments, wealth and land ownership instead of "high birth" and membership in the priestly class became the bases of qualification to rule, with the natural need for the common people (whose status of being exploited changed very little) to be educated into values that supported and accepted this arrangement, which prevails today – note how the common poor and working-class people today are conditioned to collapse in awe at the sight of the "rich and famous," just as the slaves and peasants did at the sight and mention of "royalty" and the powerful religious rulers. For those of us slaves of today, who refuse to be indoctrinated, intimidated, and pacified, the impulse to revolt and overthrow oppression is as natural and legitimate as it was for the slaves of yesterday. Indeed, it is our right and our duty.

But I've given the general outline of the character of ruling classes to reach a point. The point being that societies and masses of people became corrupt as a result of the value structure and social ethic imposed on them by those who made themselves rulers. Before monarchs and high priests consolidated their power into state structures, you had egalitarian band and village societies (what some social historians and anthropologists call primitive or rudimentary communism or communalism.) Even a cursory study of these pre-state social systems shows that at the center of these societies was common recognition of the peoples' need for social cooperation for survival, and based upon this they developed cultures that reflected mutual trust, affection, play, courtesy, loyalty, etc. These oldest of social systems completely contradict your claim that people are corrupt by nature. Self-preservation on a group (rather than an individual, self-centered) basis was the root of these societies, not "self-destructive" behaviors, as you assume has always been the case with people.

When the state-level societies began to impose upon people more and more the idea that they were dependent not upon each other for survival, but upon the rulers of the state and the wealthy elite, then people become more and more alienated from their fellow man/womyn and more and more attached to the state and the glamorized leaders. People are apt to more readily injure or ignore the needs of others if they feel no sense of commitment or attachment to them, which is why in today's society one will more readily kill a "stranger," a "foreigner," or an "outsider," than a family member, and will allow or inflict harm, oppression and abuse against such people, and "niggers," "spics," "towelheads," "faggots," "inmates," "immigrants," and others whom the rulers have taught them to fear and hate. Divide, agitate, and rule.

In pre-state societies, the entire people were close-knit, much like the nuclear family structure today. So, in those societies, people were no more prone to harm or abuse a social member than you might do to your mother today. That's how people saw each other. Which is why the Europeans and Arabs from state-level societies so easily penetrated and destroyed the pre-state and rudimentary state societies of the Amerikas, Africa, Asia, Australia, etc. (The people of such societies were not prepared for the violence and greed of these state armies, administrators, and missionaries that descended on them.) There were no police in the pre-state societies; in fact, there were no laws. There were only basic social norms that everyone recognized and respected, which one had to answer to the entire community for violating. No one wants to be persecuted, rejected, or despised by their peer group, or a group they want to be accepted by – you see this everyday in cats' responses to peer pressure, projecting images and talking in ways they expect will win them acceptance within their own peer groups.

The basis of revolution is to overthrow the elite system that dominates the peoples' access to the means of survival, and to destroy the anti-communal ethic of individualism that we've been **trained** into since birth, which has us preying on any and everyone solely for personal benefit. **This** is the root of self- and environmentally-destructive tendencies. So in the revolutionary **process**, the people must be reeducated, and social experience is the most valid educational process. Capitalism itself puts profits above humyn life and relationships, because in capitalist societies, wealth and nothing else is the basis of power. Human life, the environment, and social cohesion and welfare mean nothing. Inherent in its name is to capitalize. Capitalism exists on a global scale because of European invasions, destructions, and replacements of traditional economic and social systems across the globe with the cutthroat capitalist one beginning in the 16th century, thereby expanding the capitalist empires and developing the system of imperialism on a global scale. It was the European elites who created and imposed on people of color the notion that we were all corrupt, savage, and stupid by nature, and needed their rule and guidance to become "civilized." What they really wanted was and is the natural wealth of the world extracted by our forced labor to export back to Europe to pay mercenary armies that were fighting endless wars to overthrow other empires, to fill their coffers, and to try and satisfy the demands of the middle classes, who (then as today) were used to control the majority lower-class, laboring masses.

Your proposing to change our communities without moving beyond capitalism is an unrealistic proposition, first of all, because those who rule will not let you. Any economic system, capitalist, socialist, or pre-state, demands a **source** of wealth, and by wealth I don't mean currency; I mean natural wealth (natural resources) and mass labor to extract and work up those resources into usable and/or consumable forms. In the capitalist context, this will compel competition with existing huge capitalist enterprises, and the governments that protect them, for access to and control of large and diverse areas of fertile and mineral-rich land and large labor pools. Today, **all** of that sort of land is claimed by already existing big capitalist powers, including the land on which Black folk live in

Amerika. So to change the economic conditions of Black folk under capitalism – a contradiction in itself – you would first have to be able to enforce sovereign (that is inalienable) claims of ownership of large fertile and resource-rich land areas (much of which is already claimed by big capitalist enterprises, such as agribusiness and mining corporations, or are held in "reserve" by the federal and local governments). You must then be able to provide all needy Black folk with adequate means of meeting their basic needs. In Amerika, the job market is owned, controlled, and regulated by big capitalists. So, to do either of these things you would have to first seize your own territory, which would mean a war for national independence to seize land from the big capitalists (who themselves took all they control from us and other people of color through the force and protection of the US government and military), 'cause they damn sure ain't gonna give or sell it to you (this land is the very **source** of their wealth and power, and many being self-financing enterprises, they damn sure don't need any paper currency).

This is what World Wars I and II were all about, namely European countries and Japan competing for control and possession of the world's regions of natural wealth. In fact, Japan tried exactly what you're talking about doing – namely, using capitalism to consolidate, develop, and "improve" the economic conditions of Asia. Their reward was economic embargoes on their basic trade imposed by Amerika (economic warfare calculated to basically destroy Japan's economy), which predictably provoked a military reaction from Japan – namely, Japan's attacking US military bases in Hawaii and the Philippines where Amerika was colonizing and economically exploiting people of color in a not-very-nice way; all of which ended in Japan's defeat in World War II by Amerika's dropping nukes on two of Japan's major population and industrial centers, Hiroshima and Nagasaki (1945).

The only reason Japan's wealthy elite bounced back economically is because the US had to invest in Japanese communications (out of which grew the Sony enterprise) and transportation (Toyota) industries during the Korean War (Amerika needed a local supply base for military communications and transportation systems in a country that already had the industrial experience and infrastructure). Because of this US investment, Japan's economy has since developed under the telecommunications/electronics and auto-making industries; however, because Amerika strictly limited Japan's military power and has kept tight controls on Japan's access to petroleum supplies (oil is the lifeblood of any industrial economy), the US has always maintained the ability to shut down Japanese industries if Japan ever got out of line. Along with this, the US has used Japan as a strategic base to control and repress the spread of socialism and national independence struggles in surrounding Asian countries. Yet the living standards in Asia are still one of immense mass poverty and desperation under tiny groups of super-rich elites who own and control the economic and political systems. Under capitalism it could be no other way, because wealth is the basis of capitalist ruling power, and one cannot have immense wealth unless he takes it and keeps it from the working people. Whereas, if the working people collectively own and possess the land and fruits of their labor, then this ceases to be capitalism; this is **socialism**. And capitalists fear nothing else like they fear socialism, which is why they commit so much economic, military, and misinformational resources to distorting and demonizing socialism.

So, you cannot change the values and conditions of our communities without changing the economies of them. Your study of business, real estate, etc., will only teach you economic values and approaches that operate within and support the capitalist system, much as Farrakhan does. He criticizes Amerika and what its economic system has done, and does, to us, and people across the world, but he accepts entrepreneurial capitalism, which cannot function except within the market structure of the domestic and global capitalist system. Amerika can't employ us, indeed, it can't even employ a large segment of its white population, and with the continued advances of technology replacing large work forces, and jobs (even blue- and white-collar jobs) being steadily outsourced to the Third World to exploit cheaper labor costs and more easily exploit and repress workers, jobs are becoming increasingly scarce, wages continuously dropping, and "job security" is becoming increasingly nonexistent. Beyond this, under corporate pressure the government is cutting social spending and "minority" civil rights to the bone, leaving us all the more desperate and insecure. Increasingly, the only two options left open for our youth are prison and the military, and all of this because the capitalist "owners" do not want to share the wealth they take from the workers.

The tiny handful of Blacks you mentioned, Russell Simmons and his sort, have what they do because they work with the white capitalists; they promote and support the system, and serve as a source of extracting wealth from the Black sector and returning it to the white capitalists by creating Black-oriented entertainment, clothing, etc. markets. For the Russell Simmonses of Amerika to separate from the capital elites would be to commit economic suicide: they'd be bought out, face career-destroying bad media, find no one willing to give or continue giving them credit; they'd have outstanding loans simultaneously foreclosed on, driving them into bankruptcy overnight; they'd find themselves facing anti-trust lawsuits; no one would be willing to join them in investments, or they'd find investment partners suddenly pulling out of joint investment enterprises, etc. Some of this is what was done to Michael Jordan back when he tried to establish his own sporting franchise. He ended up depleting all his millions in savings and had to go back to the NBA as an entertainer to recoup his losses. And he wasn't even trying to help Black folks; he was just trying to become an equal to the big capitalists in the sportswear industry. They turned on him and booted him out on his head. The objective is to keep Blacks powerless, both on the individual and especially mass levels (again currency doesn't amount to real wealth – productive land and resources do.)

The establishment demonized, killed off, infiltrated, imprisoned, and ultimately destroyed the old Black Panther Party because they began effectively organizing Black folks around their cultural, economic, and political needs. Solely because of their organizing work the FBI labeled the BPP the greatest internal threat to US national security, and labeled the Panthers' Free Breakfast for Poor Children program its most dangerous activity. The danger that the BPP presented was in the mass support it was winning in the oppressed urban Black communities, and the powers that be knew that once we came to see that the establishment was unwilling and unable to meet our own basic needs, but that collectively we could do so, we would struggle to break away from that system. Likewise, any effort along these lines will provoke the same reaction – namely, attempted destruction by any means necessary by the system – as soon as it begins to show some results and gains mass support.

Amerika's hard line, and quite racist policy, has always been that, unlike what white Europe and Amerika achieved for themselves in the 18th and 19th centuries, people of color have no right to pursue national independence, and especially not economic independence. Most of the Third World just gained its political independence in the last fifty years, and this against brutal Amerikan and European resistance – especially in Asia and across Afrika. And almost none have been able to achieve economic independence – Amerika has prevented this at every turn through imposing indentured slavery on entire countries through World Bank, IMF, and WTO debts imposed on them, backing, arming, supplying, training, and financing sub-imperialist states like Israel, Turkey, and South Afrika and local death squads and mercenary forces to massacre millions of workers and peasants, political, labor, and religious leaders who have protested poverty and corruption in their 3rd World countries, etc.

It's no accident that the corporate media (entertainment) industry has taken control of our ideological and cultural systems, and through them promotes the most self-destructive and self-depreciating of all subcultures within our communities, that major labels only promote negative, frivolous or conformist images for Black entertainment and role models. We must be reeducated, Bro, and nothing shocks the consciousness or creates group cohesion like raw oppression and resistance, because under such circumstances survival turns on the people's ability to cooperate, thus bringing back to the surface our **natural** inclination as communal creatures to cooperate to survive. "Even enemies, if together in a boat tossed by waves, cooperate just as the right hand does with the left."

Rashid

33.   To Outlaw: Included is my reply to T's letter; tell him to let me know if he doesn't understand my position on anything and I'll clarify. You should read this letter too.

Rashid

34.   To Rashid: A few days ago I had identified this cynicism in T and his utter lack of faith in people as well. So I gave him *Revolution: a Blueprint* a few days ago, 'cause that essay addresses people's co-operation, group survival, and how integral it is to and has been in human history. But a discussion had jumped off and I ended up telling him to write you and get your perspective on whatever he held opinions on, 'cause my cell-partner supports some twisted concept of "people's capitalism" and "human nature is corrupt by nature," and T seemed to agree. My argument was it was too closely tied to the Christian idea of we're all "born sinners," therefore we can't govern ourselves, as they say to undermine confidence and faith in ourselves. I didn't deny slavery, betrayal, and the like amongst Blacks/Afrikans before European intervention. I looked at what was general amongst those various Afrikan tribes, their customs, especially in dealing with strangers – they welcomed and cared for (fed, adored, exalted) strangers.

Obviously my argument wasn't effective in convincing these dudes otherwise, mainly because they **see** so much "corruption." These elites have waged some intense psychological warfare on us; excluding **acting**, we don't even **think** we can operate independently of European paternalism.

Surprise – Mau Mau is next door to me. Came in on Friday. I didn't know who he was till Saturday. I have yet to mention you to him, nor has he directly mentioned you; only in passing has he referred to you, and that's something I recognized because I know your style. Well, I can't conduct a purging move at this point. He sensed something because of my "character flaw" of intolerance seeping through, or his extreme paranoia; however, to eliminate his uneasiness I explained my serious poise (which he questioned) away as being in conformance with George's description of the man-child being cool, unapproachable, and my overall frustration with various struggle-related matters. I'm making you aware of his presence 'cause, shit, I ain't got nothing to hide. I told you how I feel about informants; however, I'm thinking also in terms of how can he be useful to the cause. I guess I should be giving more attention to Sun Tzu where he discusses the "expendable agents." "Men must be pampered or annihilated." I can't or am not willing to incur the consequences of the latter (I'm speaking in literal terms) and run the risk of compromising or jeopardizing the "True Soldierz" overall objectives. Do you understand my concerns? Uhuru!

Outlaw

35.   To Outlaw: About your "new" neighbor … I fully understand your position, but I don't know how he might react if he found out my location **and** that we are in frequent contact. If he comes to feel you "hid" it from him it's likely to prompt a paranoid "reaction," but if you do mention it, the same is still likely to occur. I'm sending you that letter he sent me so you can see for yourself his rat confessions. Perhaps it'd be best to broach the topic of me to him as a passing subject. If you allow him to feel that we've never discussed him before, he may confess on his own the situation and keep his feelers out to see what your reaction is. This might come as a test of your composure in a real-life situation where an opponent must not know your state of mind. I feel you completely on not being in a position to "deal" with him – I concur with your choice, but keep mindful that dude is highly paranoid, and I don't discount that his "fear" may push him to "act first." I can only counsel you to tread lightly with him. When he sent me this letter, I didn't respond (a response is obviously what he wanted) or even acknowledge it. He got me moved out of the unit. I'd been moved into the unit where he was because they were painting the unit I was in. He'd gotten moved out of that old unit and into another one because of fingering me to the pigs. Whatever "use" you make of him, you should be certain not to give his character any credibility in the eyes of others. Dude is a rat and a mole, so you need to be conscious of all you say to and around him. It's even probable that the pigs have planted him there to probe you – they've clearly made the tie-in between you and me, and, as you know, they keep plants under me.

Rashid

36.   To Rashid: I don't know whether to describe what I'm feeling after reading this letter from dude as emotions, or as a relentless desire to rid the world of such repulsive elements! I'm seriously reconsidering my original intentions to use or even be associated with this agent. I just did some handwriting analysis for further confirmation. Even though I don't have any of his cursive handwriting, I still see the graphic, striking similarity! And other features are exactly the same as in the notes he gave me on the *Catechism* and "Che Talks to Young People." And even more convincing is his "D.T.F.I." organization. He mentioned the exact same thing to me on Sunday before you sent this kite. Though I can't give him what he deserves – death – I could rearrange his facial-structural features! I have utter disgust for his kind, and that disgust is exacerbated by the fact of our peers' overall tolerance for such actions – it's alright to snitch – and I want to separate and distinguish myself from all that. It's just like one agent down, a million to go! What to do. What to do. I feel complete allegiance and camaraderie towards you, and wouldn't mind avenging the wrongs this agent perpetrated against you, however, on the other hand, the True Soldier has objectives that weigh heavier on the scale of goals. You are exactly on point in saying do not "credit" him with anything – my thoughts exactly. This shit is surreal. I still haven't mentioned you yet. I'd rather seize an opportunity than create a "loophole" for his suspicions, but I'm working towards it. I'm just trying to calculate his responses. I can logically assume your plans for him, but at this juncture what use can he be? Give me your input, specifically.

Outlaw

37. To Outlaw: As for your neighbor, I can actually see no **use** he can be put to under the circumstances, except to be made an example of or publicly ostracized. I'm thinking to circulate copies over there of his confession note – I got eight copies made of it. Since there seems to be no progressive use that he could be made of, perhaps you should just disclose what you know to him, give him a copy of his own letter (I enclose several), and just tell him you disapprove of such conduct and disassociate yourself. Let him know that I just sent you and several others copies of the letter. Ask him if he in fact wrote it, and upon a confession let him know that you don't fraternize with dudes who conduct themselves that way and cut him off. No need for a confrontation. This mode of addressing the situation will clear your conscience and resolve the situation in a principled manner. How he may react is another question. But make sure you let him know that I sent **several** brothers over there other than you a copy of his letter. This way he can't isolate his reaction – if any – to you. I don't know though; he's likely to get himself and/or me moved to another unit. I leave the choice up to you.

There's a brother I've recently been dialoguing with. He's very astute in revolutionary theory, and is involved in some valid work. His name's BX. I'd like to share a couple of his letters with you, give you a feel for him. I'm very partial to him and his approach. Before I send you BX's letters, I'd want to know your choice in dealing with Mau Mau just in case it may lead to me getting moved or otherwise putting heat on the taxi. Folks will likely make an issue out of **how** you got the letter he wrote me, if he runs to the brass about the matter. Again, I'll leave to your discretion how to resolve the situation. Just let me know your choice beforehand.

Rashid

38. To Rashid: I got your essay "Amerika – Freedom is Slavery, Ignorance is Strength."* That was the only item sent at that time right? I will follow your suggestions in dealing with my neighbor. Just to ensure that the other transaction goes through, I will defer "exposure" until afterwards. It struck me you know how can I justify, later on, my association with this dude especially when the objective conditions are not conducive to a result in the True Soldierz favor. So, fuck it, whatever may come. I still have reservations about declaring foe with this dude, but yet living around him not knowing his reaction or what it could be … it's just something I haven't been doing consciously in previous incidents. But it will occur, all on the principle – no snitching.

Another kite I'll be sending later today is an attempt to assess a situation and put those assessments on paper, though I'm rather rough around the edges. How can dude propose your actions to be counterrevolutionary and he's a rat? The audacity of the pig agent!

Go ahead and send the letters over from BX, I would like to get a feel for him. When you initially advised me to avoid alienating individuals I didn't fully understand how not to do so. I mean, it's a case-by-case task. But somehow it's somewhat easier now, I just didn't want to support people's self-destructive actions inadvertently. It's the "how" that matters. "I'm alive and learning."

Outlaw

— — — — —

* See page 323.

39.   To Outlaw: A quick note to send these letters over from BX, a longer reply on your neighbor will follow later – I have about ten outstanding letters to reply to, one of which being one of the enclosed letters from BX, which is why I'm hurrying to send his letters to you – I need them back ASAP so to reply to this last one he wrote.

Yes, I sent that "Amerika" essay by itself, I had just gotten copies made and dropped it on the taxi while he was passing by. I'll explain later how you can tie in to BX. He promotes preparatory work in anticipation of "spontaneous" struggle, at my present stage of development I'm more inclined toward "manufacturing" struggle. But I fully support his position also.

I touched base with SK yesterday who's in your unit, and told him that you're a solid young brother. On that account he replied that with my acknowledging you, he embraces you also. I sent him some materials and referred him to you for further reading and to get an idea of the range of literature I have on hand – I have extra copies of most of what I've already sent you over. He says you two had spoken briefly, but nothing in depth. In any regard I think you two should connect. He expresses embracing an ideology similar to my own.

Rashid

40.   To Rashid: Well, I seized the opportunity. Mau Mau was viewing the board with all the residents in your unit and asked did I know W. After confirming that I do, I asked who does he know, and he said K. Johnson – Rashid. I then proceeded to find out how well he knows Rashid, to what extent, and mentioned I myself had heard about Rashid, even corresponded with him a few times. I mentioned Rashid's ideology was along the lines of his (Mau Mau). Which, as I predicted, prompted him to note the distinction. Mau Mau lacks an understanding of the necessity of practice and that people learn from observation and participation, which works toward developing the unity and solidarity so needed to accomplish the goals of liberation ideology. Whereas Rashid, on the other hand, has pursued various forms of practice in order to radicalize people by appealing to people's inherent ability to identify with action more so than words or theories, and at the same time establish and offer material support to people in times of crisis. And this material support is very much appreciated – especially when unsolicited – as has been the case whenever Rashid has intervened on other prisoners' behalf. I must note that by no means has Rashid neglected education or ideological training or failed to put "politics in command," any person engaged in exchanges with Rashid cannot deny this fact. "Practice is not only the basis, but the ultimate aim of knowledge."

Mau Mau seems to promote liberation within a vacuum. A theoretical vacuum full of intelligentsia or a vanguard who expects to have the masses support liberation upon the vanguard's command, without its prior relations to the masses, which is like producing political robots. Yes, the vanguard must play its role, but that role is nothing without the masses' support. We must relate to them. The vanguard must organize itself around the needs of the masses, upon what the masses want. To find out what the masses need and want, we must go amongst them, we must relate to them, we must protect their interests. Mau Mau has seemingly overlooked or maybe disregarded one of George's most fundamental statements or quotes from Marx, "it is the educator himself who must be educated," and where does this education come from? I think the point has been made.

You know Mau Mau expressed the feeling that your practice is counter-liberation because a social revolution won't occur inside prison, which cannot be denied, however, it's gotta start somewhere, and why not amongst people who harbor the most anti-empire sentiments? Though undisciplined, prone to diversion, and not politically conscious, they/we have potential, for under empire we have no credentials. I detect a lot of nihilism in Mau Mau's voice. Even before the revolution of 1917 the Bolsheviks still fought for better working conditions, and economic concessions. Though not the goal, still these struggles were part of the overall strategy. Likewise, we can struggle for better prison conditions, elimination of mandatory minimums, restoration of food items in segregation commissary, etc., etc. These aspects of struggle serve to stimulate and educate the masses to one degree or another, because it involves political exposure, lived experience.

None of this is to be perceived as favoritism or blind faith in Rashid 'cause of your practice, but your activity seems to be the most effective in garnering attention and support. Mau Mau said how if he was as educated as you, he wouldn't waste energy stabbing pigs in seg, he would be trying to be on the yard talking to people, which makes sense. But that doesn't preclude practice, if anything it entails practice, and I'm speaking in terms of putting up resistance in some shape or form – Mau Mau seems to want to avoid this issue. I see that you, like our predecessor George, don't plan on "leaving anything behind." In relation to which George was referring to his manhood. It makes me analyze my own position, 'cause I know I will have to take principled, practical stands whether it be against the pigs themselves or against pig tendencies amongst prisoners. An individual may end up in seg dependent upon what type of practice is applied in a situation. I'm not a self-assumed authority on politics or matters that concern the lives of millions, as you say about yourself. "I'm alive and learning."

When, to be sure, you speak about "manufacturing" a revolution, you're essentially speaking in terms of coordinated efforts, right? Whereas BX's concept of "spontaneous" revolution essentially involves a series of selective forays? I'm not clear on that point. Otherwise BX sounds seasoned and informed, armed with a coherent approach to preparation.

Remember in *Blood In My Eye* where Jonathan was discussing new recruits and he noted that an agent would be unlikely to have studied revolutionary ideology/Marxism-Leninism-Maoism in depth? That the types of texts one has read reveals what thought processes have occurred in one's mind, and that an agent won't have or it's unlikely that an agent would have an in-depth, thorough understanding of revolutionary ideology. Well, based upon this encounter with Mau Mau, there seems to be new evidence of greater desperation among the agents to thoroughly infiltrate, by bearing a heavier workload in order to understand and undermine movements. All this may hold no weight, it may not even matter about the extent of an agent's ideological education, but Jonathan did establish this point.

I'm in ideological agreement with BX for the most part, especially on the point Uncle Ho established. I conceive of politicizing prisoners nationwide. I will touch base with BX, familiarize myself with him, him with me. What did BX mean in his last letter that the groups of the oppressed nationalities "is not the vanguard role but it is important"? I'm about to give Lenin's *What is to be Done?* a lot of attention. I've been trying, painstakingly, to break down *Political Economy*. Also Mau Mau gave me this book to read, *Against Empire*, by Michael Parenti – good book, bad supplier.

Outlaw

41. To OUTLAW: I think at the core of your neighbor's thinking, indecision, and evasions is a basic confusion built on noncommitment. He's found something that (for whatever reasons) he wants to appear to be "down" with, and he wants to "adjust" the interpretations of it to conform to his own individual dysfunctions. He doesn't strike me as a persyn capable of calm, calculated, premeditated violence – he's clearly the type that needs an emotional and psychological boost: anger, fear, vengeance, peer pressure, etc. In adopting an ideology that compels – at some point – one's taking a confrontational stand against a stronger opponent based solely upon principle, one must have a certain mental and emotional fortitude and commitment – your neighbor doesn't strike me as having this sort of constitution; therefore, he will obviously avoid any interpretation of

liberation ideology that will compel him to take principled stands at times other than when he feels personally threatened.

Mau Mau always promoted himself as being a fighter, a soldier. Yet in every exchange I had with him he proved terrified of the *consequences* of militancy. What led to my originally distancing myself from him was his having admitted to snitching on another known rat (who goes by Teardrop and Black Cherry) because that pig agent threatened and convinced him that he would break out of his cell and butcher him. I asked if he proposes to be a soldier, what in hell would he do if he were captured while in the field of battle and subjected to torture by the enemy? He claimed that he'd stand firm because of his ideological convictions. Yeah right! He further claimed that the only reason he snitched about the other rat supposedly scheming to attack him was because in seg he was defenseless against cats who could circumvent "security" and catch a man in handcuffs.

I asked, did he expect that in custody of military or CIA torturers he'd be in a better position to "fight" back? Of course not, but he still returned the answer about his fortitude based on ideology. Dude is twisted. If he can't stand up under these "civilian" conditions, he'd be the first to defect under conditions of martial rule where the pigs are subjected to no oversight and no limits on their sadism.

When I speak of "manufacturing" revolution, I mean creating the objective conditions which will provoke insurrection on a mass scale, for example, provoking repression while giving an example of how, and in fact **that**, resistance can be waged. BX speaks of "spontaneous" revolution as the vanguard waiting and preparing for objective conditions, which might provoke mass discontent and consequent insurrection. He maybe rejects George's view that revolutionary conditions can be manufactured as opposed to just waiting until they arise as a matter of course in the enemy's continued expansion of repressive policies. He proposes that the vanguard agitate and prepare a logistic support base meantime, which once the masses begin rebelling, can arm, organize, and lead them in a successful revolutionary struggle instead of allowing the rebellion to degenerate into a mere riot.

I think Jonathan and George were in error in that the enemy will not study revolutionary theory in depth, and that any in-depth consciousness of these theories will prevent one from becoming or being a pig agent. One can be very class-conscious without having to commit class suicide. V and I have been dialoguing on this point in recent correspondence. He's a white intellectual, a professor of political science and Marxist theory – in his sixties. He was around and in fact involved in the various movements of the last century. Even organizing and teaching in South America. And he concedes that he's had to build many barriers around himself (organizational, intellectual, physical) over the decades to fortify himself against the tendency that he's witnessed throughout Leftist history of "conscious" people jumping ship and becoming co-opted. His making this point came in response to and in agreement with my position that education alone will not raise mass consciousness to the point necessary for resistance. That merely educating the people will not compel them to break away from the oppressive enemy order any more than educating people about AIDS will compel them to refrain from risky behavior (unprotected sex, needle sharing, etc.). If the short-term benefits seem to outweigh the fear of risk or the immediate dangers, folks will generally pursue immediate gratification and push the more remote possibilities of danger from their minds, that is, unless they've had a very personal experience (objective experience) with AIDS, say, living around AIDS patients during some very sobering stages of its development. Likewise, telling people that they are being oppressed and are living at the expense of the immediate suffering of others and future destruction of their own ecosystem, will be ineffective so long as they feel they're reaping relative immediate benefits from those conditions – one has to shock them out of their senses of comfort and privilege.

I further gave him the example of the deep infiltration of the old US Communist Party – that by 1956 some 1,500 of the remaining 5,000 USCP members were FBI informants. Likewise the Socialist Workers Party was crawling with pig agents, three of whom ran for public office on the party platform. Implicit in their party memberships is that these pig agents were politically conscious – well-versed in liberation ideology. Yet that knowledge didn't prevent them from working with the opposition. He got the point.

So your neighbor is no special case – one's knowledge of revolutionary ideology cannot be used as a yardstick to measure their sincerity and commitment. As always, it turns on practice and consistency of practice.

About BX's remarks concerning the leading National Independence mass organizations (of the internal US colonies) not serving in the vanguard role but serving an important purpose: remember that the vanguard role is that of the international working class (which is both multi-ethnic and multi-national), whereas mass-based national independence groups resisting colonialism will consist of classes other than just the laboring class, but who are members of the particular national group.

If you recognize your role and most value to be in political work/agitation, then you maybe shouldn't create a situation with your neighbor that might affect your ability to maintain the necessary contacts with our peer group. Our workers have always been surrounded by pigs – on the inside and outside – but they don't attack pigs or provoke them unless victory is assured or party ranks have been infiltrated and the enemy element must be purged. But I suppose you can break what you know to that rat and terminate interactions with him without provoking a reaction. Tell you what, holla at SK, explain your situation and get his feedback (and give him a copy of that letter).

Rashid

42.   To RASHID: Well, Mau Mau moved out of the unit tonight for some reason or another. The whole time he was over here he was trying to get me to write something down regarding ideology. It was a frivolous issue, but he wrote me and kept telling me to write my answer down, he "doesn't want to discuss it verbally." Of course I blew it off as irrelevant and rejected the proposition to participate, which evoked an unusual response – I've never seen a person get mad 'cause I wouldn't write something down that could easily be discussed. I think I handled ostracizing him well. I seized an opportunity. He gave me a book that I was procrastinating in returning while simultaneously requesting more literature, 'cause I know how much he values, or appears to value, his literature. He got irritated. So when he copped an attitude and tried to debate about my procrastinating, I brought the book out and threw it in his cell and walked off. He tried to say something. I just said, "fuck it," "fuck that shit," and didn't speak to him again while spreading the word about his agent status, which caused everybody else to ostracize him as well. He had nowhere to turn but to the pigs. So as it stands, that's the reason for cutting him off (the book) as opposed to siding with you and letting him know I know he's an agent, which definitely would have put him on the defense to the extreme. He definitely was over here for a purpose. I don't care about his response personally, but the pigs are definitely on his side. While he was over here, he used the phone anytime, with the consent of various ranking pigs. He stayed in their face, in the office with them – fuck him. It's a little after 10 PM. He left about thirty minutes ago.

George made a statement along the lines of recognizing he's fighting the TV images/media, the established "legitimate" institutions, the minds and influences of people, and that it was a trying task.

There's a white dude named ST over here – how is he? I've talk-ed to him briefly. As for you and me, I think we see eye-to-eye on a lot of things, some discussed, some not.

I know in the Republic of New Afrika's program, they call for establishing our New Afrikan national territory in those five south-eastern US states called the Black belt.* Have you ever discussed this with your Native American comrades? I get the response from our peers that we shouldn't fight for a piece of Amerika; we should just move back to Afrika and "let the crackerz have this shit," etc. It would be easier to just go back and avoid war. There seem to be some misconceptions about how we will be accepted in Afrika, its present state, and its relations to global capitalism. Our peers don't see the reality, world trade in the favor of capital. This dude told me that Third World countries' dollar value might be lower than, say, the US dollar, but that it's sufficient for the people in the Third World. They don't need as much money to survive, though their economies might be starved. "Those who mistake what should be for what is, pursue their own downfall." Uhuru.

Outlaw

— — — — —

* South Carolina, Georgia, Alabama, Mississippi, and Louisiana – terri-tory which was promised to Blacks in exchange for our aiding the US mili-tarily in defeating the confederates during the US Civil War (1861-1865), which we developed and slaved on for centuries and were the majority population of in most areas, and which we were pushed off of during Reconstruction (1860-1880) by the US army and terrorist attacks, by the Ku Klux Klan and Knights of White Camilla from which we fled and were herded into urban centers where we remain.

43.   To Outlaw: The white fella ST is solid peoples. He's one of the dudes who rolled with us when we fought the pigs last year. Tell him to holla and I'll be sending a message to him later.

Much of our peers' reluctance to fight for independence (political and economic) here on US soil and their promoting flight "back to Afrika," I interpret as stemming primarily from conditioned cowardice, fear to confront established white power. And of course that psychological conditioning of cultural imperialism, which has us seeing ourselves as too stupid and backward by nature to successfully challenge that "invulnerable" white power structure, plays a major part. But as you observed, flight to Afrika doesn't offer escape from conditioned oppression under capitalist imperialism. The western European-Amerikan powers have the continent in a state of collapse. The life expectancy rate across much of Afrika is half that here in the US. Ghana is amongst the highest at 57 years old, but the continental mean is mid-thirties: Zimbabwe 34/35, Malawi and Tanzania 33/34; Mozambique 37, etc. I'm 33 this year. In Afrika, I'd be amongst the soon or already dead from ripe old age. Then there's the AIDS crisis, and pervasive war, instigated and armed by the US and europeans and their sub-imperial lackeys, South Afrika (still owned and controlled by the white minority), Israel, etc. But their problems, their state of disrepair, comes on account of the US and its policies toward exploiting Afrika and keeping chaos as the norm so to keep her vast natural wealth flowing out of Afrika and into these western economies, and to prevent a tide of revolutionary struggle from sweeping the continent again, as occurred from the late 1950's–1970's, which threatened to unite the continent under socialist economic independence which would turn Afrika's wealth over to the benefit and development of Afrika for the Afrikan people. Those very struggles that succeeded in driving the european colonialists out, but because native puppets of the west were maneuvered into political power, allowed Afrika's wealth to continue to flow out of the continent and to the west for a small cut of the profits, and prevented the economic unification of the continent. Afrika thus remains underdeveloped and in chaos. The west fears a united Afrika, which is why they had to kill Patrice Lumumba, Amilcar Cabral, etc.

We won't be avoiding war by running to Afrika – we'll in fact be running right into a war zone, replete with genocides, pandemics, and mass starvation. Look at Sudan, the Congo. In just three years, some 2.5 million Congolese people have died, but there's a conspiracy of silence surrounding this crisis in the west – Amerika especially. This is all part of a clear US policy of Black depopulation (genocide) in and outside of Afrika. So, even those who promote flight to Afrika would need to put in work right here in Amerika if they expect to have a stable place to run to in Afrika, and overall, we must unite our struggle here with Afrika's. The US – the main backer of regional terrorist states like South Afrika, Israel, etc. – must be taken down in order to give Afrika room to breathe; to develop, instead of being robbed of her natural resources to continue enriching the west. We've got to overcome this cowardice. We must realize that the oppressed and exploited internal colonies of Amerika (Native, New Afrikan, central/south american migrants, etc.) have proven to produce the most effective fighting forces **for** Amerika. Especially us New Afrikans (Blacks). We've been **the** decisive force that has won **all** her wars for her: the Revolutionary War, the War of 1812, the US Civil War (in fact, Lincoln emancipated the slaves only in the confederate states because the US needed us to fight with the union army to turn the tide and win the war against the confederates), the Spanish-Amerikan War, WW's I and II, the Persian Gulf War, and now the Iraqi occupation. We can fight **for** our oppressors – so starved are we to win his praise, approval, and acceptance – but we cannot fight **against** him to win our own dignity, rights, independence, self-determination, and reclaim our own identity and history. We want his little toys, tokens, and status symbols, all of which he has acquired by looting and destroying the lands of people of color and enslaving them. Yet we're too timid to pursue our own collective interests, to obtain our own economic independence wherein **we** define our own values, instead of having the west spoon-feed us its own warped ones. I'm for New Afrika (whether its territory be concentrated in the southeast of Amerika or spread out in enclaves across claimed US territory). I'm for the right of our Mexican and Native American brothers and sisters to also achieve national independence, reclaiming the vast territories stolen from them by Amerikan deceit, lies and genocidal murder of millions, and I'm for any other struggle against imperialism and neocolonialism, but we must this time unite all these liberation forces into a united front (along with the international – including the white Amerikan – working class) to deal imperialism the death blow. I've shared, and there's an agreement on, these points with the more advanced Native comrades. The failure of the struggles of the First Nations and our own ancestors during our chattel enslavement can in many cases be traced back to our failure to unite our forces against the common capitalist enemy. As with today, we fought against and were used to destroy ourselves more than anyone else.

I embrace all who promote progress – as for these timid cowards who resort to escapism and philosophical excuses for avoiding the inevitable armed contest, they're to be ignored, purged, and trampled underfoot as we advance forward to crush the enemy. As Machiavelli accurately observed, one should not allow disorder to persist in order to avoid war, for he doesn't avoid war but only delays it to his own disadvantage.

We've got a Black brain trust here on US soil that can match and beat everything Amerika has. We have intellectuals, educators, scientists, technicians, and specialists of every make. Instead of being pimped of our knowledge, talents, and skills by Amerika, we need to turn them to our own benefit and that of our oppressed brothers and sisters across the globe. And what we have that Amerika can't contend with is the potential to organize and field a fighting force that will crush imperialism at its root. The only thing the US has to offer us by way of real options is the choice of which way we prefer to suffer and die, while helping to maintain the obscene wealth and dominant status of those who own and control this plantation. We have the choices of dying in the streets (the ghettos – the Black refugee camps), dying in imperialist wars while massacring other people of color and poisoning and destroying their environments, dying from medical neglect (the Black child mortality and life expectancy rate in Amerika is the same as that in many of the poorest Third World countries), dying by the millions of the AIDS pandemic which the government and big pharmaceutical industries outright ignore, dying of social neglect (aid to the poor, who are disproportionately Black, has been basically cut in Amerika, while millions of jobs are being lost to developing technology and outsourcing), or rotting in these concentration camps – dying a slow and mental death (locking away our young males throughout their most productive years in such vast numbers that young Black womyn are frequently heard to complain of being unable to find Black male companions – thus destroying our capacity to reproduce). But we don't see all this. Meantime, empire neutralizes our will to resist this fucked-up arrangement (this is, KILLING US OFF!) by advancing a handful of self-interested, opportunist, or politically confused Blacks to positions of prominence, and waving them in front of the rest of us as "proof" that the Amerikkkan dream is indeed achievable for us.

I've seen more talent in these prisons than the whole entertainment industry put together, which industry uses us as clowns and diversions for the Black masses, and then throws us on the trash heap once our use-value and profitability has been sapped; meantime our youth are in a frenzy of competing at the bottom to gain their own five minutes of fame. Brother, there's work to be done, and it damn sure ain't over there in Afrika laid back with its feet propped up.

I'm going to try and send you this Mao *Selected Works Volume I*. Hope this doesn't end up snagged.

Rashid

44.   To Rashid: I see how your thinking has developed along the lines that it has; **Mao is profound**! Talk about elucidation! His "Analysis of Classes in China," "Problems of Strategy in Revolutionary War," "On Practice," these writings stood out to me like a motherfucker! Excuse the expression. This is exactly what I needed, because I've been stuck, so to speak, in learning, but not yet understanding application. I've just recently been able to engage in some practice, but only to a very minor degree. Plus, these essays provide guidance in analyzing our "situation as a whole" here in Amerika. I would definitely like to be able to **study** this again if circumstances permit. It's unfortunate that copies of this aren't readily available at present. I wouldn't want you to jeopardize losing this book either, so it's probably best to get it to me how circumstances permit. I know you probably don't agree with Mao wholly when he says that "war can be learned only through war," but since these conditions are not present or available, to what extent can war be learned from study and in what direction due to the lack of "rich experience." I ask 'cause this is of vital importance and it's a problem, presently, to be solved to the greatest possible extent. You'll have to forgive me, I'm still in the perceptual stage, though striving to develop. There are matters that I can perceive and process mentally **involving** concepts but not yet **producing** concepts. Goddamn, Mao is on point. I see why you "religiously study" his work.

I'm assuming your conclusion of the necessity of "shock treatment" to further our aims is the result of your own "analysis of classes" in empire. But from your analysis of these classes who do you consider to be the most revolutionary, considering the majority of workers in empire are complacent to some degree or another, due to the international class relationships of empire to the Third World nations, and the conveniences proletarians, and even lumpen-pro-letarians, are afforded as a result of that international situation and relationship? This question comes in light of the present dire situation in the Sudan and in Haiti. In the Sudan, the Arabian government has displaced almost two million and slaughtered hundreds of thousands of Black Sudanese in the course of a month. This situation has evoked "public outcry" and civil disobedience among petty-bourgeois actors and intellectuals (Black and white) in the US, but that's it, nothing more. In Haiti a hurricane has ravaged the whole country, killed thousands, displaced thousands, and stagnant water (due to its lack of an adequate water-sewage system) has brought disease. However (and this is crazy), the US promised to donate millions, but has only sent $60,000 to date. International aid was sent, but obviously not enough, 'cause the natives of Haiti are fighting over the meager relief that's being sent. In the US among the Blacks, no response, only broadcasts of the situation on the news, primarily BET and the "Black Star Power" bourgeoisie outlook. No efforts whatsoever exerted by these prominent Black "leaders" like Russell Simmons (with all his millions) to bring aid to that country, or any other Black Afrikan country in crisis, but yet he has all these pseudo-political agendas and even more backward popular support to some degree. However, all these figures are bent on "get out the vote," "vote or die" (!??). These are their slogans, "Vote or Die." Can you imagine telling that to one of them starved, desperate, displaced Sudanese or Haitians ("Vote or Die"!)? These house-niggers think good ol' Massa Kerry is gonna take us to the promised land. I'm aware of the concept of living at the enemy's expense, but aren't these Black bourgeoisie types like P. Diddy, Russell Simmons, etc. my enemy too (and they're more vulnerable)?

So, back to my original question or point with the masses (of Blacks, anyway), in light of these examples of "pathetic" leadership and meaningless slogans, who is the most revolutionary, in your opinion? I mean, the working class has complaints, but the specter of losing what they have (or what they actually don't have, rather) is undesirable. The lumpen lacks political consciousness. I mean, even after the correct class analysis is made, the necessity of leadership still presents itself (our leadership, of course). But as I'm writing and thinking, the solution seems to reside in leadership/vanguard. But I still seek an analysis of the classes in empire. This is uncharted territory for me, which became significant to me after reading Mao. I understand that knowing the relations of a class to the means of production is the starting point – maybe I've answered my own damn question. I'm essentially asking, can Mao's analysis of classes be applied to our situation; is it applicable? The extent of the development and contradiction of capitalism in empire – I'm sure – have necessitated alterations of Mao's analysis, and what specific features have changed, and how.

Concerning our peers' cowardice, that's exactly what it is – cowardice. I have that same quote from Machiavelli. You should be here or should've been here when I make our peers aware of their shortcomings like cowardice; they don't like that, and I know I stand in error in general by employing criticism only because of our peers' lack of understanding, but in my view it's only **part** of the shock treatment, the need to break those psychological barriers in accordance with Fanon's views and make our peers see themselves "as they really are, instead of who they think they are," to quote Marx. Uhuru.

Outlaw

45.   TO OUTLAW: So you share my views on Mao's genius? The capitalist-imperialists are terrified of his teachings and have waged extensive campaigns in the west to malign and slander him and revolutionary successes achieved under or in coordination with his ideologies. The BPP was Maoist influenced.

That was only Volume I of Mao's selected works; Volume II is even better, particularly in the refinement of his military thinking. Volume I included his writings from the period of China's internal civil war, where the working-class Chinese Communist Party and Red Army was fighting the bourgeoisie Kuomintang. Volume II includes his writings from the period of Chinese resistance to the Japanese imperialist invasion of China – during which the CCP and Red Army were resisting a powerful imperialist army, as opposed to Chiang Kai-Chek's relatively weak Kuomintang forces. Remember that Japan was then as powerful an empire as the western ones – and the CCP was handling Japan as effectively under Mao's leadership as they had/were the Kuomintang.

The class analysis thing is **mandatory** for waging any successful resistance against imperialist forces. This is something I desire to make here, but my isolation here on the inside prevents me from being able to make an accurate analysis of actual material conditions out there. I can give a general analysis, but it would be based on what I've only been able to glean from reading about modern US economic conditions and the arrangement, sizes, etc., of the contending classes. From this position it would be somewhat difficult to conclude who is the most conducive to revolutionary struggle on a particularized level. Class conditions in modern empire are profoundly different than they have been or were during other historical stages of revolutionary struggles. For example, the US is neither a majority peasant nor proletarian society. It is principally petty-bourgeoisie.

It has an over 80% service-based economy. Remember that the proletarians are the wage-earning productive manual laborers, primarily (although not exclusively) within and around the factory set-up. Since 1973 the US has been steadily de-industrializing and replacing its manufacturing sector with a continually expanding service sector. Manufacturing jobs have been and continue to be outsourced to the underdeveloped world and agricultural manual wage-labor is steadily replaced by machinery and technological advances. So the US proletarian class is small and growing increasingly so, while the world proletariat is growing and becoming increasingly multi-ethnic. So on the international scale, the proletariat is still the leading revolutionary class, especially since the oppressive conditions they suffer in Third World countries equals and exceeds that which radicalized the working classes in 19th and early 20th century Europe and Amerika.

You should read this John Gerassi book *The Coming of the New International*.* It's an anthology of writings of the various leading revolutionary nationalist theorists and analysts of the 1950's–1970's, Mao included. It covers them by nation – for example, China (Mao, Chu Teh, Lin Pao, Chou En-Lai), India (Asit-Sen), Vietnam (Hoc Tap, Le Duan, Vo Nguyen Giap), Korea (Kim Il Sung), Indonesia, Palestine, Iraq, Afrika [Morocco, Algeria, Congo, Kinshasa, South Afrika, Guinea-Bissau, Mozambique, Angola], Cuba, Venezuela, Guatemala, Puerto Rico, Uruguay, Bolivia, Quebec, Brown-Black Amerika. Reading this book will allow you to see how George's "matured" thinking developed along the lines that it did. Most of the revolutionary nationalist thinkers of these various countries conducted analysis of their own internal classes, much as Mao did.

— — — — —

* World Publishing Co. 1971.

Amilcar Cabral is also keen – he devised an unprecedented analysis for a petty-bourgeoisie led revolutionary struggle in Guinea-Bissau, and it proved effective, which is why they had him assassinated. To succeed in his approach, Cabral required the petty-bourgeoisie leadership of the PAIGC party to develop a working-class consciousness, and ultimately commit class-suicide, since Guinea-Bissau had no real existing proletarian class and no revolutionary-oriented peasant class.

The proletariat is always the leading socialist force – as they were even in China even though China had only a very tiny proletarian class, due to a large semi-feudal economy and mass of peasants. Mao recognized the peasants (China's largest laboring class) to be natural **allies** of the proles, because of their economic oppression and exploitation, but they were not a revolutionary class. The peasants did not seek to develop the means of production, nor to take economic control and political power away from the minority oppressing class, but actually sought to return to their old feudal arrangements; therefore, as Lenin, Mao, Cabral, and others recognized, the peasants were essentially a conservative class unable to truly overthrow their oppressors and take power themselves. Not so for the more educated, organized, and disciplined proletariat.

As for the Sudanese and Haitian crises: empire and its owners are unwilling to relinquish their holds on the hoarded and mis-distributed resources needed to meet the needs of the poor and suffering within US borders. How much more do you suppose they'd be willing to provide aid to "foreign" suffering in the Third World? They send a few token crumbs as a public relations and diversionary ploy to allow them to claim humanitarian concern and aid, but never even a tiny fraction of what is needed. In fact, Amerika is **the** primary cause of the instability, extreme poverty, and chaos that prevails in the Third World. The US is the direct cause of Haiti's plight and have angled to keep it a basket case, starved of resources and impoverished as part of its agenda to keep Haiti's resources flowing out of Haiti and to Amerika and its racist plot to never allow this first Black independent nation in this hemisphere to ever appear to be a "success" in any area. Indeed, due to the various improvements that Aristide was able to institute, the US has been behind a contra war based in the Dominican Republic that has reversed Aristide's efforts and "allowed" him to be exiled (kidnapped by US military forces) from his own country.

And these token comprador sambos Puffy Combs, Russell Simmons, etc., are representatives and mouthpieces of US capital, used to influence the oppressed Blacks to seek redemption and salvation from the very forces that exploit and oppress us. Damn right those opportunist, self-concerned, self-serving "representatives" are enemy agents. They're pawns and tools of the establishment used to confuse and mislead the poor and oppressed Black folk.

As said, the proletariat essentially, by nature of its relations to the means of production, is the most revolutionary class, but the US proletariat – with the onset of globalization – is finding itself to be more and more the denizens of the underdeveloped world, while Amerika becomes increasingly the world's overseer and taskmaster (the world police – like the poor white slave patrols and slavebreakers of US chattel slavery who kept the slaves in line for the absentee plantation owner who oppressed both the poor whites he used and the slaves), expanding its dominance and exploitation to the farthest regions of the globe – globalization. I'll send you the remaining volumes of Mao in sequence.

Rashid

46.   To OUTLAW: I'm sending you a Dead Prez interview that K sent me. Also included is an essay by Victor Wallis, to give you a sense of where he's coming from. I feel that his is a valuable original contribution to developing Marxist theory. His thinking has helped me approach a solution to a dilemma I'd had – an economic one – relative to Marx's pro-industrialist position. As you know, Marx correctly promotes the proletariat as the highest and most conscious of the oppressed and exploited classes, and therefore the class that must lead any all-the-way revolutionary struggle against capitalism and imperialism.

Marx promoted broad industrialization. However, industrialization per se has proven to be a most destructive force to the environment and global ecosystem in particular, to such an extent that it seems the whole idea of industrialization must be reexamined. My dilemma came in making Marxist theory and concerns of ecological preservation compatible. Under socialist planning Victor offers an enlightening proposal on just this point.

Victor is the managing editor of a journal called *Socialism and Democracy*. It's a good theoretical media. You should contact him for a subscription. He's a good friend.

Rashid

47.   To Rashid: I've never heard of "Ecological Socialism." As Victor noted, I, like others, always separated the two. I like this though, it makes practical sense, and expounds or elaborates further on Dead Prez's statement in their interview you sent about misdirected environmentalist initiatives. I will definitely write Victor tonight for a subscription.

Dead Prez also spoke about Afrikan Amerikans largely not identifying with Afrika, and I've been pursuing open dialogue with family members about Afrika and its customs, traditions, our heritage there, etc., etc. And what I witness is a slave mentality, a domesticated, accept-whatever-Empire-does-or-says attitude. A family member told me she "don't want to know nothin' about Afrika," "white people will always rule the world." I related to the brother from Dead Prez when he was talking about his lack of influence in the home from his parents and their lack of consciousness, 'cause I grew up the same way with the same type of parents. My Moms emulated white people all my life and tried to instill those ideals and customs in me. But I ain't speaking about Afrika for the sake of Afrikanness.

On the question of the industrialization issue, have you ever thought that maybe infrastructure can be limited to basic needs itself. I'm not trying to be simplistic, actually Victor expressed it best, it's just I personally don't have a coherent picture of how that would work. What about areas of "science" such as space exploration. To my understanding, that takes away a lot of social funding and reaps no benefits for society. On the whole, do you think that the concepts and views that Victor expressed in "Ecological Socialism" implies Socialist/Communist globalization? In the beginning of that paper Victor noted he wasn't talking about "balance in absolute terms," but according to dialectical materialism in the sense of contradictions – one force predominates over the other, absolute balance presupposes inactivity and that's not in accordance with dialectical materialist philosophy.

Blacks in Amerika lack awareness about the environment in general, you do agree? I'm sure some reasons can be given why this is. But more importantly, how do we increase awareness in this area? How do we approach this problem and from what angle? I realize I've been giving people too much to look at all at once instead of "starting with what they know." I mean, this word "freedom," the meaning is too hard to grasp, for others. I'm constantly going back, reformulating, rethinking, redeveloping my approach, 'cause as it stands, I haven't gotten the responses I'm looking for. One dude told me I come across as someone who reads and reads, but the statements surrounding that imply that that's **not cool**. That's nerdy.

I'm also wondering, would our association with the ST's and Victor's (conscious whites) be accurately called a "working coalition" of some sort? Since your and my and the Republic of New Afrika's views seem to be more revolutionary nationalist than anything. I know there is a lot of work to be done.

Outlaw

48.   To Outlaw: "Ecological Socialism" is a relatively new concept. I don't see that Victor's analysis expounds/elaborates on Dead Prez's statement in that interview about "misdirected environmental initiatives." Dead Prez places the humyn condition above the environmental one. Victor, however, sees them as inseparable, namely that environmental sciences and the social sciences are interdependent. There's an essay in the last *S&D* on this point. In it the author agrees that Marx's own theories were actually compatible with promoting environmental balance.

I think we can all understand our Black Amerikan elders' and relatives' senses of pessimism and dissociation towards Afrika. All they see portrayed of Afrika are images of "primitive" backwardness, chaos, war, famine, etc. Compared with the images they have of Amerika, and seeing themselves as members of the most powerful society in history, they obviously prefer to identify themselves with the images of Amerikan wealth over that of Afrikan want. We here in Amerika are actually the modern "house niggers." We relate to and identify ourselves with the master and his wealth, which he obtains by subjugating, exploiting, and (using his hired mercenaries) violently repressing the miserably poor people of the underdeveloped world (the modern field niggers) especially Afrikans in Afrika. We get to wear massa's hand-me-downs or a comical imitation of them, and live in relative privilege above the world's field niggers, so we, in our inherited backward self-interest, care not to know about or relate to the modern enslavement of our estranged brothers and sisters across the world. I find it ironic that today many are arguing for reparations because of what western Anglo-Amerika did to our forebears and the vast empire they've acquired because of their crimes, yet they turn a blind eye to the fact that Amerika is still doing the same things today around the world and indeed maintains its predominant wealth and might on this account.*

Reparations will consist of what? The wealth that empire has, which originates from modern enslavement and bitter immiseration of the masses of laboring poor today on a global scale, a slavery which far exceeds a few million Afrikans on southern US plantations. So any gains we may win here must be used to generate a mutual exchange and benefit between us and the oppressed people of the Third World – Afrika especially.

Of course, industrial infrastructure should be limited to providing for actual social needs, instead of ones created by corporate advertisers and lying policy makers who are in pawn to the corporate powers. Indeed, the catastrophic failures and excesses of the former USSR's experiment with socialism came on account of social resources and labor having been expended toward building a vast military industry during and following the Stalinist era, instead of towards meeting social needs. The same has occurred here in Amerika since WWII. The US economy is principally a military economy. All of its main internationally competitive sectors grow out of the military system, with the Pentagon as the main financer of those sectors. This is where the money is, where a vast percentage of social wealth (taxes) is expended, e.g. military contracts, research and development, etc. NASA is a branch of the Pentagon system.

— — — — —

* In effect, the demand for reparations is a demand for a greater share in the fruits of the exploitation of the Third World. However, if used in a revolutionary manner, i.e. to create community survival programs, liberation schools, etc., reparations could truly benefit Blacks in Amerika and oppressed people throughout the world.

These initiatives (vastly wasteful of social wealth, labor, and resources) are ones that the common people can have no insight into, nor can they conceive of democratically controlling them, since they are specialized high-tech fields, beyond the understanding of the common persyn.

So, by promoting these fields as necessary (keeping the public in constant fear of created internal and external enemies – communists, Blacks, immigrants, terrorists, etc.) the establishment is able to route a vast portion of social wealth into the pockets of its high-tech and military contractors/corporations, while using government-funded universities and institutions to perform the necessary research and development. If you were to look at major science and technology magazines like *Popular Science* and *Popular Mechanics*, you will see that **all** technological innovations and developments come out of work done through or for the military, e.g., the internet, computer hardware, genetic research, etc. The Pentagon dictates US social policies and spending. Even those technologies developed by "independent" researchers, if innovative, are incorporated into the Pentagon system. How do you think Bill Gates made his fortune? This use of the Pentagon and other state sectors to subsidize private corporations with public funds has been the case since WWII when the US economy was restructured under fascist Keynesianism, namely the merger of state and corporate interests.

It is a generally correct Marxist principle that there can be no balance of anything in absolute terms, one polar force or the other is always dominant, while it is the nature of the evolutionary process to maintain relative balance, to prevent excesses.

Of course Black folk here in Amerika have no concepts on the environment, hell, we're too consumed, as Dead Prez observed, with immediate survival, and otherwise trying to measure up to and win acceptance from the dominant culture.* I think in order to increase our awareness of environmental issues we must revert back to our ancestral cultural ties to nature as an extension of and independent aspect of humynity. This will call for developing an economic order that respects and protects, rather than depletes and exploits nature and her resources.

Actually, I don't have a hard time helping our peers comprehend the concept of "freedom." They comprehend that we have nothing, own nothing, and that everything we aspire to has been defined by a culture and social order that has perpetually dominated and destroyed our innate sense of self-worth root and branch, and that this will always be the case unless/until we live up to reclaim our self-identity, independence and sovereignty. Now if we do agree that we are stupid, tricks, backwards, unintelligent and all the other degrading things that imperialism, colonialism and their spawn – racism – has labeled us and that "white" supremacy uses to rationalize and justify treating us as inferiors, then okay, we **can't** take the reins and seize our own destiny. The opposite has only been successfully done by those who've completely severed ties with western imperialism. Japan did it during the Meiji Restoration (1868–1912) – although they merely applied an Asian version of imperialism, adapting western methods of industrialization and colonizing surrounding lands. China developed independently after the 1949 revolution. During these countries' developments they shut western control and dependence out. All other countries that

— — — — —

* This was written before Hurricane Katrina hit the Southern US.

maintained economic and political ties with, and subordination to, the west became, and still are, economic basket cases, especially Afrikan ones.

I suppose you'll have to see me in action with our peers, I use a variety of approaches to draw them in: comedy, challenging their "manhood" – all subjective tactics. The raw, direct approach doesn't and won't work with most, it only makes them defensive, an excuse for them to be even more set in their ways.

Sure, when you approach and challenge them intellectually they'll promote and attempt to dismiss you as nerdy, since you're coming at them with facts and reality they can't dispute, yet which they want to resist for the sake of staying in their comfort zones. But when they present to you that books and study ain't "cool," present to them that the only people who know enough to move against our oppressors were those devoted to study and research and thereby learning the real nature of our enemy. Take for example Hubert Harrison, George Jackson, Huey P. Newton, Malcolm X, etc. Now if there's some impediment preventing them from study and learning and then conforming our practice to physical reality to challenge and change our conditions, then maybe they are that stupid, un-intelligent, childish thing that "white" supremacy has said about them. Our work should be a "working alliance" with *all* genuine anti-imperialists, no matter their race, nationality, etc.

Rashid

49. To Rashid: When I spoke about "freedom" in my last missive to you maybe I didn't correctly explain (I have that shortcoming). True, your analysis concerning our peers acknowledging our lack of ownership, lack of political rights, lack of self-worth, etc., is right on target. But there's this trend. "Freedom" has become interchangeable with "fun." See, it's like when we talk about re-establishing, re-building, restoring those rights, we're talking about work, responsibility, commitment and also being victims of empire's repression. All this excludes "fun." When our peers think of "freedom" they're thinking about the strip club or a fancy car or a pair of Timberland boots or a beach/bike fest or the Freaknik, you see what I'm saying? When we're talking about self-determination, we're talking about prioritizing, doing what **needs** to be done *first*. After we get our freedom then we can have fun. But you know like I know even after our freedom is obtained the work has only begun, again.

These are the mindsets I'm coming into contact with. "Life is too short man you gotta have fun." I don't associate liberation with fun, comedy, jokes, playtime. Now, if there was or is some way I can associate the two and still help bring about liberation then I'm all for it. Now how can I make pursuing liberation enjoyable, make it into a source of happiness for others on what seems to me a trivial level, I don't know. I suppose you have more experience and knowledge in that area than me no doubt. But again, how can I make it a source of happiness for others? That's the fundamental question of recruitment for me.

Work with me Rashid, I'm doing, "concrete analysis of concrete conditions" and this is what I see. My question concerning ST, Victor, all conscious whites, comes in light of RNA's revolutionary nationalist position and their emphasis of the errors of past movements for abandoning that **nationalist** position. And showing a lack of faith in us, the New Afrikan masses. I'm down to "work" with anybody, White, Red, Yellow or Black. But the fundamental contradiction is the New Afrikans' lack of national independence. So how do I assert my position without seeming to project or evoke racial hostility – how far does the association with whites go, and in what direction? "I'm alive and learning."

Okay, let's say our peers do recognize and acknowledge our lack of freedom (lack of power, lack of ownership, etc.). It definitely doesn't seem as important to them as going to the club, or going to amusement parks, or just kickin' it. So you mean to say our peers comprehend that we are slaves, but they're not willing or trying to get free? We might just be inferior, and, hey, slavery might've been good for us too – saved us from our own backward-ass ways, eh? Well, I feel like a black panther or some animal in captivity. I mean now that we're "integrated" and are able to participate in the same activities as our white counterparts, that has become freedom. This is what I mean when we talk about getting our freedom (i.e. political independence), then our peers responding by saying we're trying to take away their freedom (i.e. going to the club, the skating rink, etc.). They use the latter "freedoms" as an excuse for having fun to neglect getting our real freedom.

Freedom has come to be defined as integration, not in the race sense but in the class sense – we can do what the rich do or have some possibility of doing so. In general, I don't see where our peers are aware of our lack of freedom since 1) freedom has been redefined, and 2) our peers' low level of political consciousness prevents them from understanding freedom as self-determination. Then we have the rich who, to our peers, very much appear to be free too because of the almost total immunity they're afforded in the "courts of law," which leaves the impression that freedom is possible under empire.

Outlaw

50.   TO OUTLAW: The subcultural ethic that our peer group is conditioned into is one of shirking responsibility. One principal countermeasure against this is to create conditions that promote an ethics of duty, loyalty, commitment, responsibility. One approach can be found in relating to the inborn tendency of people to bow to group-based expectations – namely peer pressure. We would first have to create a peer group, or the basis of a peer group, that is appealing (objectively and subjectively) to our presently unconscious New Afrikan peers. We know that one thing our peers are drawn to is affiliation with groups that have or "exert" power. This subjective "want" which grows out of the objective human "need" for security, is what draws them so single-mindedly to people and groups that show themselves as willing and able to assert themselves with and by force (namely, the gun, the knife, the fist). This desire for affiliation with "power" is a major factor behind our peers – those who reject the street life – being suckers for the imperialist military. This all is another reason they ultimately reject those who accomplish little more than lip-service power.

A lot of this is what I believe is behind Dead Prez seeming to promote or support brothers on the corner hustling. They are expressing political and economic ideals (revolution) that the young hood denizens don't relate to because no one's backing what Dead Prez is talking with force. So there's obviously the lack of appeal to young Blacks, and the sense that they're alienated from Dead Prez's actual message that we need to *get free*. Consequently, Dead Prez has the sense of needing to connect themselves to these youth by not outrightly rejecting (or as these youths would see it: "hating on") the only role models or models of "power" that exist for them – namely the thug and gangsta image. This is likely why they pepper their lyrics with 5% wordplay. Namely, to allow our peers to feel a sense of connectedness between the 5% school of thought (which is so prominent within our peer group) and revolutionary ideology. With the result I expect of ultimately weaning them out of the 5% thinking and fully into revolutionary ideology.

In any regard, if we were to develop youth organizations and security forces – or the nucleus of viable security forces – following the line of a revolutionary political-economic platform and movement (socialist national independence, anti-imperialism, etc.), and had a message and strategy that our young peers could feel, you can believe that they'll be running to join the ranks. They identify with the thug mentality 'cause that's the only realizable image of power and respect they have to emulate within our own racial/class groups. And connected to this image is the idea of leisure that has been adopted from and imitates the capitalist ruling class culture. Therefore they identify what is socially good with self-gratifying leisure, which is positively reinforced by their peers and a reflection of bourgeoisie culture.

As for whites and what role they play here, the progressives and anti-imperialists are clearly our allies. Their work should be toward crippling empire from within in unity with our struggle for self-determination. Our struggle for independence and genuine socialism will compel toppling imperialism, which is the source of neocolonial sabotage of independence movements. Building alliances with white progressives, anti-imperialists and workers is essential to any struggle to deal imperialism the coup de grace. But of course we should not and cannot wait on whites in pursuing our struggle for independence, but it's very likely that by observing our example, whites will join and consolidate the anti-imperialist front. You might note that all of the white and European progressive movements during the early 1900's were initially pro-imperialist, from the populists to the feminists to the liberals. In the Western countries Europeans did not begin challenging imperialism and its logic until the colonized natives in the underdeveloped world began themselves resisting and struggling for independence. The only organized whites who resisted imperialism prior to this was V.I. Lenin in his *Thesis on the National and Colonial Question*, which was adopted by the Comintern in 1920. So, *until* we lead and pursue our own fight whites will accept the dominant stereotypes surrounding us and our satisfaction with and acceptance of neocolonialism and exploitation. Following the example and logic of our struggles here in the 1960's and 1970's (led by the Black Panthers for example) progressive and anti-imperialist whites and white youth came out in support of our movement, and many looked to Huey Newton and Fred Hampton, Sr. for leadership. But Huey cracked and Fred was assassinated. Whites didn't begin to resist chattel slavery as an organized movement until the slaves themselves became decidedly extreme in resisting slavery first, e.g. Nat Turner's revolt in 1831. In turn it was subsequent white unity with the Black resistance (John Brown for example) motivated by the Black initiative, that brought the broader anti-slavery white sectors to the point of willingness to adopt the anti-confederate position and back it with arms.

Rashid

51.   To Rashid: How are you? Fine I hope. Well, Bush is officially president for another four years. I'm mentioning this as an example of the statement that "Black nationalism is a response to white racism," which is in the "Notes on Cadre Policy and Development," *Vita Wa Watu* Vol. 12, p. 31. Now, in an effort to get someone in the White House who "represents our interests" (Kerry in this case), we had Blacks mobilize a massive "Get Out The Vote," "Vote or Die" campaign, which in itself along with the actual Black voter turn-out was unprecedented. All this in response to Bush's right-wing agenda which naturally, although adversely, affected Blacks. This massive effort to some degree awakened Blacks to the political process in this country and the economy, which are issues generally neglected by us. So, if Clinton (the first Black president according to some Blacks) was still in office wooing us with his saxophone and appearances in Black churches, then basically we wouldn't have given politics or economics much thought.

Statistics are often quoted that since Bush has been in office five million people have lost health coverage, which is in addition to the 40 million who didn't have coverage before Bush. What about **those** 40 million who existed under Clinton's administration. Then another statistic is quoted saying that since Bush has come to office the unemployment rate has risen by like 2 to 2.5 million, but under

Clinton there were between 8 to 10 million people still unemployed which I think is an understatement. Then I watched BET News to get the reaction to Bush's victory among Blacks, and of course they had these Black capitalist lackeys saying they're gonna put more effort into getting voter turnout increased among Blacks in the next election. Well, I'm thinking with the rising numbers of Blacks (men and women alike) being convicted of felonies and consequently disenfranchised – not to mention the daily loss of lives in Black-on-Black violence, the overall lack of faith in this political process as expressed by numerous Blacks, also the fact that Blacks make up like 12% to 14% of the population – I mean it just seems self-defeating to me. Change demands a movement.

I read a story once where someone asked some group of people how many of them wanted freedom. They all put up their hands. Think there were about 300 of them. Then the person says, "Well, how many of you are ready to kill anybody who gets in your way for freedom?" About 50 put up their hands. And he told those fifty, "You stand over here." That left 250 sitting who wanted freedom, but weren't ready to kill for it. So he told this fifty, "Now you wanted freedom and you'd said you'd kill anybody who'd get in your way. You see those 250? You get them first. Some of them are your own brothers and sisters and mothers and fathers. But they're the ones who stand in the way of your freedom. They're afraid to do whatever is necessary to get it and they'll stop you from doing it. Get rid of them and freedom will come naturally." This passage is quoted from Malcolm X and I am seeing the significance of the message.

I see what you're saying about creating that peer pressure, that social force that exerts influence on the rest in order to ensure participation (whole-hearted) and cohesion; plus, see, I used to be idealistic about the nature of Blacks. I had blind faith in Blacks, but now I'm seeing that a lot of Blacks need to be "relieved," because they're not for freedom or for us, they're in the way. It's just I don't know how I would go about that in a broader context. I think a lot of malignant, destructive characteristics exist among us, the lumpen, more than any other sector. We need more discipline than the proletariat.

What type of ideology does SB espouse? I'm running into people that he has influenced to various extents, and from what I'm getting is a Back-to-Afrika-for-capitalist-development plan. These dudes influenced by SB are denouncing socialism.

In this MIM document ("What is the Maoist Internationalist Movement?") they basically carry out an assault on George and the Foco Theory. However, they don't offer any other rational solution except waiting for the right conditions, but they did make a point about the limited impact of certain "actions" on the Establishment; something to be analyzed. But I go back to your essay on "What's Left of the Left?" and that's the critical question of the day. The million dollar question.

Correct me if I'm wrong, but doing a cursory class analysis, I think the working class has the most revolutionary capacity. I mean the working masses aren't dumb, they're just being misled by dummies or opportunists, however, they seem to be the only sector championing labor to some degree. I refrain more now than usual from "agitation" 'cause these niggaz have no "intellectual stimulation" to investigate anything further than reading a freak book story. I'm still learning no doubt.

Outlaw

52.   To Outlaw: I'm as well as can be expected under the circumstances. Bush's re-election only shows how effectively Amerikans' voting base has been allied to imperial chauvinism, or, conversely, how effectively ballots are manipulated to produce outcomes most desired by the corporate sector – the new push ballot casting system basically undermines any ability to verify poll counts. To paraphrase Joseph Stalin, "It's not those who cast the ballots that determine the outcome of an election, it's those who count them." This summarizes my whole opinion on the claim of "free elections" in Amerika.

The common attitude of our people towards politics, economics, cultural and historical analyses, etc., is one of deference to the opinions of the "experts," who typically are capitalist lackeys of US empire. To the common Black such matters are dismissed as "deep," and thus beyond their interest and capacity to analyze intelligently. "Lack of intellectual stimulation." I get exasperated frequently with hearing my relatives responding to my thoughts as "deep" and then angling to engage in trivial dialogue.

As you imply, it's not as though democrat or republican are substantially different. They merely represent two faces of fascism, one with a smile (Democrats) the other a sneer (Republican), the liberal and conservative. As Malcolm X described them: the fox and the wolf. But few explained their character and function within the imperialist system as well as did Lenin. He stated that:

> The bourgeoisie in all countries in practice inevitably elaborates two systems of government, two methods of struggle for its interests and for the defense of its domination, and these two methods now replace one another

and now interface in different combinations. These are first, the method of violence, the method of refusing all concessions to the labor movement, the method of supporting all ancient and dying institutions, the method of uncompromising rejection of reforms. Such is the substance of conservative policy. The second method is the method of "liberalism," of steps towards the development of political rights, of reforms, of concessions, etc.... A normal capitalist society cannot successfully develop without a stabilizing representative system, without certain political rights, being granted to the population ....

Bush only represents the conservative wing that's rolling back the reforms granted since WWII under the liberals in response to public demands for change. And Clinton, he did more damage to the reforms granted Blacks and other sectors of the population than anyone. He just did it with guile – smiling like a fox rather than snarling like a wolf. In a steadily contracting economy he knocked 10 million poor people off welfare – out of 15 million total recipients. This while jobs were on a decline, and he then put over 100,000 more pigs on the streets to lock up those drawn to "crime" by force of economic and emotional frustration and desperation. Meantime there was the steadily expanding Prison-Industrial Complex in place to warehouse those people. He expanded the death penalty to some sixty new "crimes," he pursued measures to bar public assistance to teen mothers, he supported measures to reverse wimyn's self autonomy here and abroad, he supported tax cuts for the wealthy, he refused to slow down executions despite revelations of dozens of innocent people on death row, he increased energy corporations' access to fuels by accelerating oil and gas drilling on "federal" lands, he funded states to cut their welfare rolls and not help people terminated from welfare to find jobs, etc. The liberals are in pawn to the same wealthy corporate powers as the conservatives, they just do their anti-people dirt wearing a friendly face. Yes, we're definitely confused. As George noted, voting for these fascists is like choosing which way one prefers to suffer and die.

This "Get Out the Vote" thing is just a diversion, a pressure release, and a waste of Black and general working-class energy. Exactly what it's intended to be. As for fighting for freedom, I'm familiar with that Malcolm X speech you quoted from, our situation and dilemma couldn't have been described any better.

I don't believe that Black nationalism is a response to white racism any more than the national independence struggle of the 13 colonies against British domination here was a race-motivated struggle. It was a struggle against imperial domination, however, the Amerikan Revolution (1775–1783) was a struggle led by the Amerikan national bourgeoisie interests in the colonies. Just as were the citizens of those British-Amerikan colonies, so are we Black folks here in Amerika today (along with other 3rd World people here) a people colonized by an imperialist empire. In our case that empire is Amerika. It robs us of our wealth, our labor, our history, our identity and our brain power, turning our subjugation to the profit of its ruling class; depriving us of all economic, political and military power; arresting our development and destroying our capacity for cultural growth and unity by imposing its own ruling class's self-serving culture of materialism and individualism on us, which we ape with a deformed subculture, conditioning us, as it has the white US working class since WWII, to accept toys, tokens and meaningless status symbols as pacifiers in place of true political and economic control and independence. Bread and circuses.

Obviously, one cannot place blind confidence into a group of unconscious and disorganized people expecting them to be able spontaneously to know how to solve complex economic, political, military, cultural and social problems, to know what changes need to be made and to then pursue correct methods of making those changes. This would be as ridiculous as expecting a mass of people to spontaneously mobilize an army and promptly defeat another well trained, supplied and properly commanded army, while the former has no strategic leadership who knew how to organize all relevant factors – tactical, logistical and strategic – to weld that people into an effective fighting force. Leadership, guidance, organization, and discipline are imperative. **This** is what we've always lacked, since chattel slavery, and continuing today. George had a clue, but his tendency toward adventurism (of the Guevarist mode) and to overreact at the enemy's prompting, also his failure to recognize how valuable a leadership element he was, allowed the pigs to destroy him. He was one of the only genuinely advanced and developed tactical revolutionary thinkers we had. He was a herd leader that the imperialist hunters recognized and destroyed, thus leaving the remaining herd members to scatter in confusion. One of the few things I agree with that James Carr expressed in his autobiography *Bad*, is that George **knew** the pigs wanted him dead and he played into their hands.

To my thinking the lumpen can be forged into a revolutionary force given the right education, practice and "compulsion." They **are** proletarians, only broken ones ("lumpen" means broken). Many can be "fixed." They're not beyond disciplining – you can see this in those that enter the empire's military forces; they're effectively conditioned to become disciplined and organized as a team. I agree with Sun Tzu in that soldiers are made and their quality determined by their leadership, and not by the individual soldiers themselves. Again, we lack leadership. As Mao pointed out and George was correctly fond of repeating "When revolution fails, it's the fault of the vanguard party."

Now, as to what class best qualifies to **lead** such a struggle here, in the sense of our national independence, I believe it would be a working-class-conscious petty bourgeois; meaning a highly conscious sector of this class who'd be willing and able to commit class suicide upon the success of such a struggle, to preclude its assuming a role of a national ruling class which would ultimately become purely bourgeoisie and pro-imperialist, i.e. they would become a neocolonial dictatorship allied with the imperialists. This was Amilcar Cabral's approach to the nationalist/socialist struggle in Guinea-Bissau, and as I see it, he was Afrika's most advanced leader in the 1960's and 70's. He implemented a revolutionary policy that brought a working-class-conscious petty-bourgeois leadership (of which class he was a member) to the head of the struggle there, and quickly crushed Portuguese rule although Guinea-Bissau came under a proportionally greater concentration of military attack by Portugal – with US support – than did Vietnam by US forces. Cabral's genius compelled his being quickly assassinated in 1973, yet Guinea-Bissau still won independence the next year. Recall, the US is an over 80% service-based (i.e. petty bourgeois) economy. It has no large and predominant proletarian class, that class has been steadily dwindling since the US economy contracted in the early 1970's and there began a consequent policy of rapid decline in manual labor-based industry which was steadily exported to the 3rd

232   PRISON LETTERS OF RASHID AND OUTLAW

World to exploit cheaper labor forces, and other "benefits" which increased corporate profit margins.*

I'd been taking the opportunity of being over here to catch up on some projects and writing. I've just completed two essays and some art, one that I'm sending you a copy of (the Middle East drawing). I'm going to renew efforts to get some practical military texts copied for you.

— — — — —

* This analysis of the US working class as being predominantly petty bourgeois is erroneous. The predominantly service sector US working class is in actuality part of the proletarian class. Some Marxist traditionalists limit the proletarian class to only manual laborers in the manufacturing and mining industries and transport. This is because in Marx's and Lenin's day these were the primary areas of industrial development. However, modern technological advances have broadened the scope of the working class. In certain trade areas productive operations have become more and more important, such as storage and packaging. Other community economic relations have also become independent industries, e.g. public catering, energy production and various other service labors. Today's service industry workers differ very little in class and professional respects from industrial workers, and their pay is no better. The industrial proletariat is indeed the nucleus of the working class, however, millions of workers not directly related to industry have joined its ranks. Also, Marx did not narrowly classify only the manual productive laborers as the proletariat, but referred to the "collective laborer," each of whom participate only in part, to a greater or lesser degree, in the manipulation of the subjects of labor. Therefore, a proper analysis of US classes finds that Amerika indeed has a predominant and large multinational proletariat, and it is this class, which must lead revolutionary nationalist and anti-imperialist struggles here. —*Rashid*

On SB, I actually never got into a dialogue with him in a way that allowed a free exchange of ideas. As I'd told you, he tends to write these complex analyses; they seem to combine a Marxist-Leninist critique of capitalism and imperialism with some Afrikan version of fascism. He seems to promote an Afrikanized imperialism in place of the existing Anglo-Amerikan imperialism. I attempted to explore his thinking on these matters but he evaded any discussion on grounds that we had no secure communication lines and he didn't want to elaborate on paper. Yet he'd send me essays he'd written, some of which I'd read before from others whom he's also given copies to. He actually emulates some of Afrika's most oppressive despots. I've also never seen him express any egalitarian ideals. Furthermore, I've heard of him writing and circulating all sorts of other things, including explicit "freak" stories.

The brother's highly intelligent no doubt, but getting a firm idea of where his foundations lie is elusive. I've only had a few opportunities to dialogue with him face to face, and, as said, our written exchanges were limited and ultimately terminated from his end. There are other things about him that elude reason. I'll have copies made of some of his essays I have and let you analyze them yourself. To me the brother's a curious specimen, but as you mentioned before, cats who he's influenced place a high premium on deception.

As you've experienced with some of the brothers you mentioned, folks tend to generalize socialism by what went down in the former USSR, and based upon bourgeoisie propaganda. There was regimentation no doubt, but it was "validated" by the sense of need to rapidly modernize the social economy and military capability of Russia in order to create a bloc that could hold its own against the western imperialists, who promptly invaded and were repelled from Russia immediately after the Bolshevik-led revolution, and never ceased in their designs to destroy the soviet bloc. With Khrushchev's take-over after many Stalinist errors, a right-wing coup took place. But you've had other non-regimental modes of popular-based socialist and New Democratic revolution that took place, e.g. in Nicaragua in 1979, in China 1949–1976, in North Korea under its juche sasan movement, Guinea-Bissau under the PAIGC, etc.

Rashid

53. To Rashid: The drawing is artistic expression at its best! The female Establishment mercenary hovering over the murdered Abu Ghraib prisoner represents the stark reality of the hypocrisy of empire's spreading freedom and democracy. Speaking of which, I just got the *Socialism and Democracy* (Hip Hop) issue.* I've just read about 30 pages. Every prisoner should have a subscription to this. I can't begin to define how enlightening this text it. I saw where Mumia Abu-Jamal made a contribution. Although short, the logic of his article was clear.

Is TK receptive to revolutionary politics? I know he was under 5% influence. It's hard to measure a person's level of seriousness, 'cause I keep comparing how I conduct myself to the activities of others. Like with TK. He's cool, he's receptive to a degree, but he still has entrepreneurial aspirations, a fixation on making parole – I don't know why. But hopefully exposing him to revolutionary ideology should clear him of any backward notions he has. He's intelligent, but essentially lacks direction, revolutionary direction that is. I still maintain relations with him. I'm not gonna alienate him, 'cause I sense potential, but that's based on his situation – amount of time and willingness to educate himself.

Right now I'm submerged in intense study. I have a wealth of information on hand to study and I'm seeking the right info, the kind that broadens perspectives by assimilating others' experiences. I'm looking for others who share our principles, who're willing to act on those principles, who're willing to reach out.

Power to the People!

——— ——— ——— ——— ———

* Volume #36.

I just got through reading this interview in the *S&D* with Todd Boyd. Have you had the chance to check it out? Who is this cat working for, the CIA? It's clear he's been co-opted. Bought off. I don't understand how these Black intellectuals could "consciously" betray the interests of their own nation. He has the audacity to say he's never heard debates about reparations until the 1980's by some hip hop artists, then proceeds to take Malcolm X's statement that revolution is based on land totally out of context into some metaphor. I have that speech and Malcolm wasn't talking in no damn metaphoric abstract sense! Then he talks about Black-on-Black crime as "part of the process." What process is he talking about? The process of self-destruction. See, this is why I advocate criticism of each other, 'cause these fallacies, these backward-ass mindsets are or have become generalized amongst us. We've internalized our own oppression as Kristine Wright observed. I just wanted to vent some frustration. I'm gonna get back into this joint.

I'm taking a break from reading and was just reflecting on the recent past. You don't know how much I hold you in high regards. I've learned so much from you sometimes it's overwhelming – the passion – I *must* channel my energy for the sake of not exploding. I was attracted to your practical-tactical aura, but your theoretical genius is what got my loyalty; you know, 'cause "being a warrior is not enough." I don't know how deep in the hole you are and, I mean, I don't know what your prospects are for release into population, but if you can get there, do it. I just happen to like challenges.

This agent Mau Mau is back over here trying to remain low. This is where that saying applies, "prison saved some niggaz," especially with this ultra-controlled environment. Maintain that discipline. "All sincere actions must be rewarded." We bear a great responsibility and with revolutionary pleasure I might add. That's what keeps me pushing on, 'cause though they may not be in my immediate presence, I know I got comrades somewhere, "struggling and studying."

Holla at me!

Outlaw

54.   To OUTLAW: I sense that this latest *S&D* will be a valuable progressive analysis of today's hip hop scene. One of the essays I just wrote is a critique of the Black entertainment media. I've yet to read this *S&D* – I'm so immersed in a variety of other matters – but I scanned it through. From what I gather Yusuf Nuruddin's seems the broadest and most comprehensive contribution, and his interview with this Todd Boyd character leaves me with the same impression that he's an Establishment toady or just an outright opportunist.

And, yes, TK is *very* receptive to revolutionary politics. He's completely rejected the 5% views as inane, dysfunctional and presenting a caricatured version of history. He's a slow learner, but he's absorbing. I'm committing a substantial amount of time to helping his development.

Rashid

55.   To Rashid: I've just finished reading both your essays – the one on the Black Entertainment Media *(see page 331 —Rashid)* and the exposé on the abuses occurring here. Not just talking, the latter essay makes me want to get my ass whooped! It reveals just how dire our situation really is and I feel like an unworthy being at times not being able to engage in "result-oriented" action. I feel like one of the petty bourgeoisie over here surrounded by TV's and radios and commissary. I've been learning (still am), but it's been in a spontaneous direction even after consistent reading. After I'm done with Mao, any psychology books you may possess, please send them.

Have you given thought to the present state of Black women and their increasing lesbianism? My own sister just disclosed to me that she is involved with another woman. Her professed reason being "all these niggaz is dogs." And I concur in addition to your own observations, it stands out more, has more validity. In years to come our women may feel no more need to seek relations with us men beyond reproductive purposes, so they and their "partners" can raise a child and fulfill their sense of being a "real" family. I don't hate lesbians and gays, but for Blacks this could and will have harmful effects. This is what I was getting at in part when I mentioned "us not having enough time." The social disintegration isn't fully complete but it's rampant. I don't think it will ever be fully complete. I do envision "socialism," but it's not the socialism we envisage. It's more a world devastated by destruction, pollution, wars and an extreme lack of natural resources; so scarce that humans are gonna be **forced** to adopt communal relations in order to survive. But this of course is in the event that our efforts fail.

Outlaw

56.   To Outlaw: You can hold the Mao till you're finished with it. I have no psychology books. K was telling me about your nearly coming to blows with some fella over there who shot some verbal bait at you challenging your "revolutionary sincerity." I agree with the advice he gave you about your larger priorities taking precedence over reacting to the emotional outbursts of a clueless peer, so long as there's no physical threat or attack. Likewise with your feelings in response to my exposé, in the context of weighing priorities, as Lin Piao (one of the Chinese Red Army's greatest generals) observed, "It is opportunism if one won't fight when he can win. It is adventurism if one insists on fighting when one can't win." Our primary objective should be to get into a position where we can struggle **and win**.

As for your question on lesbians. As said before, I have no issues with folks' same-sex inclinations. Specifically in relation to Sisters' indulgences – can you blame them? Look at what the males have been reduced to. The dominant subculture among them, adopted from this patriarchal society, emphasizes pimping and otherwise sexually exploiting and degrading sisters. As part of our subjugation and creating disunity, colonialism and capitalism and their spawn (white racism), are the conditions that divided us and keep us divided. As George observed "The Black man and the Black female must be, as I have mentally ordered things, completely joined together in the act of liberation."

Rashid

57.   To R<small>ASHID</small>: I'll have this last volume of Mao ready by dinner-time, so you can go ahead and send any other books you suggest I read. I've found Mao to be quite interesting. I've got to get these joints.

I know at times I may sound like I'm just not getting it, but I am. I just have difficulty expressing myself. Attribute that to my up-bringing. There was no room for "freedom of expression." I sent that other military text back earlier and it was crazy because I gave it to the taxi (all wrapped and sealed up) in the envelope **before** we went out to recreation. When I came back it was still sitting in the office and I was greeted by all these concerned stares; it was "all eyez on me." So I know these folks are going into the packs and piecing bits together, forming their own perceptions and simultane-ously bolstering their authoritarianism. I gotta get those psychology books.

I've attempted to write a paper about the "Intergenerational Gap" but I cancelled it 'cause I don't feel like I'm qualified plus I wouldn't have any "insights" to offer like yourself. I'd just be stat-ing simple facts. Facts that indict the Civil Rights generation for their failures and get them to acknowledge that they failed, open-ly. I just received the John Gerassi book – *The Coming of the New International*. Also, here's an article on Cuba.

Have you ever considered why people tend to take kindness for weakness and trust as naïveté?

Outlaw

58.   To Outlaw: I've received the Mao and Cuba article. I think you should pursue writing. We're *all* in varying stages of development ideologically. Just be certain that your thinking is indeed rooted in facts. And I believe I'd mentioned before, the taxi is used by his higher ups in a good cop role because it serves their interests. It's about catching flies and honey versus vinegar.

On your question concerning why folks tend to "take kindness for weakness" and interpret "trust as naïveté." This obviously results from the dysfunctional tendencies of capitalism. Capitalism has as its ethic the pursuit of profit and self-gain at the next person's expense. This generates within the capitalist society an instinctive, subconscious tendency for everyone to be forever suspicious of everyone else's motives, and to expect exploitation and competition from and by everyone else. One who is not sensitive to the next person's predatory impulses and who is trusting and open is seen as "fair game" to be targeted for exploitation. They're deemed weak and naïve because they don't exhibit the necessary defenses against becoming a victim of the next person's profit interests and schemes. In short, they're tagged as being a "sucker" to be played for all they have.

Rashid

59.   To Rashid: On the lesbian issue, I support Black females' position cause **I do** see what they have to choose from. I've discussed this with my sister. We have that understanding. But instead of promoting them turning their backs on men, I myself would advocate a "National No Sex for Black Men Day," or maybe week or perhaps month. The women would celebrate this holiday and refrain from sexual activities with Black men in order to raise the men's awareness about important issues. This would send the message that if we men can't perform our manly duties of being socially responsible to our future society, our communities, and start thinking and behaving in productive ways towards our women, then we shouldn't be allowed the privilege of performing manly duties in bed. It's extreme but it's necessary. Women use their sexuality to steer men into chosen positions, for their own purposes, and they set standards in the process, which we feel the need to live up to. Whether the standards be a balla or soldier or ball player or what have you. They thereby already use sex and their sexuality as a "behavior adjustment" tool. I think that tool can be used for more significant issues and can bring issues to the surface that we tend to shy away from. Hopefully this would bring about the "open dialogue" that's needed to develop and progress.

Somebody has to stand up and say this shit ain't right, and my doing that is somewhat at the root of the verbal conflicts with a few dudes over here, and even goes back to W. Y'know, just cause we homies or niggaz don't mean I'm gonna uncritically support everything a person does. Now when we have a "shared principle" then we both know the bounds of our actions and act accordingly. But prevailing trends show that among our peers there **are no** "shared principles" if any principles at all, considering the rampant snitching and backstabbing that's going on. I initiated a lot of dialogue where I made it easy for me to be criticized, talked about, etc. But somebody has got to speak up and break the silence, the trance. So dudes catch feelings 'cause I "break their sleep," if you know what I'm sayin'. I just be boggled at some of the comments and responses I get, which is a sign of amateurism on my part, meaning I haven't developed the methodical responses (scientific) that you're able to give. You and K. I value you all's advice, criticisms, etc.

I like this *Art of War in the Western World** you sent, but I just don't understand what the "four basic weapon systems" are, and furthermore, where a tank, a plane, an M–16 or M–4 would fit into that spectrum.

Outlaw

---

* Archer Jones, University of Illinois Press, 2000.

60.   To Outlaw: The method you promote of Black wimyn using their sexuality to address and correct our men's backward behaviors and thinking is valid. It was in fact a method used by sisters during Reconstruction to push Black men to take responsibility and advantage of our newly won freedom from chattel slavery. The results were phenomenal. In developing businesses, political empowerment, school enrollment and economic self-sufficiency, we outpaced the white southern population. Short of having a defense force we developed the fundamentals of a viable nation in the southern Black Belt states. *This* is a large part of what prompted the US government to withdraw support for Reconstruction, to withdraw the union Army from the south as our "defenders," and to condone the ensuing rampant terrorist violence of the klan and white knights of camellia which was targeted primarily at Black businessmen and politicians. The rationale used to justify this wave of white terror were false claims of Black men raping white wimyn. People like Ida B. Wells and Frederick Douglass exposed the lie for what it was and the fact that the anti-Black violence stemmed actually from white economic competition and insecurity. So, being unable to defend ourselves from these attacks our gains were lost, there was massive flight of Blacks to the north, and the prior plantation owners were allowed to take the land back which the previously enslaved Blacks had settled.

The four basic weapon systems mentioned in the *Western World* are heavy infantry, light infantry, heavy cavalry and light cavalry. In ancient warfare heavy infantry were the heavy armored ground troops who engaged in shock combat fighting hand-to-hand using spear, swords, axes, shields and such. Light infantry were the light armored and therefore more highly mobile ground troops who used bows and arrows, slings and other projectile firing weapons to attack opponents from a distance. Heavy cavalry were horse-mounted heavily armored troops who fought close with swords and such but had greater speed and mobility over infantry. Light cavalry were lightly armored horse-mounted troops who used projectile-launching weapons and had greater speed and maneuverability than all the other weapon systems. In modern warfare light infantry are ground troops armed with machine guns, mortars, grenades and other man-portable weapons. Heavy infantry are ground troops operating stationary missile and artillery. Light cavalry are combat aircraft, and heavy cavalry are tanks and such heavy armored mechanized combat systems. These are the four weapon systems and how they relate to modern warfare.

Rashid

61.   To RASHID: I should make you aware that the "hook-up" you suggested between me and SK has not been copious. I reach out but essentially we don't share the same ideological values. This proves to hinder communication (on his end). I mean it's a non-antagonistic relationship, but I get the impression he's not too motivated to "build" on these politics, economics or social issues. I'm following the principle of "keeping politics in command." I recognize the significance of this. He says it's about deception, referring to Sun Tzu's edict "All warfare is based on deception." I concur but does that preclude agitation and education, consciousness raising? From my viewpoint, no. I asked if he wanted to read the last two essays you sent but he declined on reasons of possibly going back to segregation, 'cause of enemy harassment (his record and pig fears). I understand but I hold "conscious" brothers more accountable. We have an obligation.

I might not be through with the Gerassi until next week. It's phenomenal!

Outlaw

62.   To Outlaw: It's a truism that one can't sow seeds in cold, hard earth. Some people are just not going to be receptive to progressive thinking. Many although principled (in an idiosyncratic sense), are unwilling to reject stereotyped views and values, to change with new exposures, to adapt their views when proved wrong. There are a variety of factors that cause this.

Certainly, it's true that "all warfare is based on deception," but this doesn't mean self-deception. It's the enemy that's to be deceived whereas we must know ourselves. This so we can determine our strengths and concentrate them against our enemy's weaknesses, while avoiding the enemy's strengths and concealing and protecting our own weaknesses. Knowing ourselves calls for introspection and self-evaluation in relation to external events and realities. One cannot understand reality or even discover facts by closing themselves off from evaluating and studying new things. If the brother isn't receptive that's an internal flaw that you can't force to change. Just continue with easy indirect prodding, but at a distance. I believe he has good intentions – he merely lacks correct insight.

I told you that the Gerassi is remarkable.

Rashid

63.   To RASHID: I **definitely** have to get a copy of this Gerassi. I think Amilcar Cabral added something new to conducting class analysis or maybe he emphasized something Marx didn't, namely the petty bourgeoisie's role in the more complicated, administrative, diplomatic sector or society which the proletariat generally doesn't have the intellectual experience with. I like the Tupamaros interview.* They made some good points. I'd never read any of Eldridge Cleaver's writings but the man had insight. He emphasized that the role of political institutions in society is to be at the People's service, and our entitlement to participate in the decision-making processes. That conception, that awareness is missing in general today. People don't question whether they can play a part in the decision-making processes 'cause we've been conditioned to put intellectuals, professionals, experts on a pedestal.

Considering the state of Blacks now it would be 200 years from now before we "wake up" and realize the errors of our actions in complicity with white empire. We've been so sensitive to racial issues which is understandable but not to the point where we're so afraid to "offend" Amerika by making claims to national independence. I can imagine a million Blacks and a million more Uncle Toms with influence undermining our efforts in the name of "racial harmony." I agree with the Republic of New Afrika's position that

— — — — —

* The Tupamaros, also known as the MLN (*Movimiento de Liberacion Nacional* or National Liberation Movement), was an urban guerrilla organization in Uruguay in the 1960's and 1970's. The MLN in inextricably linked to its most important leader, Raul Sendie, and his brand of social politics. Since spring 1995, it has been represented in the Uruguayan parliamant by Pepe Mujica, a former political prisoner.

we're not officially Amerikans (citizens), 'cause it wasn't a conscious and informed choice by us to be so. It was **imposed** contrary to our right to choose and the related legalities involved. Do you think we could take that argument to the United Nations and formally secede? I'm gonna write the RNA and find out what their present agenda is.

I do realize there is **a lot** of work to be done. Especially in the subjective sphere. I had neglected this area before because I focused on the rampant injustice, and assumed those objective conditions alone would produce the needed actions. Another thing, my efforts in engaging cats over here are producing some minor results. Cats have expressed in so many words they see what I've been pointing out to them **now**, although still not fully. In my view they're only grasping a sense of what's happening. But it's hard to convince someone or even to just tell them to "keep reading." That doesn't translate into a concrete objective for most of us, although it is. But the dissemination of your essays has evoked those responses.

I didn't know Communist history was so full of pacifism. I'm reading a piece that promotes the Soviet Union's line of "peaceful coexistence."

I wanted to stop and holla at you while you were outside today, but I just kept it movin', 'cause the pigs on this shift don't like me at all. They suspect me of anything and everything. A couple of weeks ago I told a dude don't talk to me until he can prove he's not the snitch people said he was. Next thing I know the sergeant's calling me in the office, addressing me about "approaching" people (read intimidating people) about them being snitches. So I be steering clear of their tendencies of looking for something. Send me some Angela Davis.

Outlaw

Amilcar Cabral

1924-1973

Guinea Bissau

RASHID
'05

"By far the sharpest fighting ideologue
in Portugese Africa - and indeed in the
whole continent - is Amilcar Cabral...."
John Gerassi

64.   To Outlaw: I received the Gerassi and immediately sent you Angela Davis' book, *Women, Race, and Class.*[*]

I think Cabral added a lot of "new" insight to revolutionary theory. Among the most valuable I see is his analysis of imperialism's role in ultimately conceding political independence to 3rd World countries, thereby allowing them to set up native-headed neocolonial governments which could rule the countries more stably (arousing less native resentment) than governments headed by Europeans faces. This while the imperialists created a labor aristocracy within their own countries, whom they bought off using the immense wealth they were robbing from the 3rd World. They used this bribed sector of the working class to undermine international working-class solidarity and turn the working class of the industrial countries against the 3rd World workers and peasants. On this point I should qualify my *full* position on RNA politics to you.

I promote New Afrikan independence – liberating the areas of empire *where we are actually concentrated* – for us as a step **toward** ultimately defeating the imperialist state. But this operates along with building active alliances with other oppressed nationalities and the multi-ethnic and multi-national working class (which includes white workers) to deal empire the death blow. Our principal struggle is the class struggle. Ignoring the tendency of the imperialists to hijack national independence struggles against colonialism (direct rule by European imperialists), only to install neocolonialist regimes (indirect European imperialist rule through native puppets), is to continue to accept economic exploitation and strangulation

— — — — —

[*] The Women's Press Ltd., 2001.

which will see any "independent" New Afrika reduced to the state of places like Haiti. It must be remembered that we Blacks are not Amerika's only oppressed internal colony.

National independence struggles against imperial domination is a means not an end in itself. Our ultimate struggle is toward achieving a classless and nation-stateless society and world. The nation-state is only a stage of historical social development, and will pass away in time as have all preceding stages of social developments, bands, tribes, villages, feudal-states, etc. In the practical context, history proves it is much easier to mobilize broad sectors of a society to accept the difficult protracted struggles of revolution in support of national independence than in support of immediate socialism. The nationalist drive of a colonized people easily extends beyond just the working-class revolution (socialism). Mao Tse-tung, Ho Chi Minh, and others who led determined struggles in their countries against western imperialist domination appealed especially to their people's nationalist sentiments in the first stage of their struggles (to obtain political independence), and then secondly to class interests for socialism (economic independence where native labor and resources were used to develop and benefit the native people and national economic development, instead of continuing to be exploited to the profit of the ruling class in the imperialist countries).

I'm always mindful that the ruling class was the one that deliberately created the classifications of "race" and this in response to struggles against it by united Afrikan and English slaves in the British colonies; specifically Bacon's Rebellion of 1676. They – the ruling wealthy elite – made us (blacks and whites) come to hate and fear each other, just as **they** created the sense of division and distrust between "pure" Blacks and those who have mixed European blood (note the Willie Lynch process[*]). Where do we draw the line? Do we also struggle for a Black versus mulatto state? What happens to the mulatto's white relatives whom s/he loves? We must also recognize that **in the real world** there is no existing nation made up of a single race. Race is a social construction not a biological one. DNA demonstrates that there has been so much blood transferred between gene pools that we are all today thoroughly mixed. And differences in features, builds and color are the result of environmental adaptations. So essentially I see our struggle towards New Afrikan independence as a step **toward** a much larger process and result.

Consider this reality: if our independence struggle gets under way full scale, the rulers of the US empire are going to try and mobilize the white population against us, which with many whites will be relatively easy to do. Now if we were trying to displace whites living in the "Black Belt" states, and they thus had **nothing** to gain from helping us run them off the land they live on, how many more do you think would rush to join ranks against us in a counterproductive race war sponsored by the ruling class? We'd be pushing sympathetic whites into a no-man's land. So focusing solely on the Black Belt and excluding whites from our struggle against imperialism and for independence would not produce a revolutionary struggle, but all-out race war and mutual ethnic cleansing, and from

— — — — —

* Willie Lynch was an 18th century businessman who served as a consultant to wealthy plantation owners. He was considered an expert on "how to break a slave," specifically in subduing slaves into a "slave mentality." He wrote an infamous document titled, "The Willie Lynch Doctrine." The term "lynching" was named after him.

the logistical standpoint (logistics determines strategy), we'd be at a decided disadvantage.

We need progressive whites to prevent any New Afrikan struggle from deteriorating into a genocidal race war that will pit one sector of the international proletariat (New Afrikan workers) against another sector ("white" workers), which is what the empire will angle to provoke once it loses any ability to neutralize our struggle with other devices. Remember it was the wealthy elite who created racism and white supremacy to undermine resistance against their domination. Progressive whites must stand to gain something from allying with our struggle. Now it's here that I see we can endanger the entire imperialist structure. We must ally ourselves to aid all other oppressed nationalities and the conscious whites to defeat empire itself, giving all exploited and oppressed elements (the neo-colonized and white workers), a tangible benefit in joining into an International Front Against Imperialism. For us there can be **no** "peaceful coexistence" with imperialism, however, there can and must be unity between us and all other oppressed nationalities and white workers. In any event, the end result will be a full scale class struggle with empire itself and joined up with struggles worldwide. This will be the international and proletarian-led struggle of the exploited classes and oppressed nations against the exploiting imperialist class and its protectors.

As far as your seeing minor results in our peers, that's good. You must remember, what you're exposing them to runs counter to all they've learned and experienced during their lives, furthermore many of them have never developed the "mental equipment" to readily comprehend complex issues of politics and economics – they've never developed their intellectual faculties and foresight, so learning for them will naturally take some time. Just remember, people learn by repetition; that's how enemy indoctrination proves so effective ... repetition of their lies and gloss over and over, day after day, like those jingles in the TV commercials one subconsciously memorizes from hearing them repeatedly. But our object is to not merely have people passively memorize, but instead to actively learn and analyze.

Enclosed are recent letters from BX and a Sista whom I've been corresponding with for a few months. I asked her input on Black/white intimacy in pursuit of writing that essay I sent you – "An Answer to Today's Black Entertainment Media." She brings out some good points. She seems to think I was expressing an interest in pursuing an intimate relationship with a white womyn. Anyway, you asked me a while back about conscious sisters and whether I know any. She's the only one I know personally, but as you can see she claims many are around. I'm sending BX's letters to allow you to scrutinize some proposals he has. Your feedback is welcome of course.

Enclosed is a book I think you'll find useful. You can have it. If you'd like I'll send you Howard Zinn's book *A People's History of the United States.**

Rashid

— — — — —

* Harper Perennial Modern Classics, 2005.

65.   To Rashid: I got the speed reading book. Thank you! It appears to be very useful. I must retract my opinion on mulattoes, that they deserve the "not thoroughly Black" treatment. Considering the pervasiveness of forcible rapes of our women ancestors by white slave owners and overseers, there's no doubt a majority of us have a touch of white in us.

Here's the Angela Davis. I enjoyed it though I expected it to go more in-depth in certain areas. It was informative.

I like BX's ideas of turning the prisons into Liberation Schools. His ideas are more coherent now that you've sent me his response. How does the line, "we must continue the Democratic Revolution that began in 1776" factor into our struggle? There was nothing "democratic" about our situation during that time, nor was there any intent to make our situation democratic. But I suppose for practical purposes, it seems less threatening to those who call themselves Amerikan, Black and white, to say we're continuing the Democratic Revolution of 1776.

Send me the Howard Zinn.

If memory serves me correctly BX was saying how an Afrikan state could be set up in Harlem and a National Coordinating Committee as well, I believe. But this leaves Blacks in the inner city, whereas RNA wants the land in the south as an agricultural base with some level of self-sufficiency, which is a plan, as you know already, I favor. However, BX's plan in Harlem is the exact opposite, how does this fare with you?

Outlaw

66.   To OUTLAW: Here's the Zinn book. On the point of continuing "the democratic revolution that began in 1776" line, I'm sending you some more material that elaborates on the idea from the Red Heart Warriors Society. I of course agree that during and about 1776 there was no existing "democracy" for us (the "Founding Fathers" vacillated on the point and their noble words were contradicted by their practicing the opposite), neither was there democracy for the Natives, nor wimyn, nor the poor for that matter. That was a struggle to institute bourgeois democracy, but it was a democratic revolution nonetheless in that it overthrew the then-existing feudalist political economy imposed by the British crown.

In order to advance the political economy of a society to socialism from a feudalist arrangement, the society has to proceed through the bourgeois democratic (laissez faire/decentralized capitalist) phase. This is what the Bolsheviks did in Russia and the CCP in China – recall you once asked why Mao proposed investments from capitalist countries and encouraged development of capitalist enterprises during the early stages of China's revolutionary development? He was steering China through what he called "New Democracy" or a bourgeois democratic stage, however, these bourgeois democratic revolutionary struggles were led by the proletariat instead of the bourgeoisie as occurred here in the US so the bourgeois democratic stages were allowed only temporarily and then transformed into socialism.

While of course the bourgeois democracy isn't democratic in the sense of empowering everyone equally, it was seen as a phase necessary to first develop and organize a proletarian class who would **then** transform China into a socialist society, namely a society run by the workers. So, while bourgeois democracy is certainly **not** an all-encompassing democratic process (i.e. it's not representative of **all** exploited classes), it is a **phase** in the democratic revolutionary process advancing towards socialism. Just as we must use state forms (socialism) to ultimately destroy the state (communism). And just as you observed, the line of continuing the revolution began in 1776, allows for winning folks over who would immediately be alienated by a line promoting destroying the social order they're accustomed to even though it oppresses and exploits them. The object is to win people over not alienate them – remember Sun Tzu ... the second most important factor in war is building alliances.

BX wasn't proposing building a New Afrikan state in Harlem, but specifically mentions the demand for land for Blacks. He proposed that Harlem could "be the likely spot for a Nation's capital." And this makes sense given that our massive urban migration last century saw us transformed from a predominantly peasant population into a proletarian one, and Harlem has been symbolic of the cultural renaissance that accompanied this transition. On the land issue the position he promotes, and which I share, is that the demand for reparations (40 acres and a mule) can be directed toward recognition of our sovereignty rights and collective land ownership. Recall, he is not merely envisioning Blacks gaining National Independence from US domination, but destroying imperialism altogether and organizing **all** oppressed peoples toward this object. At the beginning of his letter he stated, "Revolution here won't be kicking out a colonial power or breaking off a piece of the empire, it will be the coup de grace that brings down global imperialism (monopoly capitalism) and ends the Epoch of Exploitation." This organizing must begin by exploiting the limits of legality so not to provoke outright destruction by the enemy **before** a foundation is laid and so not to alienate the very people whom are the very social force that must carry the struggle forward. He recognizes – as I stated before – that Black folks are not the only oppressed nation in the US, that the US is, "a nation of prisons and a prison house of nations." He envisions not an Indian and/or New Afrikan nation co-existing with imperialist Amerika, but the defeat of imperialist Amerika (the liberation of all the oppressed and exploited internal nationalities/nations and workers) and a subsequent federation of the peoples of the various nations who were once colonized/neo-colonized by and within Amerika similar to the federation that existed under the Lenapes between the various Northeastern Indian First Nations. It's a beautiful and do-able vision. The comrade has the integrity and heart born of genuine Indian culture and the broad strategic and tactical foresight of a Marxist-Leninist-Maoist. I understand the vision completely. It's very much like what Patrice Lumumba wanted in Afrika – a fully independent and united continent of various ethnicities freed of the artificial territorial borders set up by the prior colonial powers. A truly *internationalist socialist* and ultimately communist society. Only difference here is unlike Lumumba, we are not promoting this ideal groping blindly in the dark; we are devising the means of getting from here to there.

Rashid

67.   To Rashid: I got the Zinn along with the Red Heart Warriors Society literature. I see where Lenin is quoted from his *Two Tactics of Social Democracy* in discussing bourgeois democratic revolution growing into the socialist revolution. I'm not sure where, but I know Marx said something about the transition to socialism from capitalism being facilitated and speeded up by vast stores of wealth accumulated under capitalism which would prevent economic hardships during that transition.

I know bourgeois democracy is not "all encompassing" as you noted, that's why I'm expressing my concerns and seeking a way around it. Lenin defined bourgeois democratic revolution as just instituting democratic changes, somehow that doesn't satisfy me. I mean, is this a **necessary** stage? Correct me if I'm wrong, but I feel like I'm seeing RNA's anti-Amerikanism on the one hand and BX's semi-Amerikanism on the other. Maybe it's a matter of psyche, but it's hard for me to use the Bill of Rights or the Constitution as a starting point or point of reference in seeking liberation when we were in slavery during the writing of, and included as slaves in, these "democratic" documents. I mean the HYPOCRISY of the whole ordeal is hard for me to overlook or marginalize. I don't mean to pester you with these ramblings of mine.

Outlaw

68.   To Outlaw: I'm not sure if we're on the same page on the issue of bourgeois democracy. You state because it's not "all encompassing" you're "seeking a way around it." There's no need to seek a way around it here, because here in the western hemisphere most of the existing nations have **already** passed through or exist now in the bourgeois democratic stage. The US is a monopoly capitalist country; it has passed through decentralized laissez faire capitalism into regulated centralized monopoly capitalism. There is no feudal economy here – agriculture is mechanized and wage based (no peasantry tied to feudal estates nor slaves tied to plantations) and there are wide and diverse developed industries (creating a broad proletariat). Recall, the call is to **continue** the revolution that began in 1776, meaning to struggle from slavery/feudalism, through capitalism, through socialism, to achieve communism. Revolution is a protracted process not an overnight accomplishment. Social consciousness will not change overnight from profit and property-centered to people-centered. This calls for appealing to as broad a sector of the masses of people as possible, which means presenting ideas they are already familiar with, and from there pulling them further toward total commitment to all-the-way revolution. Using the Constitution or Declaration of Independence allows us to undermine the pretenses of democracy of the established system, by exposing the contradictions between the language of those creeds and the way the rulers actually exercise their power. How unequal and anti-social the existing political economy is.

In fact Martin Luther King, Jr. used the same frame of reference to mobilize black folks around organizing against racism. He exposed the fact that the US was not "living up to the content of its creed." He gained broad appeal and support by exposing and organizing against just what you're uncertain about – US **HYPOCRISY**. Indeed if you look at the Black Panther Party's Ten Point Platform and Program they incorporated language taken directly from the US Declaration of Independence. They began with something the people were **familiar** with, could identify with, and moved them from there toward unfamiliar principles, namely revolution.

There are exceptions where some countries didn't go through the bourgeois democratic phase before implementing socialist forms. Cuba didn't, Vietnam didn't, North Korea didn't. But notice that unlike the nations who did, their socialist forms were hard to sustain when they became diplomatically and economically isolated by imperialist maneuvers.

I'm sending over another book you can have, *From Civil Rights to Black Liberation: Malcolm X and the Organization of Afro-American Unity,* by William Sales.* A good book on Malcolm's political development, work and contributions – sides of his life and work that are not exposed in his Autobiography.

Rashid

— — — — —

* South End Press, 1994.

69.   To Rashid: I get what you're sayin'. The line, "we're continuing the bourgeois democratic revolution of 1776," sounded to me like we were just gonna get back to those good ol' Amerikan values. It doesn't **sound** revolutionary. I didn't see any aspirations towards fundamental change in it. I'm being totally honest. In "seeking a way around it," I was saying that the conditions in empire being unique would allow the bourgeois democratic phase to be skipped over, because I was under the impression that we're just continuing the social forms that existed under bourgeois democracy, as opposed to saying "we're continuing the revolutionary process of social development." Sorry to put you through all that, but I wouldn't know if I didn't ask. There's an Afrikan proverb that says, "those who ask questions don't lose their way." I'm not trying to lose my way. I also want to be clear, I may have to explain to someone else and I need the correct political understanding to do so.

I'm into the Zinn. You got all the essential books 'cause you can add this to the list of "must read." I'm only on page 319 – might not get it back to you till Friday. Do you have any photocopies of this Malcolm X book? It would be expedient, I don't want to have to get rid of the book, but the condition of the book is such that I may have to.

Outlaw

70.   To OUTLAW: Don't feel as though you're taking me through "all that." Your questions are welcomed; indeed it's my duty to pass on my learning and insights. My only problem is being and remaining generally overwhelmed with a multitude of commitments, of which you are but one. For example, yes I have a copy of the Malcolm X book on hand – only one copy. So I'll have to get an extra made. Problem is, I'm constantly trying to get various other materials copied too – much of it being for you. The *one* counselor who does this sort of copying for me, I have to give small quantities of materials at a time. Then I'm left to his whims regarding whether he will copy it or not, he often brings it back without copying it with some lame excuse (such as copier's down, papers kept jamming in the machine, others looking over his shoulder, etc.). The situation's protracted further in that this isn't his assigned unit and he doesn't come in here often. So I have to catch him whenever he shows up with no guarantee of his cooperation even them. I have to use various approaches and pressures to get him to cooperate, made all the more difficult with my actual assigned "counselor's" whispering into his ear behind the scenes that he shouldn't be catering to me, doing me these favors, etc.

This is basically how all my efforts go. I'm forever trying to meet commitments and assist others but without the necessary control over resources, and I typically don't like asking people for help unless I can return them something (except in the cases of our oppressors). I don't like to feel that I'm imposing on people for my needs. Feel me? My resources are very limited, and the little help I have I must budget and juggle tightly. Not only are they limited but are often unreliable. This also stems from lack of operating within an organized structure where people have and are collectively held accountable for meeting their responsibilities. Responsibilities suited to their means and abilities. Folks out there don't see what I see, don't grasp my perspectives. What's important to me based upon my level of understanding isn't important to them, well, not to the extent that it stands out on their list of priorities. So I have to wait on their cooperation – that is, if they even choose *to* cooperate. It's frustrating.

Passing question: do you pass your learning onto your siblings? Well, of course you do. The question should be: are they receptive?

Rashid

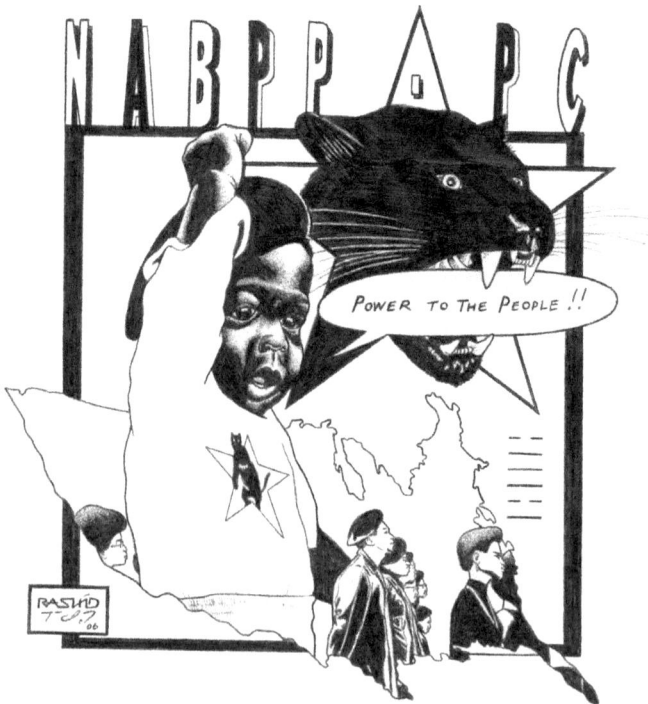

71.   To Rashid: I know I've made some requests for copies of books, but do what you need to do in order of priorities. Despite your isolation you do give the impression of being capable of getting a whole lot done from where you're at. The fact that you've gotten others to do what they have says a lot particularly in the area of these pigs and counselors. Well, unfortunately "what's important to me … isn't important to them," and in the context in which we're speaking, I don't *ever* see it to be **any** priority of theirs.

I have little to no contact with my siblings. I just resumed contact with my sister. If it wasn't for a series of unfortunate events, I might not have had that contact.

I'm completely sensitive to your frustrations and I hate to say things I know I can't readily act on to ameliorate your frustrations as well as the source. But on the other hand, we've gotta remain alert and optimistic.

I'm also beginning to understand BX's approach (and how your own is much the same in many respects) a bit more, as well as a few other things after reading the Zinn. Right now I'm checking out Del Jones' *Black Holocaust,*[*] and it's jive geared toward a "skin analysis" as opposed to a "class analysis." I noticed your handwritten notations throughout the book, so I suspect it was once yours. Well, I'm wondering, what do you consider to be the most useful aspect of this book and do you agree with the conclusions about whites' nature and "that they are socially and mentally ill and must be captured, controlled and treated from a position of power if this planet is to survive?"

Outlaw

— — — — —

[*] *The Black Holocaust: Global Genocide*, Eye of the Storm, 1992.

72. To Outlaw: Got the Zinn. I suppose that, yes, I can/do get things done from this limited position. It's just, as I said, I have no control over resources and must rely on others' resources and willingness to help. Then for obvious reasons there's my not being able to tell many of them my intentions.

Yeah, that *Black Holocaust* – I presume you got it from K – came from me. And no, I don't agree with Del Jones' conclusions about whites in general. Hell, one could say the same of Arabs that he says of whites given the way they treated us in Afrika and Asia – particularly the nomadic Muslims. We suffered brutal invasions, colonizations, slavery at the hands of the Arabs many centuries before the Europeans set upon the continent with the same designs. But, as far as the time frames he covers, I find Del Jones' historical references and the designs of imperialism to be sound.

If one actually studies and understands European history it can be readily seen that all Europeans have not been inclined to violence, subjugation, pillage, plunder, and domination. The trend grew out of the conduct of some segments of the Nordic peoples (north-western Europeans), who were a less culturally developed, nomadic people for whom hunting and male dominance were the predominant social status qualifiers. Many entered into the Roman military as soldiers and mercenaries and thereby received a high and refined training in warfare, which was unknown and unavailable to other European ethnic groups across central and eastern Europe. When Rome collapsed there remained this culture of highly trained and experienced nomadic warriors whose main conditioning in relating to others was that of military plunder, subjugation and bloodshed. So they spread across Europe conquering and destroying everything in their paths. A similar mentality was developed by the

Poles. Those warrior people created a common trend of perpetual violence across Europe and even destroyed various peace-loving and highly cultured European ethnic groups; such as the Prussian stocks. So subjugation and counter-violence became the European norm.

Among the conquered were Italy, Moesia, Pannonia, Gaul, Spain, etc. The Slavic stocks of eastern and central Europe were the principal ethnicities who were enslaved by, and struggled against, the Norse invaders. It was on the basis of this history of conquer and plunder that Hitler pressed the idea of the Germanic "Aryan" peoples being the superior "master race" (remember that the different European ethnic groups had no concept – as had been created in Amerika – of an all-encompassing "white" race back in the times of Nordic expansion), who by birthright were destined to conquer all people. And it was on this basis that the Nazis mobilized the invasions of Poland, Czechoslovakia and Austria (the old Germanic empire) on the eve of WWII, to begin a greater expansion and conquest intended to encompass all of Europe, and ultimately the world. Hitler played on the notion of the Nordic warrior people being superior to **all** other European and other stocks. So, in dealing with **real** history one can see that the so-called whites are not "by nature" a violent, conquering people, but sectors of them became that way and have been able to seize power through violence, on account of social-economic conditioning. The Europeans' mode of relating to the various ethnicities and castes within their own "white" race with violence and deceit grew out of tribalistic and military conditioning. When they began expanding outside of Europe in the 1400's, largely in response to the Turkish onslaughts, they found much easier prey for their violence and vastly greater stores of untapped natural wealth among peoples of color. So, finding a new "outside" enemy they came to consolidate their own numbers and rationalize their violence under the banner and theory of the "white" master race, and their common mode of relating to people of color, to conquer them, was via the same insensitive violence that has long become the norm of European societies. And much like the early victims of the Germanic Norsemen, we the victims of Western (as in western European) domination, have come to adopt and measure ourselves by the violence and militaristic values of our oppressors. As you noted and quoted Bobby Seale on before, all we can relate to is the gun, while ignoring the social value of community and culture. So if whites must be contained and controlled by force, so then must we, which in itself is an oxymoron since it's reactionary social groups who use force to permanently dominate others that's the very thing we're suffering from. So the object is not to continue to perpetuate a cycle of oppression based upon flesh tones, but to repress the haves who deny power and basic necessities to the have-nots, as they are the source and cause of all chauvinistic divisions to create followers whom they pit against other groups in pursuit of expanding and securing their own power. In this regard we must "take up the gun only to put it down," as Mao observed. Meaning we must repress reactionary violence with revolutionary violence, to seize power from the imperialist oppressors, and once the remnants of capitalism have been purged from societies, the masses can then put down the gun, as the need for it will no longer exist.

So what might be your perception of whites? Do you agree with Del Jones?

Rashid

73.   TO RASHID: Your posing the same question to me opens up sort of a "Pandora's Box" of my **extensive** relations with and observations of white people. Let me first say, NO, I don't agree with Del Jones' sophistry about whites needing to be ruled by force. Some of his observations about the attitudes and behaviors of whites, certain whites anyway, I believe to be accurate. My opinion here is based on my own experiences with upper- and lower-classed whites. Starting in my childhood my only "playmate" was white, but it was in an apartment complex that was majority Black; though I believe my mother influenced who I was to be "playing" with because of her own ideas about race. But later on, due to her occupation – cleaning white folks' homes in affluent (very affluent) neighborhoods – and other whites who you could say "sponsored" my family to better our schooling, housing, etc., I came to a lot of conclusions.

I think most whites controlling or having the advantage of access to profitable and prestigious positions, along with the fact that they know the system and how it works, have developed this paternalistic attitude toward us "colored" people, who more than likely don't hold the same socio-economic power and only know that this system's unfair, unequal and discriminatory when it comes to Blacks. I think concepts like "the white man's burden," "charity," and "noblesse oblige" reinforce the paternalism and condescension on the part of certain whites. They have all the levers and mechanisms at their disposal to project themselves to the world as the "god race," which they have no problem doing. Like even in their relations with animals. I love animals myself, but I've noticed whites will "love you to death." These animals are always in **need** of care and **need** to be in cages or under their watch to survive. Then they come up with a "wildlife conservation park" to try and make up for the destruction and deforestation of these animals' natural habitat. Something similar to what they did to Native Americans, destroy their food supply, way of life, societies, kill them off, run them off their land, etc., and then place them on a reservation or conservation park so they can come and "view" the Indian species at their whim and caprice. Much like a zoo. Much like they do animals in a zoo. Just like they placed us in ghettos – a reserved spot which they can contain and control. I've noticed this among certain whites no matter how benevolent or well meaning some might actually be. I think it's a psychological problem that comes from being in a dominant position for so long over a majority of the earth's population. The only opposition they've had that is/was capable of inflicting the same injury that they inflict on others are other Europeans who possess the same technological and military capabilities. I agree with you though on how they became so bellicose.

I believe all human species are based on communal relations to some degree or other. The Finns, Scandinavians, Swedes, they're socialist countries and have been that way for quite a while to my understanding. White people know the power of, if not unity, at least coordination and organization, which they are very skillful at. Now whether that derives from an urge to survive or from one to just "stay on top" of other races I'm not sure. I mean their own history tends to favor the latter. I think that's why whites feel so "shocked" and "distraught" when we reject their "offerings." They come into the relationships assuming we have no independent thoughts, ideas, culture, survival skills whatsoever. Kind of like a racist white girl who all her life had been told "niggers are animals" and a lot of other such dehumanizing, debasing shit. But when she comes into personal contact with Blacks herself and sees that the very opposite is true, she recognizes her/our humanity; she falls in love with some Black man or becomes real tight with some Black women. As for these racists who just are hard core they're just in a state of denial. They've started to believe their own lies and cling to this racism, which is quite synonymous with religious fanaticism.

I concur with the philosophy of Historical Materialism that it's the small, minority, ruling class dominating and influencing the masses. That goes for whites and Blacks. However, because some whites don't understand this and refuse to engage in any unified struggle of peoples of color, doesn't mean I'm going to seek to win them over, or, like Hubert Harrison was saying, I'm not gonna predicate my/our progress on these whites accepting or not accepting our achieving liberation. These attitudes of whites, which is the attitude of the Establishment, must be checked, tempered and ultimately stopped. They're not going to take us serious while we're talking about getting free, yet the whole time we're offering to take their coat and hat, to rub their feet and massage their shoulders, and fixing them dinner. This isn't going to work.

But their arrogance and pompousness must be checked. It's like they're withholding a certain job from someone but at the same time telling them they're not qualified to do the job. They own and control the food supply while denying us ownership and control over the food supply but tell us we're not capable of feeding ourselves. They tell us we're "terrorists" and insurgents for seeking independent political power, but yet we're not capable of governing ourselves.

But I have met and known some very accommodating and respectful whites who'd welcome you in their home as one of them without having to compromise who you are. Is that the general attitude of whites? No. But they do exist. You seem to be aware of this fact very much so. I'd assumed otherwise prior to "meeting" you and only having your actions and selected thoughts (depending on who I was talking to) vicariously presented to me.

I'd like to see a world (which I probably won't) where all races are in harmony without either of each having to compromise or sacrifice their dignity, self-determination and culture for the sake of another self-appointed race. That's why King's "I Have a Dream" speech was so appealing – because I think they did want racial harmony. But King didn't understand in/under Empire there is no harmony with certain whites except in accommodating to their rule – that's harmony to them.

There was just a catastrophic event in India, South Asia. A tsunami hit India, Indonesia, Malaysia, Thailand, Sri Lanka even all the way to the Afrikan coast of Somalia people were killed. Something like 155,000 people were killed, but the toll keeps on rising. Something else in the news gives an example of what I've been saying: a white child, a boy is missing, presumed kidnapped. There's a special team investigating and mobilizing efforts to find this white child. Okay. Now in those countries such as Thailand, Malaysia the native "colored" children have been kidnapped, enslaved and sexually exploited for years by Europeans who specifically and especially have had no concern whatsoever for those innocent children's safety and welfare. But for this one white child there's an international campaign to find and save the children, that is, be on the lookout for a white child.

But to return to previous points you made. I agree with you on the RNA question. I mean your concerns are not unfounded. "Revolutionary Nationalist **Humanism**." I emphasize the Humanism because I think that's the key factor in preventing our struggle from degenerating into a futile race war or myopic "race state." At bottom, despite our racial/cultural difference, we are all humans, and in our struggle for national liberation humanism must be kept in the forefront, the reasons for our claims to national independence along with others. It was as a "race" that we were/are enslaved, segregated, lynched, unemployed, imprisoned, deprived of healthcare, (mis-)educated, etc., etc., etc., the cost of which manifested itself in two ways, yes as a race, but more importantly as a race of human beings. Human beings who eat, sleep, shit, love, die, breathe, etc., etc. just like all other human beings on this planet. So RNA's plan should be of a dual character of liberating a race and human beings.

We could cite the long list of abuses perpetrated by empire that have decimated us and degraded us as human beings in the name of race, that we will reclaim our dignity as human beings, recognizing we are a colonized peoples. The Humanism aspect could facilitate the acceptance of socialism as well, since socialism is organized around humans' needs and not what is profitable. This in itself is a unifying element – the Humanism.

I like the part where you suggested that we ally ourselves with progressive whites as a show of solidarity with our fellow human beings, 'cause that would negate and hopefully destroy any imperialist plots to label us "mad Black racists." But even were it possible to cripple Empire without formal secession based on skin tones, I'd still support our self-governance to re-establish some self-worth through education in relation to the world, and as a safeguard against being dominated by any race again, and to preserve our culture and achievements. Yet if a pluralist (racial) state is possible allowing all races and human beings free development, I'm not against that. But I think a consensus should be taken amongst the population to ascertain whether or not this is their will.

The argument could be made that Blacks are a subjugated class, considering our lack of control over any resources or vital aspects of the economy in the productive sector as opposed to the non-productive sector. I mean there are only a few Black farmers. And how many Black shoe companies? How many Black car factories? I mean you already know we might have capital and jewelry but we must keep being exploited in order to maintain ours, whereas the whites just keep exploiting us to maintain theirs. We have some weight on paper, but in terms of concrete assets, we have none.

The Humanism aspect could help bring us "back to earth," away from these abstract concepts of thugs, hustlers, pimps, etc. I mean how much weight do you think the Humanism aspect has? We could promote Humanism, or the consequences or rewards of any of our actions from a human standpoint in terms of the human cost and loss of life in war, or a society of new, improved, concerned human beings. Frantz Fanon said, "You do not carry on a war, nor suffer brutal and widespread repression, nor look on while all other members of your family are wiped out in order to make racialism or hatred triumph." This must be our guiding principle (one anyway) and perhaps a slogan directed at whites and other races. It would need some clarification in that race doesn't determine whether I like to smoke, or how well I want to live; they may find different expressions but represent the same human desires, irrespective of race. And that extends to the desire for freedom, justice, etc. And since Blacks in Amerika have been referred to as the "moral conscience/consciousness of Amerika" it should be fairly easy for us to accept this line of reasoning.

I don't know if a national independence struggle would necessarily isolate us cause the world has watched and continues to watch the injustices we've suffered from within Amerika. I guess it would boil down to whether world opinion was on our side, which I don't see why not, why it wouldn't be. But that's where the realities of our nation or our race, nationally and internationally must be emphasized.

The AIDS cases, we hold 30 million of the 40 million AIDS cases worldwide. Afrika has no nuclear weapons, no air force, military, no means of effective defense. Shit, the French just razed the weak air force planes that their neo-colony the Ivory Coast had, in retaliation for an uprising against foreign domination. It goes back to Garvey's questioning where are our men of big affairs, navy, etc. The diamonds extracted from Afrika are refined in Europe. Afrikans should have total control over their assets, but they don't. There are some complex considerations and issues involved. I think someone like yourself is unduly qualified to bring a solution(s) to these problems. I'm just offering my perspectives from my level of development. A lot of work would have to be done to expose the fact that despite the Oprahs and Russell Simmonses we are on dependent economy status. We have **no** means of self-sufficiency in Amerika and therefore our progress as humans as a race as a nation is dependent on outside, hostile forces.

We could point out the nature of capitalism. The word itself, as you pointed out, implies capital as a priority not society (socialism). But more so, the fact that okay ruling classes, y'all are so bent on passing all these measures to "protect" us from terrorism, well how about equally "protecting" us from unemployment, rising health care costs, poverty, a life of insecurity. 'Cause they have the means and that raises the question of welfare and security, and more importantly **whose** welfare and **whose** security, Enron, Halliburton, Dow, GE, Boeing, Lockheed Martin, Raytheon, Morgan Chase, or the citizens, the working masses, the society. Arguments like that could serve to expose the true nature of the Empire. Whose interests are they really protecting? You know.

Perhaps RNA efforts, carried out properly, could be the "little motor" to the much larger process and results you have in mind, which I presume to be a harmonious world free of exploitation of man by man* in all forms and shapes. In that class/civil war Blacks would be the principal fighting force. It would be difficult to get across that it's a class struggle cause of the fact that Empire is a white empire. But that's another reason for low-income whites to question their racist white sentiments and ask those same whites how many Blacks hold dominant positions over them, who's their landlord, their employer, their president, you know.

Outlaw

---

* And of womyn by man. —*Rashid*

74.   To Outlaw: Humanism I believe is the only appropriate approach to serious anti-imperialist struggle. As for the approach to national independence, I do recognize that it has been our peculiar targeting as a "race" and the resultant destruction of our social cohesion as a people that compels our need for a movement and struggle to become a cohesive and united people. So we must of course liberate ourselves as a people and also support the liberation struggles of other oppressed peoples. Unity amongst the whole of oppressed peoples must be the basis of a socialist project in this racially and culturally diverse region. This means a federation or confederation (depending) of New Afrikans and other oppressed nations here. Remember, the ultimate object of revolution is to destroy state systems themselves, not to perpetuate them ad infinitum. The **only** reason that we embrace statehood is first to unify and liberate a colonized people, then to repress internal exploiting classes and unite with all workers' states, and ultimately to end in having the state "wither away." The only way that this can be done is that the class struggle be internationalized (Humanized, Huey P. Newton coined the term "Intercommunalism"), to undermine imperialism by united struggles of all colonized peoples for genuine independence, led by their respective working classes (to prevent reversion to neocolonialism by native bourgeoisie elements building ties to Empire and seizing power of the national political economies). If we are able to ensure that neocolonialism is defeated once and for all, we must defeat the imperialism which spawns it, which means destroying capitalism in an international workers movement. If capitalism isn't overthrown in the imperialist countries, the colonized people cannot break free of neocolonialism. **This** is why we must unite with all workers, including white workers, and our independence struggles

must be worker-led. Revolution in the imperialist countries means allying with white workers. There's no other way of defeating the bourgeoisie except by the seizure of power by the workers. If we don't defeat capitalism inside the imperialist countries we will never truly defeat colonialism. Colonialism *is* capitalism.

Rashid

The following letters are excerpts from an exchange I had with a dedicated anti-imperialist Amerikan white womyn; I felt these to be relevant to the final discussions Outlaw and I were having on Amerikan race politics.

---

75. To AZ: Race is a thorny issue in this race-sensitized society, and, in that it's such a major social reality it can't be ignored. Indeed the very foundation of the Amerikan national identity, as its founders emphasized, is one built on the Herrenvolk (white master race) concept. Race has always been US capitalists' last-ditch appeal to bring a reactionary and backward white working class (and especially the poorer whites) out in aid of them and in violent opposition to workers of color.

On the other side of the coin a lot of folks – particularly those who are members of oppressed nationalities – tend to mistakenly view race and nationality as synonymous. How this happens I don't quite understand (as far as people's tendency to distort reality). There is no nation that consists of a single "pure" race of people.

Furthermore, race is a proven unsupportable concept – in the biological context. In fact, the advent of DNA technologies has proven all humyn populations to be basically the same genetically, and the variations in physical features, complexions and constructions are the result of environmental and geographical adaptations, and that there have been so many transfers of genes from one gene pool to another that all existing populations today are thoroughly "mixed." I only tend to use the term Black in the racial context when identifying my "race" group because although race is itself scientifically unsupportable, it's a very real social concept. And it cannot be ignored or marginalized in that race is still a predominant basis for social oppression, division and therefore control, which can only be resolved as a result of revolutionary processes.

Actually, I believe you recognize at least some of this.

As for the question of nationalism: we New Afrikans must expand the features that characterize the New Afrikan and Pan-Afrikan nations. Skin color cannot be the definitive feature. We must be able to embrace any "race" of people as members of our Nations, and the defining characteristic is instead of being skin color, that of having or embraced an Afrikan heritage. So under this broader and more realistic concept of nationality you can be embraced as a member of our nation regardless of your race, just as Native Americans adopt people of any and all races into their nations. In fact many Indian Nations have survived intact till today, despite enduring continued policies of oppression and genocide, due to this practice.

Rashid

76.   To Rashid: One reason I could/would **never** attempt or claim to understand the impact of "race" on a Black person (especially a Black womyn), is because I know how deeply "race" has affected me and I'm of the oppressor race. I am not and would never claim to be *oppressed* by whiteness, but I do feel fucked by it – mind-fucked. Maybe tormented is a good way to put it.

My perception of race has been formed by being a white minority (not in the usual oppressed sense of the word) in communities of color. Thus, I've been in situations where, being white, I'm not accepted by people – but for the most part I've felt, and was, accepted. I attribute this to my physical build, my ability to code-switch (flow easily between speaking $$ English and Black English depending on my surroundings), my tendency to defend myself, to earn people's respect and sometimes surprise people by coming back at them when jokes are made, and the fact that most people can sense a genuine spirit and will be open to that despite skin color. And of course, I'm nasty at spades. Oh, and also the fact that I don't get defensive about being white – something that I'm conscious of, and is hard in a world where everyone is judged by the color of their skin. But I try to recognize that, and squash it if it ever arises. This has left me at times in a position of feeling loyal to and comfortable with communities that, because of race, I will never "belong" to.

So a friend might say, "I hate white people! AZ, you're different, but white people … " going on to describe some fucked up situation they were just in. But I'm **not** different. I mean, in some ways I am, but no one can transcend race. Not as long as they interact with the world. So instead I embrace my position. I accept my place as an outsider with a backstage pass – not getting hurt when my friends disapprove of interracial dating or when there are certain events that we all agree I shouldn't go to. I genuinely believe that Black unity needs to be built and strengthened and that there are places where whites **should not** be. In fact, I think it's a shame that Black people are labeled "prejudiced" when they don't want to involve white people – even radical white people. Shit, we get to be involved in everything else in this world, why we gotta get jealous about not being a part of something that's not for or about us?!

In a discussion about the possibility of creating a Black nation – with geographically defined boundaries – within the current Amerika, my friend CC once said that she wouldn't wanna move somewhere I wasn't welcome. I kept quiet (didn't feel it was my place to take part) but thought to myself that as sad as I'd be to say goodbye to many friends, such a place sounds much better than what we got now, and who am I to protest because I'd be left out. But at the same time I was filled with love at the fact that CC said that, and filled with sadness at the thought that the solution does not include me. So my logical side and my emotional side differed – but I try to stick with my logical side. Personal attachment is rather insignificant in the grand scheme.

I've never fully understood the point that there should be a generation of "pure Blacks" as some have said. Because in the race game the rules say: one drop of Black blood and you're Black. And of course, it's a socially constructed game, not biological. So the rules create the reality. So why then does "white blood" equal an "impure" Black person? Wouldn't it actually create more Black people if two Blacks had kids with two whites instead of those four remaining racially segregated?

I don't mean to say that Black men should necessarily father children with white wimyn. It **is true** that there's a lack of Brothers!

(You know this, 'cause they're in there with you.) So the available ones, especially the conscious ones, should be available for Black wimyn. There are a lot of Black wimyn who have been hurt by Black men, which conscious Black men like yourself are in a position to heal. There's just a need for many, many more conscious Brothers able to make themselves available. I just wonder often where I fit into the struggle against imperialism here.

AZ

77. To AZ: You asked where you fit in here in the struggles against imperialism. That's a broad question. I expect a large part would be in working to raise the consciousness of other whites (especially youth), particularly in the context of having them understand imperialism, class, and the extremes of struggle likely to be made by folks of color (domestically), and which have been made, and why such drastic measures were/are necessary. Most whites have been conditioned to perceive any independent initiatives by Blacks, and especially any with a militant orientation, to be anti-white schemes which will ultimately see Black violence targeted against them. This is the mindset cultivated in whites since race became the principal tool of social and class division used by the ruling classes here since the late 1600's. They conditioned the poor whites to feel any struggle of Blacks against oppression were fundamentally anti-white – thus whites must subvert all such efforts and be at the head of any Black activities. Then there's the sense of paternalism and condescension developed in the white subconscious after their remaining so long

in a position of social, political, economic, cultural, and military domination over Black people, which is threatened by our seeking to pursue our own best interests independent of, and in pursuit of achieving independence from, such white domination. This likely answers your question regarding whites' seeming jealousy or hostility towards being excluded from any Black activities, and not being always in control. I think with certain projects where you can serve in support areas to help the work of oppressed nationalities and races, you can set an example that whites can be supportive of work that expresses and pursues radical perspectives and initiatives of people of color, and to educate others through your own practice that we all have a gripe that grows out of a common system of imperialism/capitalism. We must remember that the fundamental contradiction in the world is privatization of the means of production and the socialization of labor, while the main contradiction is between imperialism and everyone else on the planet. As Mao observed, we must unite all who can be united to drive the imperialists out.

ALL POWER TO THE PEOPLE!!

Rashid

A few months after Outlaw and I exchanged the last letters included in this book, Comrade Shaka Sankofa Zulu and I came together to found the New Afrikan Black Panther Party–Prison Chapter (NABPP-PC). The NABPP-PC has since developed branches in various prisons across the U$ empire and has its own newsletter, *Right On!*

Though an embryonic form of a genuine vanguard Panther Party, the NABPP-PC aspires to rebuild the original Black Panther Party (BPP). Our efforts in this regard will be based on learning, applying and advancing the lessons and successes of the BPP, but, more so, we are giving special attention to studying and correcting the errors of the BPP, especially errors made in its organizational structure, (the BPP erroneously combined both a Vanguard Party and a mass form of organization in its structure), and its decision-making process, which it *called* Democratic Centralism (DC), but was actually a form of Authoritarian Centralism (AC).

Many sincere comrades have confused DC and AC, and mistake the corrupting and "commandist" practices of AC for DC. AC is the tendency our comrade Maroon criticizes but mistakes for DC. Since he wrote the Foreword for this book, I have elaborated more fully on these subjects in a separate article, entitled "On the Roles and Characteristics of the Panther Vanguard Party and Mass Organizations."

Many of the thoughts and ideas that went into the formation of the NABPP-PC and its mass organization, the New Afrikan Service Organization, can be seen in their developmental stages in my letter exchanges with Outlaw.

Not everyone is willing to submit to the discipline or sacrifices demanded by the struggle for genuine revolutionary change, but there are many who are. There are comrades like Maroon, Sundiata Acoli, Mumia Abu-Jamal, Tom Big Warrior and others who continue to "soldier on" in the struggle. They are living martyrs who've given their lives over to the people and the struggle for mass liberation from capitalist imperialism, and the self-determination of oppressed nationalities. They provide the example, history and ongoing work that inspires, informs and guides the younger generations, mine included, and those yet to be born.

The struggle continues!

—*Rashid*

PART THREE

"THE PRINCIPAL RESERVOIR OF REVOLUTIONARY POTENTIAL IN
AMERIKA LIES IN WAIT INSIDE THE BLACK COLONY"
GEORGE JACKSON
BLOOD IN MY EYE

See: "Right of
Revolution" BLACK'S LAW
DICTIONARY (7th Ed.)

Born
Criminals

RASHID
7-8-7'02

KEVIN (RASHID) JOHNSON

WHAT'S LEFT OF THE LEFT?
A CRITICAL QUESTION

We are living in what is obviously a decisive point in history. We stand as witnesses to the super-consolidation of global empire and the militarist super-state. We in Amerika live within this monolith's very nerve center. We therefore stand at a decisive point in relation to how or if we will ultimately confront this situation. We can either be the hope for the survival of future generations, or we can be enemy collaborators – tacit or otherwise – and aid in nailing the coffin shut for humynity. Which course we take will largely depend on whether or not we can rise above capitalist, anti-humyn, individualist influences and cooperate towards human and environmental survival.

With China on the capitalist road; with the Soviet Union having collapsed while traveling the same road; with the non-aligned progressive leaderships neutralized, killed off, co-opted, or demonized; and with all other remaining anti-capitalist nations rendered irrelevant and impoverished due to economic and diplomatic isolation by the West, imperial Amerika faces no meaningful threat to its security except from those who live within its own territorial borders.

The domestic upheavals of the 1960's and 70's taught empire some valuable lessons on just how dangerous an informed and discontent population can be. As a result, and through a steady application of misinformation, carrots, and sticks, empire has worked steadily to drain the focus, resolve, and militancy of the informed and discontented. From that point to this, empire has manufactured a discontinuity in popular struggle, while maintaining continuity in its own growth and consolidation. One of the empire's principal tools and weapons has been its prisons.

After constant failures of empire to deliver promised changes, during the 1960's and 70's, Amerikan Blacks became radicalized in opposition to abject poverty, systematic economic exclusion, political impotence, racism, police brutality, and colonialism in general; Native Americans were radicalized on much the same bases in addition to the denial of territorial rights. Wimyn were mobilized in opposition to gender oppression, and a cross-class mobilization erupted on account of the war against Vietnam. In pursuit of reaching my point in this paper, I'll limit my focus primarily to the Black resistance.

In response to the Black insurrections and mobilizations, empire had influential and genuine Black leaders imprisoned and/or assassinated, and their politics and meanings rewritten and distorted. The image of Dr. Martin Luther King, Jr. has been represented as pro-middle class and pro-integration of Blacks into the US capitalist empire. These were the views he perhaps held during the August 1963 March on Washington when he gave his "I Have a Dream" speech. However, deliberately obscured are King's increasingly radical views, his public opposition to the Vietnam War, his preparing a Poor People's March on Washington set to occur in 1968, and his adopting socialist economic and political views in repudiation of capitalism, all of which developed toward the end of his life. In the latter half of 1967, he expressly rejected the idea of Black integration into the Amerikan capitalist empire.

Following a continuous FBI campaign of threats, hounding, stalking, and intimidation against him, King was conveniently murdered just months before the Poor People's March was set to occur. That march was intended to effectively shut down all movement and operations within Washington, DC, just as the 1963 March on Washington was originally planned by its original grassroots organizers to do, until President John F. Kennedy and his financial backers used the then pro-empire King to subvert the March and transform it into a benign, peaceful affair.[1]

Similarly, Malcolm Shabazz (X) has been wrongly portrayed as a disjointed radical with very little political vision and development, who ultimately became pro-integration into empire. Mainstream accounts of Malcolm avoid his work toward his life's end to organize an anti-colonial Pan-Afrikan Internationalist Movement. His Organization of Afro-American Unity was patterned after, and planned to work to advance the objectives of the Organization of African Unity, and to operate as an anti-colonial movement to unify the world's Black people and build economic and political ties with other Third World, progressive, and socialist leaders and ultimately came out challenging capitalism as the true enemy of Blacks and all poor. He was subjected to relentless FBI surveillance, stalking and harassment under its COMINFIL program and also conveniently murdered. And as civil rights leader Bayard Rustin predicted, imperial powers, and "not Negro people, will determine Malcolm X's role in history."[2]

As scholar and writer William Sales, Jr. observed of the treatment of leaders like Malcolm, Martin and others, "once the images of these leaders can no longer be suppressed or ignored, their value and their significance are distorted, often by being reduced to slogans, which satisfy temporarily but whose superficiality masks the deeper meaning of the issues and analyses these leaders try to convey."[3]

Empire's subversion of the 1963 March and other channels of Black popular resistance to oppressive conditions between 1960 and 1964 prompted the armed urban uprising which empire called "riots" by the disgruntled urban Blacks between 1964 and 1968; the uprisings of 1967 being the greatest "urban riots" in US history.[4] Consistent with what both Malcolm and Martin had come to realize at just the times they were both killed, the economic and political needs of Blacks and all poor people could not be solved under capitalism and compelled fundamental change of the political and economic structure of Amerika, i.e. revolution. And it was their demand for this sort of change that drove the Black uprisings. However, the empire had other ideas.

The 60's rebellions compelled empire to study and develop tactical methods to convert the Black revolutionary initiative. It had to divert the collective attention of Blacks away from issues like poverty and disparities in wealth to more controllable issues, like voting and civil reforms, and it had to crush the much more uncontrollable danger of Black armed struggle.

The Kerner Commission was put in place to study the Black "urban riots" to determine their cause (!) and provide "appropriate responses" to prevent future uprisings. The Kerner Report devised both military-police (repressive) methods and socio-economic (pacification) schemes, calculated to undermine and neutralize mass revolutionary awareness, potential and activity; to keep such energy repressed and diverted; and to prevent its resurgence on mass levels.[5]

With the implementation of these policies targeting grassroots political elements, which were seen as fueling the flames of mass Black discontent, many of these elements who were not neutralized or intimidated were forced underground to evade capture or assassination. The latter measures were used with increasing frequency against the Black Panther Party, which developed in 1966 as a Black self-help and self-defense organization in response to both the assassination of Malcolm X and the continued government violence against and disregard for the needs of Blacks. The Party further sought political independence for Blacks.[6] These elements, having been forced underground, then resorted to armed strategic defensives, for the sake of personal survival and resistance, while empire was busy neutralizing all aboveground political workers. These initiatives were implemented through the counterintelligence program COINTELPRO – white house, FBI, CIA, and local police collaboration.

Subsequently, Daniel Patrick Moynihan counseled Richard Nixon in 1970 to implement measures to isolate this growing "armed front" from the masses. (Quite obviously because mass involvement or sympathy with organized tactical armed resistance is the one form of struggle that truly endangers empire's power.) Moynihan prescribed such methods to accomplish this objective as "criminalizing" their image (all truly revolutionary activity became "terrorism")[7], refining policing methods, and creating a buffer by undermining and replacing lower-class grassroots influence, and pushing the middle class as a model of social conformity. It was pure neocolonial strategy, adapted to the US. It was also Moynihan who counseled Nixon in the 60's to implement policies which would dissolve the grassroots elements of the "lower-class strata" that were so prominent in the urban rebellions.[8]

One example of empire's criminalizing tactical armed resistance at this stage (and exposing its recognition of educated Black youth as a leading revolutionary element) occurred upon the capture of Black professor Angela Y. Davis in October 1970 – she was accused of supplying George Jackson's seventeen-year-old brother Jonathan with the guns he used in the Marin county courthouse raid where he armed and attempted to free several Black prisoners. Richard Nixon quickly denounced Davis (who was ultimately acquitted by an all-white jury) as a "criminal" and "terrorist."[9]

While the Kerner Report was a principal tool used in the late 60's to destroy grassroots-level "political leadership," it was, however, focused mainly on the unorganized masses and "urban riots." Thus by 1970 the task force on Law and Law Enforcement of the National Commission on the Causes and Prevention of Violence was developed to confront the more organized underground armed resistance, such as the Black Liberation Army, Revolutionary Action Movement, Weather Underground, and other "small but increasing number of Black militants," who "actively espoused and sometimes practice illegal retaliatory and even guerrilla tactics against existing social institutions, particularly the police and schools." The taskforce was concerned with "stopping the spread" of such "purposeful violence" which it recognized to be "potentially even more destructive than the urban riots have been."[10] It was in this vein that Nixon first coined the "war on crime" agenda, with a focus on "violent crime" and urban youth in particular.

Under these policies, empire, by the mid-1970's, was well on its way to destroying the active radical youth forces of Black Liberation. It was also preparing to develop schemes to neutralize all independent Black organizing, because although empire had passed various civil reform laws and spouted rhetoric about racial equality and justice, there was no intention of enforcing them, nor of allowing any foundation to remain for a renewed round of Blacks organizing for resistance.

With revolutionary forces in Amerika on the rise and joining forces (e.g. Blacks, Native Americans, Wimyn, Students, anti-imperialists, poor whites, anti-war elements, etc.) the wealthy elite had to change the face of the empire's administration to a more modest, conciliatory and humane one, so they offered a democratic presidential candidate of "humble" origins (a peanut farmer) to promote a pretended policy of diplomacy, racial sensitivity, and concern for humyn rights – Jimmy "Ethnic Purity" Carter.

Carter began his presidential term by pardoning most Vietnam war draft evaders (pretending to be a friend of the social forces who'd forced empire to abolish the draft in 1973), acting to broker peace in various Third World countries, and promoting his administration's agenda as one of supporting and protecting "humyn rights." However, events on the ground and policies implemented by Carter showed his concerns for decreasing US militarism, for people of color, and for humyn rights to be very different in reality.[11]

Pertinent here are the secret measures passed under Carter to permanently destroy the US Black movements for civil and humyn rights. Under counseling of Zbigniew Brzezinski, Carter and the US National Security Council devised and implemented a policy and study under National Security Council Memorandum 46 (NSC 46), in 1978.

The stated objectives of NSC 46 were to prevent domestic Blacks' awareness of and organizing against US economic, diplomatic, and military ties to the openly racist apartheid regime of South Afrika; to prevent Black Afrikan governments from coordinated protests of this US/South Afrika relationship at the United Nations; to prevent "discussions on the US racial issue at the UN ... "[12]; to reduce and contain activities in the Black Movement that were once nationally coordinated to merely local levels; to destroy all "organizational unity in the movement"; to create "sharp social stratification of the Black population and lack of policy options which could reunite them"; to "prevent" the development of "a national leader of standing comparable to Martin Luther King."[13]

Specific methods proposed in NSC 46 to accomplish these ends include: developing "a special program designed to perpetuate division in the Black movement and ... to encourage division within Black circles ... to preserve the present climate which inhibits the emergence from within the Black leadership of a person capable of exerting nationwide appeal"; to prevent the development of any "durable ties between US Black organizations and radical groups in African states," to "sharpen social stratification in the Black community, which would lead to the widening and perpetuation of the gap between successful educated Blacks and the poor, giving rise to the growing antagonism between different Black groups and a weakening of the movement as a whole"; the creation of a broader Black middle class to play against the masses of poor Blacks; to "take every possible means" to work through white labor unions "to counteract the increasing influence of Black labor organizations ... including the creation of ... adverse and hostile reaction among white trade unionists to demands for improvement of social and economic welfare of the Blacks"[14]; and "support the nomination at the federal and local levels of loyal Black figures to elective offices, to government agencies, and to the court." The objective of the latter being "it would be easier to control the activity of loyal Black representatives (sic) within existing institutions,"[15] and so "the idea of an independent Black political party ... would soon lose all support."

Following the pattern from then to the present, we can very clearly see how – and that – these policies undermined and de-popularized truly revolutionary activities which posed a genuine danger to empire's power (e.g. how middle-class Black "elites" were created and used to replace and undermine grassroots leadership, how the practice of armed struggle was demonized, how divisive schemes were implemented, etc.). These government tactics also demoralized the progressive movement.

So, early on, the imperialist US empire struck back against Blacks not only with misinformation and noble-sounding rhetoric, but also with the stick (military policy initiatives) and with the carrot (such initiatives as "community action programs," the Equal Opportunity Act of 1964, the Voting Rights Act of 1965). It then used the co-opted token Black middle class model (dark faces in high places) to parade before the poor Black masses as the only viable avenue out of economic and racial repression, and as an example of the "character" which Blacks must assume in order to win even marginal assimilation into the empire and live the "Amerikan Dream." The promise became that those Blacks who broke their ties with the poor Black masses and disavowed any connection with the world's people of color, and thereupon adopted the cynical, cutthroat, backstabbing and individualist values of the empire, would then be judged as acceptable based upon the co-opted "content of their character" instead of based upon "the color of their skin." For a still relatively small number of Blacks, Martin Luther King, Jr.'s 1963 pro-empire dream was to be fulfilled, but only upon them literally selling their souls. It was just on account of his realizing that this was the only basis upon which Blacks would be marginally accepted in Amerika (and only a few at that) that he broke with his 1963 views, characterizing himself as having been "naïve and deceived" and remarked in 1967 that "you've heard me say before that I have a dream; well, I woke up and found out that it was a nightmare."

There was a general lack of understanding of what the role of the armed underground should be in relation to the legal aboveground movement and vice versa. Nobody seemed to have a clear idea or strategy on how to move towards preparing urban revolutionary base areas and doing revolutionary work in a pre-revolutionary situation. Thus they fell into reformism and co-option on the one hand and adventurism and "revolutionary suicide" on the other. As a result both legal and underground revolutionary activity in the inner cities was defunct by the early 1980's.

By that point (after Jimmy Carter was used to effectively implement measures to undermine Black organizing, and to pacify the Amerikan public in the wake of mass resistance against the war, and other conditions already spoken of earlier) Nixon's "war on crime" agenda, which came in answer to mass Black rebellions, became a central policy of Ronald Reagan in the 1980's via the methods prescribed by NSC 46. The ensuing mass incarceration, criminalization, concentration of police and surveillance, and the vast Prison-Industrial Complex targeted especially at poor, urban Blacks, has been a conscious tactical response of empire to repress anti-colonial, anti-capitalist, and revolutionary fervor amongst the oppressed classes.

It is no coincidence that during the Reagan/Bush, Sr. era, during which the incarceration rate quadrupled, these administrations initiated an outright attack on domestic social programs while simultaneously and effectively criminalizing the character of Black youth, knowing that urban Blacks would suffer the most under cuts to social programs; leading to greater levels of frustration, desperation, and insecurity within Black communities. But with the schemes implemented under NSC 46, any Black reactions would likely take the form of Black-on-Black exploitation and violence within their communities instead of conscious resistance against empire. In 1982 Reagan cut $44 billion in social spending and another $19 billion the next year. Under Bush, Sr. this line of attack continued. By 1992, Reagan and Bush had succeeded in transforming the previously liberal Supreme Court into a conservative one that has proven most hostile to civil rights for Blacks and prisoners. Under Bill Clinton ten million poor people were kicked off welfare with little option for finding work in a continuously shrinking job market; he then put more police on the streets than any previous administration to ensure the steady disposal of the desperately poor into the nation's vast prison system – indeed, the world's largest prison system.

It is worthy of note that Reagan ushered in and the commercial media popularized the "war on drugs" initiative (as a major component of the "war on crime" scheme) just before the crack epidemic swept the urban Black communities in all major US cities. Criminal laws were on the books specifically targeting this drug before it was even in widespread use. There is certainly no lack of evidence and admissions of CIA, DEA, and White House involvement in trafficking tons of narcotics into the US on the one hand, while professing to outlaw it on the other.[16] Human Rights Watch noted in a 2000 report that one fifth of the states in Amerika incarcerate Black males on drug charges twenty-seven to fifty-seven times the rate of white males. HRW attorney Jamie Fellner observed that "most drug offenders are white. Five times as many whites use drugs as Blacks."[17] This targeting of Blacks (young Black males in particular) for such disproportionate imprisonment is a conscious political tactic of empire.

Addictive drugs have long been tactically used as "chemical weapons" to effectively destroy cohesion and organizing unity and potential within societies. An early example being the British saturation of China with opium in the 1800's to destroy Chinese resistance to forced trade relations with Britain, which was followed by Christian missionaries pushing morphine (which the Chinese called "Jesus Opium") claiming it to be a "cure for opium addiction." Another early example that continues today was the destruction of the Native American societies with alcohol (rum), which allowed for an effective campaign of genocide to be waged against them by the US in pursuit of stealing their land.

Indeed the esteemed US founding father and co-author of the declaration of independence, Benjamin Franklin, openly acknowledged and promoted the use of rum as an ethnic cleansing weapon to clear out the Native Indians who were seen as impediments to US land seizure and expansion. He stated, "If it be the design of Providence to extirpate these savages in order to make room for the cultivators of the earth, it seems not improbable that rum may be the appointed means!" In fact, the rum produced through the slave colonies of the Caribbean was the principal drug trafficking of the British/Amerikan colonial system. As W.E.B. DuBois wrote, "the West Indian Islands became the center of the British Empire and of immense importance to the grandeur of England. It was the Negro slave who made these sugar colonies the most precious colonies ever recorded in the annals of imperialism. Experts called them 'the fundamental prop and support' of the Empire."[18] But what must be understood is what made these sugar colonies so profitable was the sugar's being the base ingredient for production of rum, i.e. sugar-cane turned into molasses and distilled into rum. This rum was used to destroy Indian societies and trade with Afrikan chiefs for slaves. Similarly the thriving Black and Puerto Rican working-class Bronx, NY communities of the 1940's and 50's were decimated by the influx of heroin introduced by the Mafia with complicity of empire. In fact, the CIA reestablished the Corsican Mafia in France, and in exchange for the Mafia's smashing the working-class resistance of dockworkers there, it was allowed to set up the largest post-war western heroin racket – the famous "French Connection." During the Vietnam War the CIA routinely smuggled heroin into South Vietnam using planes from Air America (its own airline) to addict both US soldiers and South Vietnamese, leading to a national scandal surrounding the "GI heroin epidemic."[19]

From all of the above, at least four things can be concluded. First, whether you agree with their politics or not, the Black Panther Party failed in their strategic revolutionary goals, because, although as a political group they were able to rally mass support and sympathy by providing community support and self-support programs – which empire could not and would not – amongst the targeted group (i.e. poor urban Black masses), they failed at the same time to prepare for and implement military and counterintelligence (as well as their own intelligence) initiatives to protect themselves and their programs, to ensure the continuity of their organization, and to organize and arm the masses. Second, by splitting into re-formist and adventurist factions and failing to continue to combine *Serve The People* programs with revolutionary political education, the Party became utterly vulnerable to government repression and internal disintegration. Third, modern imprisonment and its targeting of the urban Black masses in particular is a tool and weapon, the increased use of which has been to dispose of the most expendable and potentially revolutionary sectors of a superfluous population; to undermine dissident political awareness, organizing, and most importantly, tactical dissident action of a militant nature (the unspoken sides of the strategic demonization and mass incarceration of Blacks are the genocidal implications – this is especially apparent in the deliberate imprisonment of Black males throughout their reproductive years, which is the effect of mandatory minimum, three strikes, and parole abolition laws).[20] The fourth point is that empire does not fear mass rallies and marches (in fact it will support, infiltrate, and control them), speeches and pamphlet-passing, so long as these activities remain peaceful; and it has proven able to ultimately contain and repress unorganized riots. What empire does fear, however, is tactical and strategic mass-based resistance – in conscious preparation for revolution.

As a modern example of how effective mass peace rallies truly are, consider that ten million people worldwide assembled in opposition to the US invasion of Iraq in early 2003 – with not the slightest deterrent effect. On this point I quote a cohort's comments in a recent letter about his experience in the 2003 anti-war rally in Washington,

> Can you imagine being part of a mass turnout of two hundred thousand people in DC and feeling completely disempowered, and at times even bored? If the left learned anything from opposition to Vietnam, it should be that it took all facets of resistance to halt the war machine – and a full decade, no less. There seems to be some heavy-duty revisionist history that the left writes of as factual these days that states that through the constant vigils and peace marches and letter-writing campaigns and enough happy, gooey, pacifist spirit we overwhelmed the government and forced them to react to the voices of the people. Resiliency of the Viet Cong and the NLF, assassination of out-of-control commanders by common troops, armed clandestine organizations operating here in the US and abroad, diplomatic pressure. All of these key elements vanished into the memory hole, à la 1984.

We can now objectively recognize the political motive behind US mass incarceration targeted against specific classes for what it actually is, viz., low-intensity warfare against Amerikan Blacks among others. Thus, any genuine resistance to empire from within must target its prisons – among other things – with more than rallies, meetings and lobbying protests. The Animal Liberation Front (ALF) has undertaken many clandestine animal rescue operations; however, these animals, unlike desperate, radicalized, liberated human beings, aren't likely to also become active freedom fighters. Similarly, the Earth Liberation Front (ELF) has undertaken innumerable clandestine operations to sabotage equipment and projects of the empire, which they recognize endanger the environment. Yet, where indeed is the People Liberation Front (PLF) – the clandestine group liberating captured people and sabotaging projects of the Prison-Industrial Complex? The animals have allies, as do the trees, but what about the humyn beings? Especially noteworthy are those who are the victims of genocidal tactics, i.e. Blacks and Native Americans.

Multitudes of youth (of no uncertain potential) have been drawn toward such dissident organizations and groups since the 70's, but drift in and back out without purpose. Many are drawn by searches for momentary recognition in being affiliated with groups that receive some media attention for their images of rebellion and confrontation. But such cynicisms serve no long-term interests and certainly do not provide solutions to the problems of the oppressed classes, here or abroad.

There is a vast difference between rebellion and revolution. Rebellion is little more than resistance – usually reactionary and not necessarily result-oriented (i.e. it lacks tactical approach and strategic objective). Revolution, however, is a protracted tactically organized struggle to accomplish totally changing and replacing socio-economic, political, and cultural arrangements, and changes the logic upon which the old order of exploitation justified itself. Revolution doesn't work by folks drifting in and out of "the movement" and/or a collective, as soon as there is a disagreement or injured feelings. Such ego-oriented, superficial commitments are nothing short of reactionary.

Rebellion is the stage that disoriented teenagers typically go through when they claim to reject their parents' or dominant authority's culture, control, and influence, only to find themselves becoming duplicates or retaining dominant traits of what they professed to reject. So, while it is, and always has been, the youth that possess the greatest potential and energy for social change, it is the same youth that most commonly drift in and out of "the struggle," start up, join, and abandon various activist, dissident, resistance, and so-called revolutionary groups. Next to the so-called minority and prisoner classes in Amerika, the youth are the ones most hostile to the present system. Unfortunately, because of community alienation and imitation of negative media images, they are most lacking in revolutionary values. Thus, their potentially revolutionary energy is spent in individual explosive rebellions.

The youth's lack of focused commitment imitates what they see of the old left. They see movement "veterans" merely floating from rally to rally, chasing the emotional impact of each meeting, not focused on working toward building collective struggle but instead on their personal, momentary, individual feelings. Power reacts to all threats, and we can determine by the reactions of empire to various dissidents and their activities whether or not their efforts threaten its stability. Furthermore, history demonstrates for us what kinds of resistance Empire cannot sustain.

The Vietnam War opposition and Amerikan Black Liberation struggles exposed its weak underbelly. The national independence struggles of the Afrikan peoples in the 1950's, 60's and 70's (which ejected the European colonizers and their armies from the continent) also exposed imperial weaknesses. The courageous struggles of the Vietnamese for cultural and national independence against the French, Japanese, Chinese (before the 1949 revolution and after 1976), and Amerika exposed empire's weaknesses. The struggle of the Lebanese against the US/Israeli occupation that forced Amerika's retreat in 1983 exposed empire's weakness. The Chinese peasant army that defeated the Amerikan/British armed, backed, supplied, transported, trained, and financed Chinese nationalist army in 1949 exposed empire's weakness. The three dozen Cubans and Grenadans who held off seven thousand "elite" US troops for three days during the US invasion of Grenada in 1983 exposed empire's weakness. The North Koreans and Chinese who fought the US to an armistice and retreat from North Korean territory in 1950–53 exposed empire's weakness. The Cuban defeat of the US-trained, backed, advised, financed, and supplied mercenary invasion at the Bay of Pigs in 1961 exposed empire's weakness. The unwinnable quagmire that the US is now tied up in, in Iraq is exposing empire's weakness. That empire only selects the weakest of opponents to cluster bomb into oblivion and then claim military supremacy over, exposes empire's weakness. For empire to apply such methods within and against its own nerve centers with its light infantry forces tied up and over-extended in a foreign occupational war half a world away would be an act of suicide. (Revolution?)

Empire has never had the stomach for protracted, unconventional, people's war. In every theater, poor people's war has proven superior. Ho Chi Minh described it as a struggle between the elephant and the tiger. The tiger avoids the superior tusks of the elephant by hiding in the trees, dropping down on his back from the dark heights and slowly bleeding him to death by ripping out chunks of flesh. As Sun Tzu observed in his *Art of War*, and has been proved time and again, "when the [state's] army engages in protracted campaigns, the resources of the state will not suffice ... there has never been a protracted war from which a [state] has benefited." As an example of this fact, the protracted Vietnam war denied Amerikan military morale, discipline, public support, and the national economy to such an extent that the Lyndon Johnson administration had to fund the war with budget deficits, weakening the dollar to such an extreme degree that the US had to abandon the gold standard in 1971, causing loss of control over international finance policy and various economic decline, compelling the complete restructuring of the US economy. Empire further implemented policies to limit the US public's media exposure to military atrocities committed against civilians and body counts.

Similarly, today Amerika is imposing on its population an unprecedented deluge of cuts in social support programs and job benefits, reduced wages, massive unemployment and job loss, increases in labor hours, an influx of immigrant hiring and prisoner slave labor to cut labor costs and drive down wages while instigating division and hostility within the working class, all in efforts to reallocate public funds to finance the Iraq war, which is running at an annual cost of half a trillion dollars. Empire is furthermore struggling to man its occupation forces in Iraq, by forcing multiple extended tours of duty on its soldiers, forcing injured and over-aged retired soldiers back into the field, depleting its national guard and reserve forces, etc., and this war of occupation is only two years in the making as compared to the Vietnam war that spanned over a decade. The time for revolutionary organizing couldn't be more ripe!

It is for these reasons that empire spends so much energy, time, and resources on diversion (manufacturing non-stop toys, tokens, and sensational, sensory gratifying entertainment) and undermining

the resolve of its domestic masses against genuine struggle, channel-
ing the people's energy towards activities that do not threaten its
security. And many of us, having absorbed the empire's cynical and
self-absorbed values, feel ourselves too valuable to commit our en-
ergies and our lives toward valid revolutionary activities; this while
empire serves us up a society of relative abundance at the expense
of inhumane suffering, the lives and compulsory cheap labor of the
world's people and increasingly ourselves. The schemes of counter-
revolution applied by empire work because we in the know allow
them to. Yet we stand on the sidelines like mindless spectators and
share in the spoils. Which begs the ultimate question: despite all of
our years of protestations, posturing, claims of moral outrage and
critical analyses, whose side are we really on?

Endnotes

1   In his November 1963 "Message to Grassroots" speech,
Malcolm X scathingly described and criticized how Kennedy and
his backers financed and created a Civil Rights Council, put King
at the head of it with five other Blacks who were initially competing
for Black civil rights leadership (the "Big Six") and used them to
take control of and subvert the 1963 March. In his *People's History
of the United States*, Howard Zinn quotes Malcolm on this point
and then quotes White House advisor Arthur Schlesinger Jr. as
admitting also that the US government used King to subvert the
March and divert the attention of the poor Blacks to voting issues
and incorporated "the Negro revolution into the democratic coalition … " Just as Black "leaders" like Al Sharpton, Jesse Jackson,
et al. are used today to manipulate Blacks to spend their energy in

voting and looking to the "democratic coalition" for solutions to their never changing poverty and abuse.

2   Manning Marable, *On Malcolm X: His Meaning and Message* (1992).

3   William Sales, Jr., *From Civil Rights to Black Liberation: Malcolm X and the Organization of Afro-American Unity* (1994).

4   Malcolm X predicted that the US was in for a "long, hot summer" at the hands of urban Blacks for repeatedly stifling and subverting their demands for change, and attempting to replace them with empty reforms. As Howard Zinn observed, "the civil rights bills emphasized voting, but voting was not a fundamental solution to racism or poverty. In Harlem, Blacks who had voted for years still lived in rat-infested slums."

5   Mwalimu Shanna, et al., "Notes on the Transition of the 'Black Liberation': Phrase, Concept and Movement," *Vita Wa Watu*, Book Eight (1986).

6   As John Gerassi pointed out in *The Coming of the New International*, the system could easily sustain and tolerate individual and isolated acts of dissent, but it could not sustain and tolerate class war. He gave the reaction to the Black Panthers' political programs as an example. "As long as their militancy was directed against individual police forces, the struggle (and empire's reaction) was relatively mild. Huey Newton was framed on a manslaughter rap and various other Panthers were arrested, but once

the Panthers began to lead a class war by confronting the whole system (for example the breakfast program which made two crucial points: white society cannot feed Black children; the Black revolution can), the harassment of the Panthers changed to attempted extermination: cops raided Panther offices in San Francisco, Los Angeles, Seattle, Denver, Chicago, New York, and other cities, killed twenty-eight Panthers by the end of 1969, jailed hundreds, and [wiped] out the whole leadership." See also, Ward Churchill, et al., *Agents of Repression: The FBI's Secret Wars Against the Black Panther Party and the American Indian Movement.*

7   Empire, just like Malcolm X, recognized that only the most committed and extreme resistance would undermine its control and lead to its overthrow, so it had to demonize all such activity. As Malcolm stated, "You'll get your freedom by letting your enemy know that you'll do anything to get your freedom, then you'll get it. It's the only way you'll get it. When you get that kind of attitude, they'll label you as a 'crazy Negro,' or they'll call you a 'crazy Nigger'– they don't say Negro. Or they'll call you an extremist or a subversive, or seditious, or a red or a radical. But when you stay radical long enough and get enough people to be like you, you'll get your freedom." And just as Malcolm X observed, the empire attempted to implement a program to stigmatize the urban youth who engaged in the urban uprisings of the 60's as being mentally impaired and proposed brain surgeries to "correct" them. And while public protest defeated this proposal, it was substituted by a preemptive program of targeting urban youth with "behavioral disorder" diagnoses and sedating them. See note 8 below.

8   Mwalimu Shanna loc cit. (note 5). In his book *The War Against Children of Color*, psychiatrist Peter Breggin and his wife expose a scheme implemented under federal funding for experiments in psychosurgery to "control violence" targeted specifically against urban people of color initiated in response to the 1960's urban uprisings. The three Harvard psychiatrists behind this program were commissioned to write a paper in 1967 in the *Journal of the American Medical Association*, entitled "Role of Brain Diseases in Riots and Urban Violence," which much like today's policies on violence claimed individual fallibility rather than economic, social, and political factors as the cause of urban rebellions and violence. Public protests that these proposals were reminiscent of Nazi experiments led to the abandonment of the scheme to bring back lobotomy and brain surgery to be used against urban Black youth; however, these initiatives were still implemented using the "less invasive" measures of targeting urban youth with newly devised behavioral disorders diagnoses of Attention Deficit Hyperactivity Disorder (ADHD) and Attention Deficit Disorder (ADD), and doping them into mental stupors (chemical lobotomies) with speed and brain serotonin enhancers like Ritalin and Prozac. It is no coincidence that these measures are targeted at youth who don't show sufficient deference to empire's "authorities" and schooling. In the report of the National Advisory Committee on Urban Disorders, the 60's rebellions were found to have "involved Negroes acting against local symbols of white American society," and the "typical rioter" was a young male high school dropout, but "nevertheless, somewhat better educated than his non-rioting Negro neighbor" and "usually underemployed or employed in a menial job ... A new mood has sprung up among Negroes,

particularly the young, in which self-esteem and enhanced racial pride are replacing apathy and submission to the system." So what is admitted here is that the empire knew it was not crazy, but intelligent, Black youth who'd become disillusioned with poverty and racism, and that it had to target them for destruction. Hence came narcotics, infestations, mass incarceration, inner-community rivalries like gang warfare (see NSC 46), and ADHD/ADD diagnoses targeted at young, urban, Black males – in short, low-intensity warfare.

9   See note 7.

10   Mwalimu Shanna loc cit. (note 5).

11   Carter repeatedly praised the "human rights" records of such bloody dictators as Anastasio Somoza in Nicaragua who frequently massacred and tortured peasants. While Carter pretended to deplore and sever all diplomatic ties to Guatemala's Lucas Garcia regime, he continued throughout the last two years of his term to send over $34 million in military aid to Garcia directly and more indirectly through US mercenary state ally Israel. This "aid" was used to indiscriminately slaughter civilians, religious leaders, and Garcia's political opponents. Carter's administration, taking over where Gerald Ford's had left off, supplied arms to the admittedly illegal Indonesian invasion of East Timor which began in 1975 and led to the senseless massacre of hundreds of thousands of East Timorese. While these massacres reached a peak in 1978, the US media stopped reporting on them, and Carter continued to supply Indonesia arms to continue the killing of a defenseless

population. In fact, Daniel Patrick Moynihan praised the killing, comparing it to Nazi massacres of Soviet Union civilians during WWII. The same sort of praise and support was given to the Shah of Iran by Carter as he slaughtered hundreds and ultimately thousands of Iranian demonstrators in 1978. Carter expressed, "there is no leader with whom I have a deeper sense of personal gratitude and friendship" than the Shah, who'd receive "no lecturing on the question of human rights" (!) but only "a sympathetic ear" for a request for hundreds of millions of dollars worth of military hardware. (Geoffrey Godsell, *Christian Science Monitor*, March 2, 1978). Carter similarly backed bloody Philippine dictator Ferdinand Marcos, despite massive human rights violations. (See Richard Burt, "Carter Asks for No Cut in Arms Aid to Marcos Despite Negative Human Rights Report," *New York Times*, February 6, 1978). And on and on.

12   This stated policy agenda explains the US attitude towards the August 2001 United Nations Conference on Racism. It forbade Colin Powell – its loyal Black, ranking official – from attending and sent only a low-level delegation that walked out of the conference. It threatened to boycott the conference if the issue of reparations for African slave descendants and Zionism as a racist Anglo-Jewish policy were not removed from the discussion agenda. And before walking out, the US delegation vowed never to give Blacks reparations and along with the European Union delegation regarded Blacks as "psychotic" for wanting reparations. See note 13 below.

13   A most telling admission in NSC 46 is its stated concern for preventing a domestic Black struggle for political, economic, etc.

independence because such a struggle "would do grievous harm to US prestige, especially in view of the [pretense of] concern of the present Administration with human rights issues. Moreover, the Administration would have to take specific steps (i.e. violent repression) to stabilize the situation. Such steps might be misunderstood (!) both inside and outside the United States." So empire's position is that in order to protect its artificial image of having granted Blacks racial, economic and political equality, it will militarily repress Blacks struggling to free themselves from oppression by a racist politico-economic system.

14   Here we have the US government who professes to champion racial harmony and equality proposing to instigate racial animosities between white and Black workers and to use white workers through government manipulation of labor union leadership to repress Black economic gains. Yet, Black folks are still duped by Black "leaders" to look to this same government to solve their problems of poverty, racism, police brutality, etc. What is most telling is that it was just such race antagonism of white workers against Black ones that led to the 1926 Labor Act in South Africa that barred Blacks from skilled and semi-skilled jobs and ultimately led to the racial caste system of apartheid. These are facts that empire was conscious of upon promulgating NSC 46 and it should be reemphasized that a major factor behind NSC 46 was to protect US/South African friendly relations from challenge.

Lest it escape the reader's attention, it should be pointed out that the central basis of the apartheid structure was to maintain a white minority in a position of political, economic, and military domination over a Black majority. This is the exact same model that the US heads and maneuvers to maintain on a global scale, viz., maintaining a world white minority (European and North Amerika) in a position of political, economic, and military domination over a colored majority. This race-based policy has been at the center of US policy since it emerged as the world's dominant economic and military power at the close of WWII (1945). The only countries that it provided economic aid to for industrial development after WWII under the Marshall Plan were European countries (1948–51). The "aid" that the US extended to the underdeveloped nations of people of color came in the form of minor technical assistance in agriculture and health care and developing western educational systems, all at exorbitant loan rates calculated to keep these nations hopelessly indebted, while offering them no industrial development aid even approaching that given to Europe. Not only has empire and its European "allies" maneuvered to maintain economic domination, but military domination as well by scrambling at every turn to prevent nations of colored people from obtaining nuclear weapons. So note when Amerika makes decisions in the world, such as the invasion of Iraq, Vietnam, Korea, etc., it typically consults only its "European allies," i.e. apartheid on a global scale with only white governments consulted in decisions that affect the world.

15   This portion of NSC 46 is cold water in the face of those Blacks who've believed that the appearance of dark faces in high political offices is evidence of Blacks being finally given a share in power. Indeed, as this portion makes clear, the term "representative" does not mean a person who represents the interests of poor Blacks but someone who's "loyal" to the forces that have

historically maneuvered to keep Blacks in subjugation. So much for the farce of representative democracy in Amerika.

16   See William Blum, "The Real Drug Lords: A Brief History of CIA Involvement in the Drug Trade," *Slingshot*, Early Spring 1997 (http://www.csum.edu/communicationstudies /ben/news/ cia/970130.beg.html); Ron Chepesiuk, "Are the CIA's Hands Clean on Drugs?" *The Herald*, January 30, 1997 (Rock Hill , SC) p.11A; Alfred W. McCoy, *The Politics of Heroin: CIA Complicity on the Global Drug Trade* (2003); James Mills, *The Invisible Empire*.

"[T]he court finds the actions of the government to be most egregious, indeed appalling." Judge Patrick Kelly, *Midland National Bank v. Conlogue.* 720 F. Supp, 878 (D. Kan. 1989), regarding CIA/DEA flying cocaine into US for Reagan/Bush White House with full knowledge of bank and insurance company who were arguing over who would pay for aircraft "shot down" by US customs agents.

"Our system of justice (sic) has been perverted, that [US covert intelligence agencies have] converted themselves into channels for the flow of drugs into the United States." Senator (later presidential candidate) John Kerry, *Kerry Committee Document on Drugs Law Enforcement and Foreign Policy*.

17   http://www.hrw.org/reports/2000/usa/

18   W.E.B. DuBois, *The World and Africa* (1996) p. 58.

19   Ron Chepesiuk op cit. (note 16). The US "war on drugs" is clearly a war on poor people of color in Amerika. Indeed,

the booming US drug trade has long served as an indispensable component of the US economy, and big business has a deep involvement in the racket. In the mid-1990's the Organization for Economic Cooperation and Development did a study of the global drug trade and found that over half a trillion dollars in drug money is laundered per year, with half done through US banks. A major crime, yet no bankers have been jailed, whereas an urban Black or Latino is subject to a life sentence for possessing a small quantity of cocaine base (funneled into their community by the CIA/DEA). One measure implemented that could have easily traced such laundered money – a project called "Operation Greenback" – was cancelled by Reagan's vice-president and "drug czar" George H.W. Bush at the early height of the so-called "drug war." Furthermore, the CIA found in a study in the 1980's that ninety percent of the chemical exports to Latin America by US chemical corporations are not of the kinds used for industrial production but for drug production. Again, no chemical corporation CEO's or directors are in jail.

20   Both US Law (18 United States Code, section 1091) and the international Convention Against Genocide outlaw genocide and include as acts of genocide any "measure intended to prevent births within [a national, ethnic, racial, or religious] group." Amerika forbids its prisoners to interact sexually with members of the opposite sex, thus consciously preventing procreation within the group of Blacks targeted for imprisonment. Genocide is also defined as causing "imprisonment of mental faculties of members of the group through drugs, torture, or similar techniques." On this point I'd like to refer the reader back to note 8 and something that cannot be a coincidence. The active ingredient in Prozac is a brain

serotonin enhancer L-tryptophan, which has the effect of making the patient lethargic, groggy, and mentally passive by increasing his/her level of brain serotonin. I am writing this essay from the confines of a Virginia supermaximum security prison – Red Onion State Prison. At this prison the meals' main course at practically every meal consists of turkey. Turkey has a high concentration of the same serotonin-enhancing ingredient as Prozac, and it is recognized by medical and educational experts that the reason that people tend to become lethargic and sleepy after eating holiday meals where turkey is consumed. In fact, consumption of turkey is discouraged for people from whom mental alertness is required. So, essentially, this prison, and likely many others, is giving its inhabitants a continuous regimen of Prozac-like treatment reducing them to mental passivity. (I bring this fact to most of their attentions – I am myself vegetarian.)

THE TRUE SOLDIER ACCEPTS NO WAGE, NOR AND NECESSITY, HER/HIS ONLY REWARD IS THE HEALTHY SURVIVAL AND UNCONDITIONAL LIBERATION OF THE PEOPLE....

B52

S/HE ACCEPTS NO COMPROMISE.

COUNTER-INSURGENT-TRAINED BY C.I.A.

Real Soldier

RASHID 7-07-'02

The True Soldier

The True Soldier accepts no wage, nor searches for honors or praise.

Born of desperation and necessity, her/his only reward is the health, survival and unconditional liberation of the People.

Motivated by a complete love (for the People) and a pure hatred (for the imperialist invader and new colonizer who rule by violence, fraud and artificial prestige; who would reduce the world to a toxic desert of blood, bones and ashes to feed their short-sighted greed and over-inflated egos).

Caring nothing about the judgments and promises of the enemy – accepting no compromise.

Refusing to share in the spoils taken by force and deceit from the world's poor. Blood money.

Conscious to avoid falling victim to the enemy's schemes that would divert her/him into fighting futile, divisive and fratricidal wars against other poor people.

The True Soldier is the eternal enemy of capitalist political and economic totalitarianism – knowing them to be the sources of the People's suffering.

Ever on the defensive – surviving by wit and craft – alert and focused. Outmanned ten to one. But the adversary is mechanized, without imagination, stifled by bureaucratic bumbling, using calloused brutality to compensate for stupidity; the reactionary idiot.

The True Soldier's tools – ambush, infiltration, camouflage, mobility, ingenuity.

His/her lifestyle knows no romanticism, few games of fun and pleasure. The only enduring game is that of guile. The monkey and the weasel.

Mere words do not serve the material needs of survival, nor do prayers protect the dying masses.

The True Soldier unites all who share the cause, who prove and distinguish themselves with action – by sacrifice.

S/he knows that social divisions and group competition are the creations and tools of the enemy. Racism. Sexism. Jingoism. Parochialism. Cartels and gangs. Class society – capitalism. Humyn life and relationships subordinated to property interests. Millions of lives extinguished to protect the obscene wealth and property holdings of a few, to preserve hierarchical prestige.

The True Soldier knows the experience of being the outsider, of being excluded from the dominant culture. Despised. Marginalized. Demonized.

The True Soldier's actions are driven by the demands of humyn survival, which can only be achieved by ultimately winning self-determination for the oppressed working class and poor masses.

The True Soldier's greatest good – to live her/his life for the People.

So long as there is class and national oppression, the blood of the People will continue to give birth to the True Soldier.

So long as there is mass oppression, the True Soldier can never be defeated.

ART-ATTACK

REINS OF FREEDUMB

REINS OF Freedumb

ACQUIESCE OR ELSE...

RASHID 7-02 02

KEVIN (RASHID) JOHNSON

Amerika – Freedom is Slavery, Ignorance is Strength

It is my purpose here to demonstrate that the typical Amerikan wageworker is both a slave and a victim of involuntary servitude. In demonstrating this, I will refer primarily to "established" authorities, which are not subject to dispute by the "mainstream."

Definitions of Bondage

We first begin with the definition of servitude, slavery and the like. The following definitions come from the *Merriam-Webster Dictionary*:

> **Slave:** 1. A person held in servitude as property.
> **Slave:** DRUDGE
> **Drudge:** To do hard, menial, or monotonous work.

The following definitions are taken from *Black's Law Dictionary* (7th edition, 1999):

Involuntary servitude: The conditions of one forced to labor – for pay or not – for another by coercion or imprisonment.

Slavery: 1. The situation in which one person has absolute power over the life, fortune, and liberty of another. 2. The practice of keeping individuals in such a state of bondage.

In the case of *United States v. Kesminski*, 487 US 931 (1988) at page 932, the US Supreme Court defined servitude as follows: "Servitude means a condition in which a person lacks liberty, especially to determine one's course of action or way of life."

In the remainder of this thesis, I will show that the condition of labor under which the Amerikan wage laborers find themselves conforms to all of the definitions of bondage.

The Amerikan Conditions of Bondage

In his famous treatise, *The Wealth of Nations*, Adam Smith makes three things clear about "developed societies," viz.: 1. that the industrially compelled practice of division of labor is indeed drudgework, 2. that this sort of drudgework destroys the workers' mental faculties, and 3. that this drudgework is a form of labor into which the poor working family is *forced*. Smith states as follows:

> The understandings of the greater part of men are necessarily found by their ordinary employments ... the man

whose life is spent in performing a few simple operations, of which the effects are perhaps always the same, or very near the same, has no occasion to exert his understanding ... and generally becomes as stupid and ignorant as it is possible for a human creature to be ... but in every improved and civilized society this is the state into which the laboring poor, that is, the great body of people, must fall ...

While Adam Smith is hailed as a fountainhead of modern economic thought, this observation made by him is always avoided in mainstream discussions and writings on him and economics.

The above quote from Smith establishes that the modern working conditions of industrial capitalist nations is that of slavery (monotonous, menial, and drudge work) over which arrangement the labor class has no power to change or avoid (involuntary servitude) and therefore renders the labor boss's position one of total power over the employed workers' livelihood.

These points are brought into much clearer focus by another writer who was dedicated to the common man and opposed to the labor bosses enough to make the wage worker's conditions of bondage clear and plain. In his book *Soledad Brother,* George L. Jackson makes the connection between the system of bondage of past agricultural chattel slavery and modern industrial wage slavery here in Amerika. I quote him at length:

"Slavery is an economic condition. Today's neo-slavery must be defined in terms of economics. The chattel is property, one man exercising the property rights of his established economic order, the other man as that property. The owner can move that property or hold it in one square yard of the earth's surface; he can *let* it breed other slaves or *make* it breed other slaves; he can sell it, beat it, work it, maim it, fuck it, kill it. But if he wants to keep it and enjoy all of the benefits that property of this kind can render, he must feed it sometimes, he must clothe it against the elements; he must provide a modicum of shelter. Chattel slavery is an economic condition which manifests itself in the total loss or absence of self-determination.

"The new slavery, the modern variety of chattel slavery updated to disguise itself, places the victim in a factory or, in the case of most blacks, in support roles inside and around the factory system (service trades) working for a wage. However, if work cannot be found in or around the factory complex, today's neo-slavery does not even allow for a modicum of food and shelter. You are free – to starve. The sense and meaning of slavery comes through as a result of our ties to the wage. You must have it; without it you would starve or expose yourself to the elements. One's entire day centers around acquisition of the wage.

"Others determine the control of your eight to ten hours on the job. You are left with fourteen to sixteen hours. But since you don't live at the factory, you have to subtract at least another two for transportation. Then you are left with thirteen to fifteen hours to yourself. If you can afford three meals, you are left with ten to twelve hours. Rest is also another factor of efficiency, so we have to take eight hours away for sleeping, leaving two to four hours. But one must bathe, comb, clean teeth, shave, dress – there is no point in protracting this. I think it should be generally accepted that if a man (or woman) works for a wage at a job he doesn't enjoy, and I am convinced no one could enjoy any type of assembly-line work, or plumbing, or hod carrying, or any job in the service trades, then he qualifies for this definition of a neo-slave. The man who owns the factory or shop or business runs your life, you are dependent on this owner. He organizes your work, the work upon which your whole life source and style depends. He indirectly determines your whole day, in organizing you for work. If you don't make any more in wages than you need to live, then you are a neo-slave. You qualify if you can't afford to leave California for New York. If you cannot visit Zanzibar, Havana, Peking, or even Paris when you get the urge, you are a slave. If you're held in one spot on this earth because of your economic status, it is just the same as being held in one spot because you are the owner's property. Here in the black colony the pigs still beat and maim us. They murder us and call it justifiable homicide. A brother who had a smoking pipe in his belt was shot in the back of the head. Neo-slavery is an economic condition, a small knot of men exercising the property rights of the slave as if he were, in fact, property. Succinctly: an economic condition which manifests itself in the total loss or absence of *self*-determination. Only after this is understood and accepted can we go on to the dialectic that will help us in a remedy."

Labor Forced

This all brings us to the central contradiction between Amerika's economic arrangement and the political rights it professes to give its citizens, demonstrating that the highest laws of Amerika take a back seat when opposed to the ruling class's interests in exploiting the masses for private profit. That contradiction is found in Section One of the Thirteenth Amendment to the US Constitution, which holds that all slavery and involuntary servitude is forbidden except in cases of those convicted of crimes. I here quote that provision: "Neither slavery nor involuntary servitude, except as punishment for a crime whereof the party shall have been duly convicted, shall exist within the United States, or any place subject to their jurisdiction." It must then follow that *every* so-called minority and poor working-class Amerikan is presumed by the government to be guilty of some criminal violation, and without any opportunity to prove his or her innocence. We might now have an explanation as to why those who overflow Amerika's prisons are near exclusively members of the so-called minority and poor white working classes.

If the average Amerikan worker took the notion to refuse to participate in the wage slavery economic arrangement, he will be inevitably left and forced by the system to become a vagrant and resort to other "criminal" acts in order to survive. And if a large number of workers elected to also abandon the wage system, they are subject to being forced *by the government* back to work under such laws as the Taft-Hartley Act (29 US code sections 141 et seq.) under the penalty of imprisonment or fines should they refuse to obey. The worker has *no* discretion in the matter. Amerika's economic system rides upon the enslavement of over half the population, who've been conditioned by the corporate media, universal compulsory educational system, political mouthpieces, and the indoctrinated nuclear family from birth to believe that their slavery is freedom and that the erosion of their minds under divided labor is conducive to strength.

As the foregoing demonstrated, the oppressive social contract of Amerika is organized around slave labor, while it professes to be based upon principles of liberty and self-determination for every Amerikan. Amerika's character as a society of slaves and enslavers did not change with the close of the Civil War (1861–1865), nor in the enactment of the Thirteenth Amendment (1865). Indeed, it has rendered the *entire* labor class into slaves with no alternatives for acquiring "freedom," except that these slaves may compete against one another to acquire more privileges and a small increase in wages with which to gain more diversionary toys and tokens. As long as such economic opportunism and exploitation exist, no one can claim with any degree of honesty that the Amerikan system is based upon principles of liberty and democracy. In fact, it is the social majority – the poor workers – who are the very slaves of society, upon whose backs the economic and ruling class is saddled. As one writer observed, "true liberty is based on economic opportunity. Without it, all liberty is a sham and a lie, a mask for exploitation and oppression. In the profoundest sense, liberty is the daughter of economic equality."

An Answer to Today's Black Entertainment Media

I write this as a brother confined in prison, isolated a hundred miles from the nearest urban center, sitting atop a remote mountain in a rural, white-populated region of the South. Here, the overwhelmingly Black prisoner population has little to no contact with the ever-flourishing Black urban subculture.

By happenstance, I found myself in possession of and reading cover-to-cover the November 2004 issue of *Sister 2 Sister,* a magazine that has the professed motto "Givin' it to ya straight, no chaser." Well, to put this motto to the test, I've asked them to print this essay – which likely they won't. I'm writing this essay because my reading of that and similar magazines leaves my heart heavy; some of the reasons are what follows.

From the editor's interview with actor/comedian Jamie Foxx, (pp. 62–73), one could see the still-pervasive tendency in Black folks here – continuing since slavery – to try and measure up to the white supremacist, capitalistic elite status quo, to prove that "we" are just as good as "them" by winning acclaim and recognition in fields that they've told us are important, to acquire material tokens and status symbols they've manufactured and that they've trained us to think are measures of humyn worth, to seek advancement and acceptance always with heads bowed and feet shuffling. Meanwhile, we're dying – both as a race and as a culture.

The only remnants of a culture we have left are steeped in our aping the dominant material-worshipping one, a deformed subculture imitating Mr. Charlie.* Our only use-value here in Amerika still remains that of being clowns, (entertainers), and servants, while our brain trusts, (Black intellectuals), are distanced from the needy Black masses, co-opted into white suburbia, and then sapped of their talents and skills to refine and keep Mr. Charlie's system steadily expanding and running smoothly and to keep him saddled at the cost of human suffering the world over and within our own poor communities.

From rap diva Lil' Kim's interview, (pp. 40–51), I see a confused young sister being drained, tossed, and used by a greed-motivated industry she doesn't understand, a sister who's been used to, among other things, perpetuate the idea in Black minds that for us to amount to anything in this world we must become white. Supporting such

— — — — —

* When I make reference to "Mr./Massa Charlie," this is not a term that generalizes and embraces all whites, but refers to the capitalist plantation/corporate elite, (who happen to be a minority white male class), who own and monopolize the US economy, government, and influential social institutions, through which they manufacture a white-supremacist, material-worshipping, individualist, jingoist, chauvinist, and competitive dominant culture within US society. Likewise, when I refer negatively to poor whites, I am not referring to all but to those "Crackers" who were employed as agents of repression by the slave owner class.

racist notions by undergoing surgeries and cosmetic changes that dilute and disguise racial and ethnic identity, projecting the image for our young sisters to emulate and imitate that the extent of their worth is determined by their physical assets, (breasts and asses), and their willingness to flaunt them in skimpy garb.

Do we care that the images promoted by celebrities, who are in fact seen as role models, create cultural norms that our children imitate, that they come to perceive as the essence of their humyn worth? Our people are being pimped and misled by an industry that cares nothing about the destructive effects the images it portrays have on us as a people. The CEO's and CFO's of Warner Bros., BMG, Sony, EMI, and Universal don't live in the hood and don't visit the hood. Theirs is an industry that cares about nothing but market shares and maximizing profits. To them the hood represents a vast market of consumers, and Black entertainers are their means of routing Black dollars into their own coffers. They are motivated by the same insensitive, greed-based self-interest that motivated white male plantation elites to subject our forefathers and mothers to 250 years of the most savage, brutal, and inhumyn form of enslavement ever suffered by any people in history.

We've ended in adopting the very same opportunistic, anti-humyn, insensitive, and greed-driven values that we've long been victims of. On one hand, we passionately criticize what was done to our ancestors during chattel slavery as one of history's worst evils, yet on the other, we're oblivious to the fact that all of the vast wealth that Amerika maintains today, (centered in its elite, white male-monopolized, multinational corporate powers and military industry) – spoils we aspire to share in – come from the enslavement of people today – people of color in the Third World.

The Third World is underdeveloped today solely because Amerika and other western nations force their people, under violent compulsion, by propped-up puppet governments and militaries, (armed, trained, supplied, and advised by the US), to mine and farm and then export their own natural resources and agriculture to these western countries, while preventing them from accessing the technologies and developing the skills needed to industrially develop, and thus compete economically with the western powers, meantime being forced to grow crops to be exported to these dominant countries and forbidden to grow foods needed to feed their own people.

These people live in slavery, (in many instances as brutal as what our forebears suffered). And when these people rise up to take control of their own lands and lives, to try and feed their families, the Amerikan-backed militaries massacre them, (men, wimyn, children and the elderly), indiscriminately. We need not even travel outside this hemisphere for clear examples of such. Take the hundreds of thousands of common peasants slaughtered with official US backing and arms in Central America during the 1960's, 70's, and 80's in Guatemala, Nicaragua, and El Salvador. The same policies are playing out today and are behind US financial and military aid to Colombia. The US is also ready to back an attack on Venezuela's popularly supported Chavez government because it rejects the FTAA and US domination of its economy and resources.*

But like the "house niggers" of old, we choose not to know or see this, because we want to be accepted by "Massa Charlie," to

— — — — —

* Venezuela has the world's sixth largest oil reserves and is one of Amerika's top suppliers, yet over 70 percent of its population lives in miserable poverty.

share in the spoils he's gained at the misery of our brothers and sisters. In fact we're in Iraq now, massacring people of color, primarily civilians – women and children – to aid Amerika's white male ruling elite to take control of the world's second largest oil reserves, (located in Iraq), so they can monopolize the world oil market, and thereby regain dominant control over the transnational capitalist economy, a position the Amerikan wealthy elite lost in the 1970's and who've been steadily losing ground on account of competition from the expanding Euro-based capitalist bloc in Europe. We remain enslaved to a political and economic system that we don't understand. We're being wooed and confused by "Massa Charlie's" lackeys who look like us and talk with oiled tongues, while pretending to represent us.

Then we cannot forget that the US exists on the land that it does today because it massacred and forcefully relocated millions of natives to clear them off the land, much as Amerika has militarily and financially backed Israel in doing to the Palestinians since 1948. This genocidal policy against the Indians continues today through outright racist cultural genocide and destruction of their communities with alcohol and casinos, (for us it's narcotics and the club.) The Indians have been reduced to less than one percent of their own land and population. Amerika is a land of settlers living on territory, much of which was never legally ceded by the First Nations. And like the Palestinians today, those Indians who fought back, resisting genocide and forced removal from their land, which the whites sought to settle and claim as their own, were demonized as being uncivilized aggressors and terrorists.

Were it not for us, (Afrikan people), there would be no Amerika. We taught the early European settlers how to till the land and to

KEVIN "RASHID" JOHNSON   335 tend livestock and to openly graze cattle, skills which were alien to the Europeans, skills they sorely needed when they were on the verge of starvation here, following their back-stabbing the Indians who first welcomed and aided them. It was we who left the southern plantations in droves, (causing them economic chaos), and fought with the Union Army, leading to the Confederate defeat. Yet the US promise to us of land in exchange for our military service was broken. The Union Army, in complicity with the Ku Klux Klan, drove us off the promised land we began occupying and developing, from whose violence and terror we fled north to the cities, (and to the West), as refugees and were there herded into the ghettos where we remain today – the hood.

But for us, Amerika would never have become an advanced industrial nation. It was our free slave labor in cotton production that allowed the US to undergo the Industrial Revolution, which grew out of the cotton-based textile industry that flourished in the northern states, the very industry around which the Union was built, and which provided factory work for the vast numbers of poor European immigrants. In fact, it was the competition for dominance between the northern industrial elites and the southern plantation elites in their westward expansion that prompted the Amerikan Civil War. But today, after all the years of slavery and service, death, and misery, we have nothing to show for our ordeals and contributions, except a subculture of materialism and individualism which apes the dominant culture of our historical oppressor.

In fact, we still contribute the earning of our hard labor to maintaining a social order, (through compulsory taxation), that refuses to use those contributions to improve our overall quality of life and living standard, cutting our access to social benefits, denying our access to healthcare and job security, etc. Indeed, Bill Clinton, the pretended champion of Black Amerika, knocked 10 million people off welfare, (out of 15 million total recipients), driving more poor people to compete in a steadily shrinking job market, and then put some 150,000 more police on the streets to lock up those driven to "crime" by force of economic and emotional desperation and frustration. Meantime, you had and have the steady expansion of the largest prison system in the world to warehouse those people.

The interview with singer Monica, (pp. 90–97), painfully bought home the fact that whatever the apparent financial achievements of a few celebrity Black individuals, life for us as a people here in Amerika is a never-ending tragedy, plagued with insecurity, violent death, and police oppression. This theme was consistent in all three of the interviews with Jamie Foxx, Lil' Kim, and Monica. The lives of Black "celebrities" being no exception. That despite our claims to material accomplishment in the US, we own nothing, control nothing, and remain adrift in a society that we neither know nor understand. A condition that will remain unchanged as long as we continue to accept rule by outside forces, forces alien to us, that mislead and misrepresent us, exploit and neglect us, profit off us, use us to conquer others, to hate and destroy its foes, (including ourselves), distorts and conceals our history and struggles, jails and kills our true leaders, leaves us a confused and insecure people who vent our pain, frustration, and desperation against each other, gives token positions of political power to self-interested opportunistic Blacks who pretend to represent us, and warehouses us in prisons.

During the 1950's through the 70's, the people of Asia and Afrika waged determined military and political struggles to win national independence and to overthrow European rule over them.

The various politically independent countries in Afrika today are the result of those struggles. As already noted, the ongoing political, military, and economic turmoil in those countries today stems from continued western interferences, interventions, and manipulations in their political and economic affairs, so to keep their vast stores of natural wealth flowing out of their countries and to the west, much as US corporate power keeps the wealth, labor, and brainpower of the Black communities flowing out of those communities and into its power centers here in Amerika – leaving our communities in poverty and chaos.

Yet we Blacks here in Amerika never even crossed that first hurdle of winning political independence. The US government brutally repressed our national independence struggles in the 1960's and 70's, killing and jailing our leaders, sowing division within the movement, and replacing them with integrationist civil rights reforms, (to appease us because we were tearing shit up in major cities all across Amerika), reforms which today are being systematically rolled back.

All we've gained is the ability to ape "Massa Charlie," to wear his clothes, to buy his cars, to whiten our appearances with surgery and cosmetics, to die in his wars and on street corners, to fill his prisons, to persist in proving to ourselves and anyone who might take notice that we ain't as stupid and backward as his racism has always projected us to be, because we can imitate him and thus be recognized as "the first Black to ...." We perceive such "accomplishments" to be an honor – historically significant moments in Black achievement. But unlike "Mr. Charlie," we have no political power, no sovereign territory, no one to enforce our demands, no military, no dominant culture, and no economy. We only have the privilege of trying to fit into "Mr. Charlie's" world. And somehow we fail to notice that none of those Blacks who've gained positions of political power have changed conditions in favor of the masses of poor and economically insecure Amerikan Blacks.

No wonder "Mr. Charlie" is so arrogant and has such an over-inflated ego. By dividing and individualizing us, he now has an entire race of people, whom he once had to fight tooth-and-nail to control, willingly under his thumb, accepting and promoting his politics, competing against and killing themselves, entertaining him, acting as his political running dogs, serving as his mercenaries, slave breakers, and cannon fodder to repress their own brothers and sisters in the Third World, and all just to win his acceptance and approval – again, to eat at his table, to wear his clothes, (or a comical imitation of them), and to be like him. And his reward to us has been perpetual economic insecurity, premature death, substandard healthcare, (even for those of us who can "afford" it), media stereotyping and misrepresentation, police brutality, racial profiling, social division, and political impotence, (voting means nothing when we do not choose the candidates, when "our" candidates are chosen for us, when we are thrown off the ballot as occurred in the last two presidential elections, and when we have no part in counting the ballots – "It's not those who cast votes that determine the outcome of an election but those who count them.")

When one partner in a relationship suffers continuous humiliation, abuse, neglect, degradation, and disadvantage, common sense and humyn right drive that partner to demand separation. It must be remembered that in our case we were not willing and voluntary partners to this relationship to begin with – indeed, this forced coupling was something akin to rape, and somehow we've come to embrace our attacker and his ethic. But as with any divorce, that partner who demands separation has a right to a share of the wealth that s/he helped to produce. If that share is not relinquished voluntarily, then s/he has a right to take it by force.

In that November 2004 issue of *Sister 2 Sister*, in the "letter to the editor" section (pp. 104–110), I found particularly disturbing the grievances of some sisters, specifically concerning the "trend" of brothers passing them up for womyn of other races – the white race in particular. I first found a fundamental contradiction in that there was no criticism of Black womyn's own roles in promoting this trend by their projecting images, which imply that white and white-like features embody a standard of "beauty" superior to genuinely Afrikana features, e.g. the trend of wearing straightened and blond-dyed hair, light-colored contact lenses, etc. This tendency on both sides of rejecting Afrikana beauty are but expressions of self-hatred, insecurity, inferiority complexes, and negative self-images instilled in us during the processes of chattel slavery, Jim Crow, etc.

But let me not seem to deny the fact that all sisters are sisters whatever their complexion. To accept otherwise would be to pander to the same dangerous racisms that fueled the genocidal war in 1994 between Rwanda's Hutu and Tutsi people, leaving hundreds of thousands dead, while the west sat by as spectators.

Beginning in 1916, when the Belgians, (Europeans), brutally colonized that region of Afrikan, they instigated a division between the then-united Hutus and Tutsis, by telling the Tutsis, (who had lighter skin, taller statures, and thinner features than the Hutus), that they were more European-looking and thus should see themselves as the Hutu's superiors, much the same scheme that was done during, and since slavery to divide Mulattoes against dark Blacks, and in

North and South America to divide Mestizos against pure Indians. The Belgians rewrote those Afrikan peoples' own histories to falsely project the Tutsis as a noble class and the Hutus as an underclass. Only Tutsis were permitted to attend Belgian schools, being educated into the values of their oppressors, resulting in an antagonistic divide being created between the two groups that exist till today.

When the wave of national independence struggles swept Africa beginning in the 1950's, the more educated and organized Tutsis agitated for independence from Belgian rule. The Belgians then backed and organized the Hutus to repress the Tutsis. Rwanda still gained political independence in 1962, but the newly organized Hutus took government power and stripped the Tutsis of land. The fratricidal war in 1994 was a struggle by the Tutsis to retake power in Rwanda, all of this resulting from the Belgians' creating division within a common racial group so to secure their own power. A similar device exists between Blacks here in Amerika. Indeed, Jamie Foxx in his interview described an incident where he and his sister were beaten up by some light-complexioned Black cops working in an uppity casino who were notorious for abusing darker Blacks. These same tendencies are played up by Black entertainment media who tend to project only light-complexioned and surgically and/or cosmetically whitewashed Blacks as attractive, leading us to forget that we are a common people with a common heritage and history of oppression.

Just as many, (but definitely not all), of today's Mestizo descendants from the native peoples of South, Central, and North America no longer recognize their Indian ancestry, and instead identify themselves as Latino/a. They forget that the Latin people were/are the Europeans, (Spanish and Portuguese), who invaded, conquered, and colonized their lands, destroyed their civilizations, enslaved and massacred their people, and even completely exterminated some of the native ethnic groups – as was done by the celebrated Spaniard Christopher Columbus to the peaceful Arawaks of Hispaniola, (modern day Haiti and Dominican Republic, both of which are today majority Black because of Afrikan slaves having been brought in to replace the decimated Arawaks). Now, many of the native descendants today have taken on the identity of their historic Latin oppressors.

Our knowledge of world (and our) history is shallow, our attention spans short. All we've been conditioned to care about is losing ourselves and our minds in entertainment and gratification. On the same hand, we're selling our youth a dream that the entertainment industry, (becoming clowns), will provide us a foot-up in the world. We saturate them with images of obscene wealth that they cannot obtain except by treading on others and through illegitimate capitalist channels, channels that have us dropping like flies in the streets, overflowing these prisons where we cease to be able to reproduce, and destroying what's left of our communities. And the images, the role models presented in them by the entertainment industry only encourage this self-destructive behavior.

Neither will "Mr. Charlie's" schools provide us upward mobility. They only train us to think like him, to support and accept his claimed right to rule and dominate us, (as the Belgians did with the Tutsis), to forget our community-based culture as a people, to care nothing about anyone but our individual selves. Straight A's and college degrees may provide a few middle-class options for a few of us, but these few will still be living only a paycheck or two away from poverty. They will have little to no options for spending quality time with their children, and they will still be perceived and treated as second-class citizens. Even those who find wealth are still targeted with attacks from police, trumped-up lawsuits, derogatory media stereotyping, and general humiliation. In his interview, Jamie Foxx made this quite clear. In order for Black celebrities to find recognition and respect, they've had to create a Black-only celebrity circle and counterculture that imitates "Mr. Charlie's." Why? Because they are not accepted as peers and equals by and within "mainstream" circles. Yet we're still skinning and grinning, begging to be accepted, proving our moral superiority by taking shit in the face with a smile, as "Mr. Charlie" trained us to do long ago in order to make us passively accept our enslavement.

Indeed, I shook my head sadly at Jamie Foxx's unembarrassed description of himself sitting by passively, trying to reason philosophically with pigs as they beat him and his little sister in a racially motivated attack, this while she stood alone exchanging blows with them in defense of them both. For us, cowardice has become honorable, despite the fact that passive resistance proved a failed tactic for us long ago. Even Martin Luther King, Jr. admitted as much after years of promoting this tactic. He stated on November 11, 1967, to his longtime friend and Southern Christian Leadership Conference (SCLC) board member Revered D.E. King, "I have found out that all I have been doing in trying to correct this system in America has been in vain. I am trying to get at the roots of it to see just what ought to be done. The whole thing will have to be done away with."

Then, for those of us who do find work, job security is nonexistent, particularly in this contracting economy where there are not enough jobs to employ even the white workers who have union backing. And when invoked by whites, this union power basically eliminates the possibility of Blacks competing with them for "respectable" work and "good" wages, leaving us to do exactly what we are doing now: overflowing US prisons – the irony being that as we languish, forgotten and with minds rotting, inside these steel and concrete humyn warehouses, the government will provide us freely with the very necessities, (food, clothing, shelter, medical care), that it denies us out in society; the denial of which drove most of us to "crime" in the first place.*

It seems likely that in a few generations we will cease to exist as a people here in Amerika, as would very likely be the case today for the small numbers of remaining Native Americans, had they elected as a people to accept integration into Amerikan values and culture. Our brothers are abandoning our sisters, and in turn our sisters are doing the same, especially in the cases of us locked behind prison walls. Today's trend with our youth is that of pimping our sisters, regarding them as property, objects to be bought and sold on the market, which is the very way that we were regarded during slavery – viz., as property.

Martin Luther King, Jr. foresaw things coming to pass for us just as they have, which is why during the final three years of his life he came to reject our integration into Amerika absent fundamental

— — — — —

* In the column entitled "The Name Game," by Russ Parr, (pp. 80-81), Black parents are encouraged to cater to racism in US corporate hiring by not naming their children in ways which allow them to be identifiable as Black on job resumes submitted; job applicants having Black-sounding names are routinely passed over for hiring consideration. For us, there is no option for fair access employment and integration. For us, integration into a society that demonstrably does not accept us as equal means both ceasing to be and wanting to be identifiable as Black people.

change. His views of Amerika at the time of his death in 1968 were vastly different from those he held in 1963 when he gave his "I Have a Dream" speech during the Washington March. But the US corporate media will only give us the 1963 version of King. In November 1967, he announced to a new SCLC program advisory board: "Something is wrong with capitalism as it stands here in the US. We are not interested in being integrated into this value structure." That same month he expressed at his Frogmore retreat, "The decade of 1955 to 1965 … misled us … we must formulate a new program, and we must fashion new tactics which do not count on government good will, but instead serve to compel unwilling authorities to yield to the mandates of justice."

In February 1968 he told a Selma, Alabama rally, "We're dealing in a sense with class issues … with the problem of the gulf between the haves and the have-nots."* He therefore organized a

— — — — —

* King came to totally reject capitalism, yet realized that he could not openly expose this to the masses of people who looked to him for guidance, because the US and its corporate elites were waging brutal wars directly – as in Vietnam – and indirectly, to violently crush all who resisted capitalist domination and who fought for national independence from western political, economic, military, and cultural domination. He knew that to openly promote this would mean imminent death. Speaking in 1968 to staff members of Jesse Jackson's Black capitalist Breadbasket program, a staff member recalled, King "asked us to turn off the tape recorder." He talked about what he called democratic socialism, and he said, "I can't say this publicly, and if you say I said it, I'm not going to admit it." Then he talked about the fact that he didn't believe that capitalism, "as it was constructed, could meet the needs of poor people," and that "what we might need to look at was a kind of socialism, but a

"Poor People's Campaign" set to march on Washington, but this time to shut the capital down. In the "Statement of Purpose" document issued by the SCLC explaining the march's objective, it was stated: "We are now more sophisticated," because "we can now see ourselves as the powerless poor trapped within the economically oriented power structure. The right to vote or eat in any restaurant, while important – does not actually affect conditions of living," and that the campaign hoped to force economic empowerment of all poor people, "enabling them to control their own lives." King expressed, "our economy must become more person-centered than property-centered and profit-centered … It must therefore not think of our movement as one that seeks to integrate the Negro into … the existing values of American society." Only months before the march was set to occur, and after being relentlessly threatened, stalked, and hounded by the FBI, King was assassinated.

Today, we are divided sharply against ourselves, confused and diverted, while the US rulers systematically invalidate and revoke

---

democratic form of socialism."

Another example of King's position was recalled in a conversation between him and William A. Rutherford, a Chicago native and Europe-based businessman who volunteered his skills to the SCLC. Rutherford criticized Black capitalism and its basic objective being "to replace white bastards with black bastards. If the whole thrust of assuring oneself profit is to exploit whoever's there, what the hell are we doing with black people, trying to put them in the same position where you have to exploit someone else to turn your profit?" King replied, "Bill, there's so much to be done that people are not ready to do right now. Obviously, we've got to have some form of socialism, but America's not ready to hear it yet."

the civil rights reforms passed to pacify us over 40 years ago. Self-hate is a principal tool used to drive us to kill, exploit, and oppress ourselves, much as was done during our chattel enslavement, except then it was the poor whites who were used to violently contain and repress us and to kill those who rebelled. This was done by the ruling wealthy white class, (which needed Afrikan slave labor to keep them enriched and their economy running smoothly), conditioning the poor whites to fear and hate us. Originally, both the Afrikans and poor European immigrants shared a common status of indentured servitude. However, the wealthy whites had to create a division between the two, because united rebellions of these servants threatened to destroy their rule. In fact, Bacon's Rebellion (1676) temporarily overthrew the colonial government in Virginia and captured the capital at Jamestown. Thereafter, a permanent hereditary slavery of Afrikans was codified (1682), and white bond-slavery phased out. The resultant poor whites were given a sense of superior societal status over the Afrikan chattel slaves and thereupon used as a colonial police to violently repress, break, and control the Afrikans. It was in this process that racialized white supremacy was born here in North Amerika, and prevails until today. The plantation elite used the same divisive scheme here as did the Belgians in Rwanda, the Spanish and Portuguese in Central, South, and portions of North America, and European imperialism throughout the Third World: divide, agitate, and rule.

The poor whites were given to see in any Afrikan slave revolt a threat to white civilization, and a desire of Blacks to stop at nothing until they'd killed all whites – rich and poor. Our national independence struggles in the 1960's and 70's were painted to the public in the same light by the US government and corporate media, in order to alienate whites and many Blacks against our struggle. During slavery it was inconceivable to the plantation-owning "Mr. Charlie" for us to break away from him and his rule, just as it is inconceivable to the big business "Mr. Charlie" for us to do this today. Then, as now, his created racism claimed us to be too stupid and backward by nature to do such a thing, and that without his tutelage, guidance, rule, and economic domination, we'd self-destruct. With this reverse-psychology, we were made to feel dependent upon him and thus to willingly remain his servants, which is why he will not expose the fact that only since we, and the peoples of Afrika, Asia, Australia, and the Amerikas, fell under just such rule and domination, have our people and societies become self-destructive, and all to the exclusive profit and expansion of western capitalist power.

Those we see today as our heroes, who fought and died against chattel slavery, were then classified by "Mr. Charlie" as terrorists. They were violently stalked, hunted, mutilated, killed, and put down by poor whites and the US government, but this did not discourage them. Yet today we are used to brutally repress the Third World people in order to keep them in conditions of slavery, enriching western powers and impoverishing themselves by extracting their natural wealth for and selling their hard labor dirt-cheap to the west. Those who resist these conditions, (those who strike back at "Mr. Charlie," his mercenaries, and his collaborators), are labeled terrorist threats to western civilization. It's the same old wine in new bottles.

We've gone from a race of rebellious field niggers to one of collaborating house niggers. We're so proud of being able to rub shoulders with "Massa Charlie" and his elite underlings, to receive his pat on the head for being loyal and obedient to him. So desperately do we desire his acceptance and approval and fear provoking his displeasure and criticism, that we go to any lengths to please him, including destroying our children and killing ourselves and others in the process.

But when reality sets in a little too painfully for our liking, instead of taking courage in hand and confronting the problem at the root, we limit ourselves – as our enslaved ancestors were expected to do – to looking to the sky for deliverance, while accepting the lash with the complacent and mindless dignity of trained mules. Thus the religion taught to us by the old slave master "Mr. Charlie," (which we still practice today), conditioned us never to resist or question anyone whom the old slaver appointed as a claimed authority over us. It became, and still is, for us a tranquilizer that robbed us of the will to fight back, a narcotic to keep us in a mindless stupor, a pressure release that had us singing, shouting, screaming, and crying out our pain and desperation in the all-Black churches, and a source of hope for a more fulfilling existence in another world. The modern alternative pressure release for the less religious amongst us is the weekly all-night booty-shaking sessions at the club. In place of the dignifying big flashy hats and special tailored suits and dresses that distinguished us in churches, in the club scene we've substituted equally flashy but more revealing hip-hop or casual ensembles. Little has changed for us, except that today, like happy lemmings, we are marching toward a mass grave bling-blinging and booty-shaking to the rhythm of our own death-drum, while the mainstream Black media adds gloss and glitter to this mindless death parade.

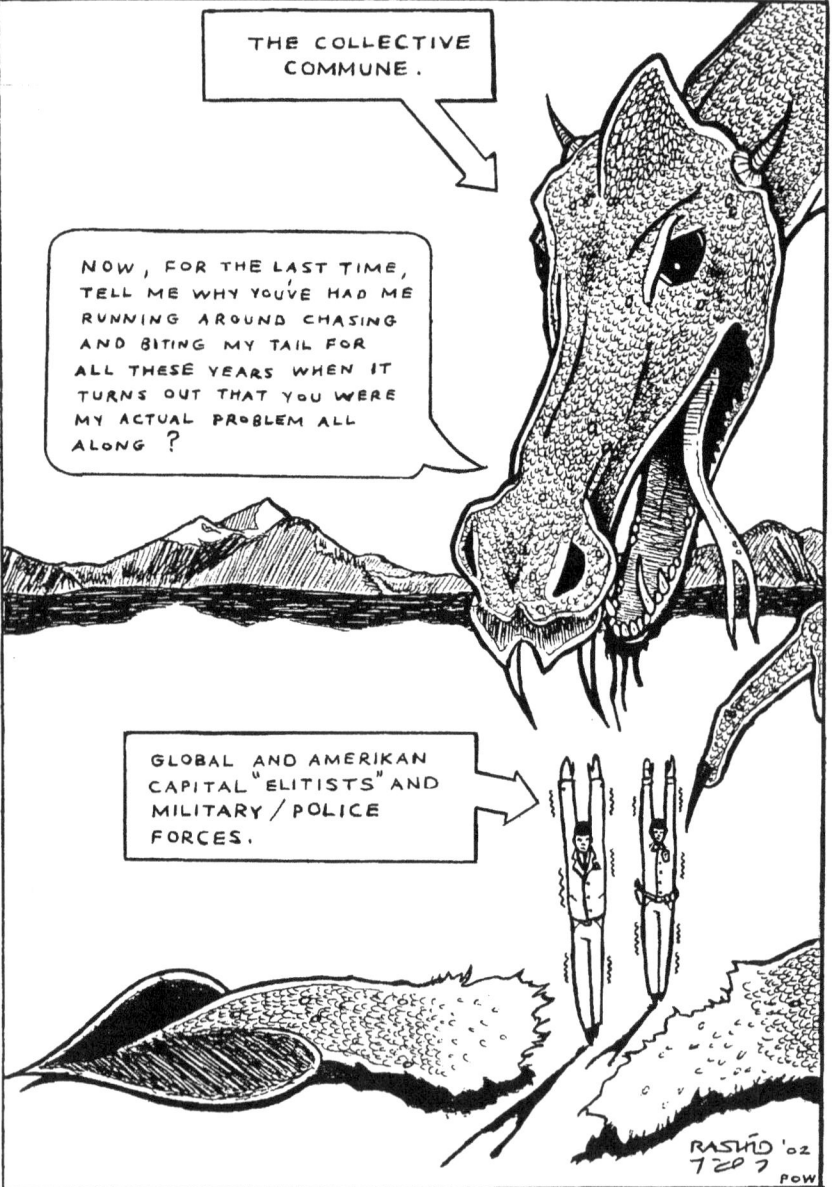

On the Roles and Characteristics of the Panther Vanguard Party and Mass Organizations

[T]he existence of a political vanguard precedes the existence of any of the other elements of a truly revolutionary culture.

George Jackson, *Blood In My Eye* (1971)

A revolutionary party cannot be built on the quicksand of ideological confusion. Obviously there are a lot of people in the Black movement whose political positions are dead wrong, and someone has to have the courage to say it, even if it busts wide open the façade of unity. A political split, like a divorce, is often healthier than trying to live together in the same house when you have fundamental differences ... There are political differences inside the Black Movement representing different socio-economic layers inside the Black community. It is better to start the vanguard party from scratch with the serious few ... than with many assorted persons who are all going in different directions and who are therefore bound to split at the moment of crisis, just when the need is for maximum organizational strength and unity. This does not mean that those who cannot or will not accept the ideology and discipline of the vanguard party cannot play a role in the movement or in concrete struggles for liberation that will culminate in the taking of power. But their place is in the various organizations of mass struggle, not in the vanguard party.

James and Grace Lee Boggs,
The Role of the Vanguard Party (1970)

Recurring criticisms and questions have been raised about the New Afrikan Black Panther Party–Prison Chapter's organizational structure. Most of these criticisms and questions have come from veteran comrades of the original Black Panther Party, (and those they've influenced), whose negative experiences under the leadership of Huey P. Newton, (the BPP's co-founder and Minister of Defense), has led them to reject both the need of a vanguard Party and the decision-making process of democratic centralism (DC), both of which we believe are absolutely essential for the success of any revolutionary struggle. Our purpose here is to answer those criticisms and questions.

In order to address these issues, we must begin with analyzing what type of organization the BPP really was and what sort of decision making process the BPP leadership actually applied.

Was the BPP a Vanguard Party?
While we believe the BPP contained many genuine vanguard elements, (comrades who had cultivated a revolutionary proletarian outlook), it also contained many elements who maintained and cultivated un-remolded lumpen class values and perspectives. In fact, BPP leaders Huey Newton and Eldridge Cleaver in 1970 and George

Jackson in 1971 proudly identified the BPP as being a lumpen party. Furthermore, as pointed out by Charles E. Jones and Judson Jeffries in chapter one of *The Black Panther Party Reconsidered* and by Comrade Sundiata Acoli in his *A Brief History of the Black Panther Party*, the class backgrounds of BPP members spanned from petty-bourgeoisie, to lumpen proletarian, to pre-class high school and college students and many were in fact employed workers. There was no requirement within the Party that its members commit "class suicide" or otherwise develop proletarian class consciousness, despite the fact that in the Black communities different classes, with various different ideological and political views, were contending to influence the direction of the movement.

Membership in the BPP was generally open to all members of the Black communities. All one had to do was walk into a Party office and sign up. This allowed raw elements to join who were not trained and prepared to lead a revolutionary movement, and offered no protection against infiltration by disruptive elements and enemy agents who would undermine the Party's ability to operate at a high level of ideological, political and practical unity.

So, in essence the BPP, while operating under the banner of a vanguard party, actually combined the features of both a vanguard party and a mass form of organization. This occurred because the BPP's leadership failed to make the distinction between the different natures and roles of a vanguard party versus a mass organization. They thus combined both organizational structures into one with the result of having many different tendencies pulling in different directions inside the Party. So, while a strong sense of cultural unity and collective willpower was able to hold the Party together in many ways, it ultimately blew apart as a result of the pigs' inciting these different internal tendencies into factionalism, competition, envy, paranoia and distrust, à la COINTELPRO. This sort of division would have been much harder to accomplish within a genuine Vanguard Party that practiced DC.

What is a Vanguard Party? What is a Mass Organization?

In order to understand where the BPP went wrong in its organizational structure, we must examine the difference between the Vanguard and the mass organizations. We must also understand that the kind of organization that an oppressed people needs is determined by what the people are ultimately trying to accomplish. As Chairman Bob Avakian of the RCP–USA has stated:

> If the goal is simply to fan dissent and protest, or to build a movement that may take militantly to the streets around particular outrages, but does not aim to overthrow the system, then one can dispense with revolutionary organization; a vanguard is not necessary, and for that matter there's no need for revolutionary ideology.
>
> But if the goal is to mobilize the masses to seize power from a murderous ruling class and to establish a new power that enables the masses to run and transform society, then you have to act on the implications of this: a vanguard party becomes essential.

How else can the masses defeat a highly organized oppressive system controlled by a united class enemy? Accomplishing this requires a highly disciplined, organized and united revolutionary party; one that understands the underlying nature of class society and imperialism, and the stages and forms of struggle necessary to overthrow such an enemy order and replace it with a system that genuinely implements the will of the masses. This form of organization is the revolutionary vanguard party.

The vanguard party must consist of the most ideologically and politically united, advanced, disciplined, and dedicated class-conscious elements of a people's revolutionary forces. These elements must have developed the class perspectives of the revolutionary proletariat, and apply the scientific method of *Historical and Dialectical Materialism* to its analyses and practice and to educating and guiding the less-advanced masses in solving socio-economic problems.

The vanguard party must be able to investigate material conditions and social contradictions, taking in a broad view of all relevant factors, drawing their information from *all* areas and sectors of society, high and low, at home and abroad. This data must be analyzed, then synthesized to draw conceptual conclusions and implement programs and policies that organize the masses to solve their own economic and political problems. The vanguard party must be united in theory and practice in the highest sense, and aspire through guiding and educating the masses to raise mass consciousness up to the level of the vanguard elements. The vanguard party does not seek to be a specialized group operating above and out of reach of the common people, instead it actually lives and struggles alongside the people and educates them in the process of struggle so that they too will become vanguard elements. The ultimate objective is to make the Party and the people one and the same.

Until the masses of people are raised up to the level of the vanguard elements, they are organized into mass organizations. The mass organizations represent and include people of various different political, cultural, ideological and class backgrounds, views, influences and levels of awareness. In the case of New Afrikans, for example, our mass organizations like the New Afrikan Service

Organization (NASO) include New Afrikan people of different political, cultural and spiritual persuasions. But they are united by a common objective of carrying out programs that serve the needs and interests of the Nation of Afrikans in Amerika. Many of the members of mass organizations are not even revolutionary minded, but they do recognize a burning need to change and improve the social-economic conditions of Black people.

So, mass organizations will include some open proponents of capitalism, liberals, reformists, activists of various persuasions and everyday apolitical people. But also spread throughout these organizations are cadre of vanguard elements whose role within these organizations is to struggle alongside and learn from the people, to materially serve their needs and interests, to educate, lead and advance their levels of political and ideological consciousness, and to ultimately develop the masses from within these mass structures, to become themselves vanguard elements. As people's consciousness and understanding are raised, and they prove their dedication through their work and study within the mass organizations, they are recruited into the vanguard party where they become fully committed leaders, educators and servants of the People.

The reality is that no people have *ever* made a spontaneous and leaderless revolution. In *every* case where any revolution succeeded (Russia, China, Angola, Mozambique, Guinea-Bissau, Cuba, Vietnam, etc.), there was a party of vanguard elements that led and organized them. It is unrealistic to suppose that a people can spontaneously unite, rise up and overthrow and then themselves replace the institutions of a highly organized economic system and state. Many ultra-Leftists theorize about the possibility, but no one has ever achieved it in practice. It is therefore an idealistic and materially unsupportable premise. (Theory, to be accepted as "truth," must be proved in practice.) It is no more realistic than expecting that a person with no mechanical study, training or experience could spontaneously build a modern car engine. To develop such a skill, one must be actively instructed over a period of time through study, practice and guidance by others who *are* advanced in the appropriate technical fields, or they must have had plenty of leisure time, opportunity and hands-on access to the necessary technical information and tools to learn the skills themselves. They must be exposed to or studied in the practice itself to become capable and effective in applying it.

So this is to say that yes, the common persyn definitely *can* learn to build a car engine, however, they *cannot* develop the ability instantly and spontaneously without practical exposure or instruction. To claim otherwise would be absurd and we dare say improvable. The same reality exists for a people consciously struggling with a society's highly developed and complex economic, political, military and cultural processes, in pursuit of first seizing power from the bourgeoisie, and then effectively operating these institutions themselves. This is why the masses need a revolutionary party to lead, organize and raise their collective consciousness to achieve and then successfully administer a revolutionary seizure of power.

In this regard, the vanguard party must consist of a hard core of committed revolutionaries who scientifically understand the various economic, political, military, cultural and historical conditions that underlie present society and its various levels of development; who recognize the changes and forms of struggle necessary to overthrow the oppressive system in the ebbs, flows and weaves inherent in the developments of revolutionary struggle; and who have the ability to organize the masses to seize the reins and administer the institutions of the new mass-based society that must smash and build itself upon the ruins of the bourgeois society. As Amilcar Cabral pointed out, while the vanguard party is needed to lead a revolutionary struggle, "our problem is to see who are capable of taking control of the state apparatus when the colonial power is destroyed." This is a key question. The answer, as Cabral observed, is the mass-based revolutionary party.

So, in essence, the vanguard party is the administrative nucleus of the aspiring and rising revolutionary society. When out of power, the Party acts as the political embryo, which guides and organizes the people's struggle to ultimately seize power from their bourgeoisie and imperialist oppressors.

And of course we do not claim that less-advanced elements won't find their way into a vanguard party, because they will. Unity of opposites and uneven development exists within all social phenomena, including a revolutionary party. People are always going to have different levels of understanding of *Historical and Dialectical Materialism* and how to apply it. What is important is that the center is consolidated while uplifting and educating the cadre and party rank and file in an ongoing way. Envision an escalator where people get on at ground level and go up in stages floor by floor. There will always be new people getting on and therefore unevenness at each successive level of a vanguard party. The deeper understanding will be at a higher level.

These are the distinctive features and functions of the vanguard party versus the mass organizations. The fact that the BPP failed to make these distinctions and organize the Party accordingly, created the internal conditions that allowed the government to destroy it.

Actually, despite his organizational genius, Comrade Amilcar

Cabral made a similar error in structuring the vanguard party of Guinea-Bissau, the PAIGC. Too many aspiring bourgeois elements were allowed to enter the leadership levels of the PAIGC. Therefore, all these aspiring capitalist elements had to do was neutralize the advanced class-conscious elements like Amilcar, (through assassinating him in 1973), and his brother Luis Cabral, (through a coup that sent him into exile), and these elements took over the Party and derailed Guinea-Bissau's revolutionary advances.

Did the BPP Practice Democratic Centralism?

The questions remain whether the BPP applied DC and whether DC is the correct decision-making process of a vanguard party.

> Every comrade ... should help the masses to organize themselves step by step and on a voluntary basis to unfold gradually struggles that are necessary and permissible under the external and internal conditions obtaining at a particular time and place. Whatever we do, authoritarianism is always erroneous because, as a result of our impetuosity, it makes us go beyond the degree of the masses' awakening and violates the principle of voluntary action on the part of the masses.
>
> Mao Tse-tung, 1945

Quite a few BPP veterans, especially those on the East Coast, are still smarting from Huey's unilateral purges of committed Party cadre, beginning in 1970 when the BPP split into the pro-Huey West Coast and pro-Cleaver East Coast factions. Huey had reached an icon status as a result of the massive nation-wide campaign led by BPP cadre

(1968–1970) to free him from prison on charges of killing a cop. An unintended consequence of this campaign was a centralization of the Party's decision-making powers in Huey. As some Comrades point out, the BPP became in reality "Huey's Party," instead of the "People's Party." What's worse, is that many of these Comrades mistakenly equate Huey's centralized power as an *expression* of DC, when in fact the BPP *did not* practice DC. Indeed, Huey's purges of BPP cadre occurred because he was unaccustomed to, and unwilling to accept, criticisms from the Party's rank and file. Whereas criticism of this nature is an *essential* feature of DC. What Huey practiced was a form of Commandism or Authoritarian Centralism, which is the very opposite of DC.

BPP veteran Mumia Abu-Jamal described the process aptly:

> Despite the ideological claim that the Party functioned under the principle of criticism and self-criticism, the Party hierarchy in fact functioned much like any other group in bourgeois society, that is, according to the principle of power dynamics: those who have power strive mightily to keep it—period.
>
> So when Huey received letters full of criticism of his leadership, he struck out at those he thought were angling to undermine his rule of the organization. When Eldridge received letters critical of Huey's leadership, he felt a sense of affirmation. Neither apparently questioned the authorship of this critical correspondence.
>
> Why would they? Why *should* they?
>
> *We Want Freedom:*
> *A Life in the Black Panther Party* (2004), p. 208

In answer to Brotha Mumia's closing questions, we must point out that *if* the BPP was accustomed to practicing DC, then Party leaders would not have taken offense to criticism nor would they have allowed it to generate factionalism. Indeed, secret criticisms of the sort described by Mumia would not have been tolerated, but the letters would have been turned over to the Party's Chief of Staff (Bobby Seale) for investigation as attempts to incite inner-Party rivalries and factionalism. DC demands that criticisms of Party members be made openly, and assures all Party members at all levels the right to criticize any other member's actions. The very object of DC is to preserve unity and prevent divisiveness and factionalism.

That the BPP did not practice DC is further demonstrated in Huey's belief that he *owned* his leadership position in the Party; that he was not subject to recall or being held accountable for his actions; and that he could unilaterally expel those who criticized or exposed his conduct or failure to meet the obligations of his leadership. Under DC, Party leaders are *elected* to their leading positions and are likewise *subject to recall by vote.*

So that we don't repeat the errors of the past and so that comrades today can dispense with the mistaken view that the BPP practiced DC, it is *essential* that we explain what DC is.

What Is Democratic Centralism?

The basic principles of DC are expressed in V.I. Lenin's slogan, "freedom to criticize, unity of action." I repeat, *"freedom to criticize, unity of action."* The *Democratic* component of DC means *all* Party members are free to criticize, debate and discuss internal matters of Party decisions, policy and direction in open sessions, and final decisions on such matters are reached by majority vote of all Party members. The *Centralism* component of DC means that once decisions are reached by majority vote, all members must uphold that decision. Those who disagree with the decisions must still abide by them, they must reserve their personal opinions, but they are free at the next session to raise the issues again and struggle to change the Party's views and vote on the matters.

Furthermore, *no* individual party member has unqualified power. Indeed, all party members must answer to the party itself and to the public criticism of the masses.

Many sincere comrades stereotype and reject DC as an organizational fetish of "Leninist" parties, based upon the practices of parties who've *claimed* to practice DC but *actually did not.* Many Leftist parties applied commandism much like Huey did and *called* it DC, leading many to erroneously equate DC with those bourgeois forms of *authoritarian* centralism.

Many on the Left also reject DC as a peculiarly "Leninist" ideology, not realizing that not only did the concept pre-date Lenin, but that DC was an organizational form embraced and practiced by Lenin's opponents such as the bourgeois liberal Mensheviks who adopted it in November 1905, a month *before* Lenin's Bolsheviks adopted it. Indeed, in its 1905 resolution, "On the Organization of the Party," the Mensheviks state that, "the RSDLP must be organized according to the principle of democratic centralism." The Bolsheviks, a month later, elaborated on DC in their resolution, "On Party Organization," and gave a very different picture of DC than what the Left depicts it as today. That resolution states: "Recognizing as indisputable the principle of democratic centralism, the Conference considers the broad implementation of the elective principle necessary; and, while granting elected centers full powers in matters of ideological and practical leadership, they are at the same time subject to recall, their actions are given broad publicity, and they are to be strictly accountable for these activities."

In fact, DC was *never* in dispute between the opposing Bolshevik and Menshevik wings of the RSDLP (Russian Social-Democratic Labor Party), neither in definition nor practice. At a 1906 unity conference both the Bolsheviks and Mensheviks adopted a resolution by vote that stated "All party organizations are built on the principles of democratic centralism." The committee report adopting this resolution was written by a Menshevik, Zagorky-Kokhmal, who stated that all Mensheviks and Bolsheviks accepted this resolution, "unanimously."

In actuality, none of Lenin's contemporaries in the Social Democratic movement criticized DC, not even Rosa Luxemburg, who strongly opposed features of "Leninist" organizations. Features, which her failure to adopt into her German Communist Party, left its entire Left wing – Luxemburg included – open to assassination.

At bottom, corruption and abuses of power are essentially impossible when DC is observed, since all Party members, leaders especially, are subject to criticism, exposure and recall through open democratic processes. Leaders are *elected* to their positions based upon *demonstrated* qualifications and integrity, and are subject to having their powers *revoked* for *failure* to live up to their responsibilities, also by majority vote.

So, in summing up the errors of the BPP's organizational practices, and recognizing the *actual* role of the vanguard party and its appropriate decision making process, we must disagree with those comrades who reject the need of a vanguard party and the role of DC as such a party's correct method of deciding its policies and practices. In actuality, what these comrades oppose from their experiences in the BPP are tendencies that we too oppose, and were not genuine examples of the type of party and practices that we promote as essential for leading an oppressed people in a revolutionary struggle.

This is not to say the BPP got it all wrong, because it didn't. Actually, the Party was right on in much of the mass work it accomplished – in mobilizing the people around their needs and showing them through example and participation that we can solve our own problems, that indeed *we must*. It was just in its internal organizing and in its attempts to perform as both a vanguard party *and* a mass organization that it erred. The Party came into being spontaneously, in response to immediate crisis in the New Afrikan communities, and consisted primarily of youth. It didn't have the time, experience or prior examples to rigorously work out its program and structure, but today we do. And we are determined not to repeat yesterday's mistakes.

A Consensus on the Need of a Revolutionary Vanguard

The essential need of a Vanguard Party stands above all other organizational forms in revolutionary struggle. This has been acknowledged and proved by the successes of all revolutionary movements.

Lenin recognized it, and committed most of his work to building the revolutionary Party.

> What few people realize is that until 1917 Lenin rarely addressed himself to a mass audience, either in writing or speaking, nor appeared on a public platform. Instead, he concentrated his extraordinary abilities and energies

on the task which he concluded was decisive to the success of the Russian Revolution: the building of an apparatus of dedicated, disciplined revolutionaries to lead the masses in the struggle for power.

For the revolutionary movements developing today in every country, the great contribution of Lenin was the clarity with which he put forward and acted upon his fundamental convictions regarding the vanguard party: 1) that the purpose of a revolutionary party is to take absolute power in order to revolutionize the economic and social systems as the only way of resolving fundamental popular grievances; 2) that it is absolutely essential to build a revolutionary vanguard party if you are not just playing with the phrase; and 3) that a revolutionary party can only be built by a) unceasing ideological struggle, b) strict discipline, c) organized activity of every member, and d) merciless self-criticism.

James and Grace Lee Boggs,
The Role of the Vanguard Party

Lenin's organizing work paid off in dividends enabling his Bolshevik Party to not only seize power in Russia, achieving history's first working-class revolution, but it survived the most extreme repression at the hands of the Czar's secret police, and the world's imperialist powers that promptly invaded Soviet Russia (1918–1920).

Why was it that the Bolsheviks (for example) could be so heavily infiltrated, suffer many busts and setbacks of all kinds, and yet remain strong enough – effective enough–to seize power in 1917? There's probably no single or simple answer, but a few things stand out:

There was a significant level of ideological training and consistency among leadership and cadres, and extensive political education.

There was a certain type of organizational structure, disciplined practice of principles, methods and style of work.

There was a relatively secure system of communications.

There was a mass-based infrastructure, and broad, active connections to the mass movement.

The party construction began at the center, and spread outward.

Vita Wa Watu: a New Afrikan
Theoretical Journal, Volume 11, p. 30 (1987)

In pursuing the anti-imperialist and New Democratic aims of the Chinese Revolution, Mao Tse-tung acknowledged the essential role of the Vanguard Party.

If there is to be a revolution, there must be a revolutionary party. Without a revolutionary party, without a party built on the Marxist-Leninist revolutionary theory and the Marxist-Leninist revolutionary style, it is impossible to lead the working class and the broad masses of the people in defeating imperialism and its running dogs.

"Revolutionary Forces of the World Unite, Fight Against Imperialist Aggression!" (November 1948)

A well disciplined Party armed with the theory of Marxism-Leninism, using the method of self-criticism and linked with the masses of the people; an army under the leadership of such a Party; a united front of all revolutionary classes and all revolutionary groups under the leadership of such a Party – these are the three main weapons with which we have defeated the enemy.

"On the People's Democratic Dictatorship" (June 30, 1949)

Mao's vanguard party walked its talk. Not only did it repel a Japanese imperialist invasion, defeat the imperialist-backed puppet bourgeois KMT army and seize power in 1949, empowering and improving the living conditions of China's millions, but with a peasant army – and fresh from a civil war – it repelled the day's most powerful combined military forces, (the US and UN), from its borders in the Korean War (1950–1953).

In Guinea-Bissau's revolutionary struggle for national liberation from Portuguese colonialism, Amilcar Cabral acknowledged the essential role of the vanguard party.

[W]e must try and unite everybody in the national liberation struggle against the Portuguese colonialists. It is imperative to organize things so that we always have an instrument available which can solve all the other contradictions. This is what convinced us of the absolute necessity of creating a party during the national liberation struggle.

The Politics of Struggle (May 1964)

But as Cabral admitted, "we are not a Marxist-Leninist party." The fact of Cabral's failure to organize the PAIGC as a Marxist-Leninist Vanguard, left it internally weak and vulnerable to destruction by bourgeois elements as occurred when he and his brother were neutralized by the rightists inside the Party.

George Jackson acknowledged the indispensable role of the vanguard party in any people's revolutionary struggle, and especially the one that must occur here in Amerika. In fact, all of Comrade George's military proposals surrounded protecting the vanguard elements at their work in organizing and educating the masses.

> Recall: our Mao teaches that when revolution fails it isn't the fault of the people, it's the fault of the vanguard party ... There have never been any spontaneous revolutions. They were all staged, manufactured, by people who went to the head of the masses and directed them.
>
> The liberalist slogan "you can't get ahead of the people" is meaningless. From what other position can one lead? From the rear? Rearguard leadership?!! A typical Yankee innovation .... In all the successful class struggles and colonial wars of liberation, the vanguard elements did get ahead of the people and pull. There is no other way in forward mass movement ....
>
> I'm not implying that the vanguard party act out the people's role. I'm not implying a "society superior to society." We must never forget that it is the people who change circumstances and that the educator himself needs educating. "Going among the people, learning from the people, and serving the people" is really stating

that we must find out exactly what the people need and
organize them around those needs.

George Jackson, Blood In My Eye (1971)

The same was acknowledged by the Vietnamese, the Colombians,
and every other movement for revolutionary overthrow of oppressive conditions under capitalism and imperialism. And every reverse in the gains of those movements took place because of capitalist elements infiltrating and subverting the vanguard parties, or
errors in their internal structures allowed external forces to cause
internal destruction. Comrade Mao was the first to point out the
importance of waging ongoing struggle *inside* of vanguard parties
to prevent their subversion and destruction by bourgeois elements,
or bureaucratic errors. The vanguard party is indeed the motor of a
people's revolution.

Is the NABPP-PC a Vanguard Party?

The NABPP-PC was founded under uncommon conditions. Being
based as we are amongst prisoners confined across the US Empire,
it is difficult, if not impossible, to function as a genuine vanguard
party that can lead and organize the masses on society and practice
DC. We are not idealists, but dialectical materialists, and therefore
do not deceive ourselves and the people about our practical limits.

Because of our material limitations, we exist in reality as only
a pre-party formation: the embryo of a genuine revolutionary vanguard. The scope of our work is limited and defined as it should
be. As set out in one of our founding position papers, "Our Line,"
we aspire through our practice and example to develop the actual NABPP on the outside within our oppressed communities, and

ultimately into a Vanguard Party of Afrikan people worldwide. Our Party will take root as our cadre re-enter society. As Uncle Ho once wrote in a poem, "what becomes of a Nation when its people come out of confinement? ... when the prison gates open the real dragon will fly out!"

The NABPP won't be real until it can hold a founding Congress, draft a Party Programme, and elect a free world Central Committee and Politburo. Then DC can be fully implemented. At that eventual stage, the Prison Chapter will be one of many Chapters within the Party.

At the present stage, we *are* able to practice limited forms of DC, with our focus on *Transforming the Razor Wire Plantations into Schools of Liberation* and organizing around serving the material and spiritual needs of oppressed people in the inside.

As a pre-Party structure, we are struggling to outline a blueprint of the ideological and organizational basis upon which our broader struggle must be built. Earlier efforts gave us examples and lessons to build on – our object is this time to get it right, and organize to win!

As we've stated before:

> We who are inside the "Belly of the Beast," may perish inside these razor-wire fences and stone walls, but not without first illuminating the path forward for our sisters and brothers, our sons and daughters. If we can offer nothing but our dying breath, it will be to say: "DARE TO STRUGGLE AND DARE TO WIN!"

ALL POWER TO THE PEOPLE!

PAID IN FULL!

Nat Turner was captured by Benjamin Phipps on October 30, 1831.

HARRIET TUBMAN

Hasan Shakur
(AKA Derrick Frazier #999284)

The Night of Fire, Saint-Domingue, August 22, 1791.

Ida B. Wells-Barnett

BEGINNING OF HAITI'S REVOLUTION

Black Panther Love in honor of yesterday's Red Heart Warriors. May their examples and memory inspire Red Hearts today. We unite with you in struggle. Power to the People! NABPP-PC

RASHID 7-07'06

AFTERWORD

by Tom Big Warrior, Founder and Chief, Red Heart Warrior Society

The monopoly capitalist ruling class of Amerika is indeed "at war with the universe," but with no one more vigorously than the impoverished, young Black males of this country. Rashid and the other comrades of the New Afrikan Black Panther Party–Prison Chapter are all POWs of this war. They were fighting back before they knew what they were up against. Only after imprisonment did they have access to literature that shed light on what they were experiencing – the writings of Malcolm X, Huey P. Newton, Eldridge Cleaver, George Jackson and other revolutionaries.

The progression from simple reaction to conscious revolutionary commitment took place in a pressure cooker. The very tactics of repression intended to break their spirits and make docile slaves of them inflamed their outrage and determination not to be broken. It is a maxim that "repression breeds resistance," but only the infusion of revolutionary theory enables resistance to make a qualitative leap to conscious revolutionary commitment. This element was introduced to the US prison system by the many political prisoners/POWs incarcerated during (and since) the high tide of the Black Liberation struggle in the 1960's and 70's: in particular the comrades of the original Black Panther Party (BPP) and the Black Liberation Army (BLA).

Most impressive of this generation are the writings and example of Black Panther Comrade, George Jackson, who, like them, was imprisoned as a youth for a petty crime but transformed himself into a revolutionary in prison and became a legendary leader who was martyred because he could not be broken. His books, *Soledad Brother* and *Blood In My Eye*, have been the primers of a generation of revolutionary prisoners.

It is not surprising that the penitentiaries are at the center of a new wave of revolutionary upsurge in Amerika. For the past decades, imprisonment has been Amerika's "solution" to growing social problems. Prisons have always been the "universities of the oppressed," and swollen with populations many times the number imprisoned just 30 years ago, as a result of the ruling classes' "war on the poor," the "curriculum" has increasingly shifted from "professional criminality" to "revolutionary science."

Many "schools of thought" are contending, from Anarchism and Afrocentrism to Radical Islam. Rashid and other comrades of the NABPP–PC have decided on "Pantherism," as defined by the original BPP in its most revolutionary period, which they are advancing and applying to the conditions of today.

This was not a random selection. The Black Panthers were the most revolutionary and successful part and movement of the Left in US history and represented the "high water mark" in the struggle of Black people against white supremacy and national oppression. Before spinning off into two basically incorrect directions, the Panthers were making ideological and political breakthroughs in the application of the "Science of Revolution" (Historical and Dialectical Materialism) to the problems of preparing to make socialist revolution in Amerika.

Many of the veterans of the BPP/BLA are still caught in the inertia of that split and are still in reaction to the effects of the government's "Secret War," code-named COINTELPRO, directed by the FBI. Though, it is impressive how many continued to be oriented toward serving the people and who remain in their hearts "ready for revolution."

What was not apparent (or understood enough) in the 60's and 70's was that even though we were in a high tide of revolutionary consciousness and struggle here, internationally the tide was ebbing. Mao Tse-tung was leading a heroic struggle to go against the tide with the Great Proletarian Cultural Revolution in People's China, but modern revisionism and capitalist restoration were spreading like cancer throughout the socialist bloc and newly liberated Third World countries. Objectively, even while it was losing the war in Vietnam, US imperialism was moving toward victory in the Cold War with its now "social-imperialist" (socialist in words, imperialist in reality) rival, the former Soviet Union, and was on its way to becoming the sole imperialist superpower.

The anti-colonial struggles in Afrika were succeeding in large part because they served the interest of US imperialism to displace its European rivals and allow the US to substitute its own neocolonialism. Genuine revolutionaries who recognized this were targeted by the CIA for assassination or at the least neutralization by co-option or coups. The fragile socialist and anti-imperialist states lacked a proletarian base and were dependent upon a vacillating petty bourgeoisie with strong bourgeois aspirations.

Even the concessions being won by the Civil Rights and Women's movements were useful to the neo-liberal strategy of the imperialists and provided fertile ground for co-option of the movements' leaders. Cold war liberalism called for the bribery and bourgeosification of the unionized workers after the unions were purged of communist and leftist radical leadership and the overthrow of overt Jim Crow segregation.

But the Black Panthers and the emerging young communist movement they helped inspire were viewed as a major threat. Malcolm X was tolerated until his trip to Mecca consolidated his anti-imperialist drift and broke him out of the grip of reverse racism. The Black Panthers continued his work that was cut short by assassination. Martin Luther King, Jr. was himself getting hip to being played and was swinging to a revolutionary stand when he was cut down, and many in the Civil Rights movement were now "ready for revolution" and aligning with the BPP.

Returning veterans from the Vietnam War, counter-cultural youth, Mexican-Chicanos, Puerto Ricans, Appalachian Hillbillies, Filipinos, Chinese and American Indians in the urban ghettos were all inspired by the BPP to form their own revolutionary parties and organizations allied with the Black Panthers. As Eldridge Cleaver, the BPP Minister of Communication, pointed out in "Education and Revolution" (*The Black Panther*, June 28, 1969), " … in reality there is no such thing as a black movement and a white movement in the United States. These are merely categories of thought that only have reality in terms of the lines that the ruling class itself has drawn and is implementing amongst the people. The United States is controlled by one ruling class. It's one single structure, and the whole drama of the black liberation struggle and the revolutionary struggle in the white community is being played out on one stage …. There's one single ruling class that rules all, that controls all, and that manipulates all, that has a different set of tactics for each group, depending upon the tactics used by the groups, in the struggle for liberation."

In opposition to the Panthers, the government called out counter-revolutionary, cultural nationalist gangs, like the group United

Slaves in LA, to harass and even murder Black Panther cadre, like John Huggins and "Bunchy" Carter. An army of informers, infiltrators and provocateurs were recruited to spy upon, sow disruption and dissension, misdirect and even set up and assassinate Party leaders and activists. Hundreds of COINTELPRO operations were carried out against the BPP and allied parties and organizations and to prevent other alliances from being formed.

Moreover, from the 70's on, the government has pursued a deliberate policy of criminalization of the younger generation in the oppressed communities, flooding the ghettos and barrios with drugs and military grade weaponry and promoting fratricidal gang violence and thug-life, lumpen, "gangsta-ho" culture of low morals, crass materialism, cynicism and nihilism. The "War On Drugs" was instituted as a thinly disguised "War on the Poor," and the "Prison-Industrial Complex" was created to cash in on the creation of hundreds of new prisons and millions of new prisoners to be exploited as "slaves of the state."

"Spatial deconcentration," (the breaking up of large concentrations of Black people), has been a consistent aspect of government strategy since the 60's urban rebellions. Out-sourcing of industrial jobs, (both away from urban centers and overseas), is not only a matter of seeking cheaper labor but also of pushing Black workers, (and youth particularly), into permanent unemployment. It also served to nip the growing young communist movement of the 70's in the bud before it could sink deeper roots among the industrial proletariat.

To understand all of this, it is important to firmly grasp what George Jackson had to say about fascism reaching its highest state of sophistication here in the USA. Instead of one party rule it has two, and the mantle of "Democracy" protects it from the formation of a vigorous anti-fascist opposition. Two and a half million people, (the majority of them people of color), can be imprisoned without any great public outcry. Comrade Maroon's analogy with *The Matrix* is very apt, the facts are evident for those who look hard enough, but for most the illusion is preferable.

Part and parcel of the counter-insurgency has been the neutralization of the Left in Amerika by promotion of every "alternative" to genuine revolutionary theory and practice imaginable. This has not been difficult as the Amerikan Left has traditionally not been revolutionary but reformist to begin with. Fascism took the form it did here because the Left could be co-opted into support for the "New Deal" and World War II, and barely resisted "McCarthyism." The CPUSA was never exactly a "Leninist" party even at its most militant moments.

As Bob Avakian, Chairman of the Revolutionary Communist Party, USA, pointed out in "Doing away with classes and what a proletarian state is good for" (*Revolutionary Worker*, August 17, 1997):

> … where anarchism grows as a trend among people radically opposed to the status quo, this is often partly as a result of the fact that what is supposed to be the most revolutionary ideology and program, namely communism, is not revolutionary itself, or not thoroughly and consistently revolutionary, but instead some variant of reformism wearing the mantle of Marxism. This is what Lenin meant when he said that, in part, anarchism is "payment for the sins of right opportunism."

The comrades of the NABPP–PC are being very careful not to "throw the baby out with the bath water." The decision to adopt the principle of democratic-centralist style of organization within the Party does not stem solely from the fact that this is the tradition of the original BPP and the BLA but because no revolution has gotten very far without a vanguard party based upon democratic centralism leading it. Despite the extreme difficulty of applying it under the present conditions, the comrades are looking ahead to when the "Prison Chapter" is but a part of a much larger NABPP centered in the oppressed communities, when it will be able to hold party congresses and elect its politburo and so on. Under the present circumstances there must be an emphasis on central control in formulating the Party's line, and there must be extreme self-reliance and initiative by the cadre and membership in applying it to build the Party.

In no way can the central leadership micro-manage the work of the rank and file, even if they wanted to. The recruits must build the Party where they are in order to join it. They must establish study circles from scratch and use available materials to illuminate their practice and develop their theoretical understanding. They must organize under the scrutiny and repression of the prison systems. This is difficult, but it will make the Party hardy as a weed and more capable of regenerating itself than any carefully tended, "hot house" grown beauty.

Just knowing that there is a center and a strategy being implemented is important. Our conditions are not worse or more challenging than those in Czarist Russia when Lenin devised the method. But the method is no guarantee of success. It is ideological and political line that is the determining factor. Without a correct ideological and political line, there will be no vanguard party and no revolution. All that will be possible is to protest, and protest alone will not bring down the empire, not even the most militant "armed propaganda by deed" or other half-baked strategies.

The masses alone are capable of making revolution, and the role of the Party (and revolutionaries in general) is to make them conscious. The masses need a revolutionary headquarters and a vanguard party, mass organizations and a revolutionary united front that is both nationally and internationally led by the international proletariat, which is the only all-the-way revolutionary class. A correct ideological and political line reflects this and illuminates the strategy and tactics employed by the conscious forces in waging the class and national struggles.

The "Science of Revolution" – "Historical and Dialectical Materialism" – which in this period is represented by Marxism-Leninism-Maoism – is based upon the summed up experience of all of humanity and particularly the struggle for socialist revolution and the advance to communism. The ideological and political line of the NABPP–PC is "Pantherism" – revolutionary Black Nationalism and proletarian internationalism illuminated by Marxism-Leninism-Maoism (MLM). The Party is not a communist party per se, nor does it see itself in competition with or a substitute for such. The Party supports the establishment of revolutionary communist parties in every country and an international committee of MLM parties to give global leadership to the world proletarian revolution.

The NABPP's particular role is to be the vanguard of the Black Liberation struggle, to advance it and link it to the overall struggle for socialist revolution. It is the merger of these struggles that is the core of the United Front Against Imperialism (UFAI) that will bring down the system of monopoly capitalism. It is the intention of its founders that the NABPP will spread to wherever Black people are concentrated – in the US and internationally – to promote Pan-Afrikanism and Proletarian Internationalism, to create and build "Serve The People" (STP) programs to meet the people's basic survival needs through self-reliance and promote the building of "People's Power" from the grassroots up while conducting anti-imperialist revolutionary education, agitation and organization.

Most particularly, the Party promotes "Revolutionary Culture" in all forms and mediums to uplift the people, raise their sights, and bring them together in community and in solidarity with all oppressed people. It opposes the poison of racist white supremacist culture, bourgeois culture, the culture of exploitation and degradation in all the forms that it takes. Black people need pride, but not pride based on hype or inverted racism. Pantherism celebrates Black culture in all its many splendid styles and the Afrikan heritage, which is so rich in culture and is the root of all cultures, but it rejects "Cultural Nationalism" which is counter-revolutionary and escapist. To substitute the lie of "Black Supremacy" for the lie of "White Supremacy" is a flight from the truth that "We Are All Related" and part of the same human family that originated in "Mother Afrika," and racism is an invention of colonialism and capitalism to facilitate our exploitation and enslavement.

Black people need to resist and stand up to their oppression as Black people, expose the lie of white supremacy and lose the slave mentality. Historic destiny calls for stepping up to provide leadership – to other oppressed people and also to the oppressed white people and proletarians. The NABPP–PC has initiated the formation of the White Panther Organization (WPO) as an arm of the Party to win white prisoners, poor whites in the oppressed communities and white youth and people generally to support the Party's 10-Point Program and rally to its leadership in the fight against all oppression. White and Black Panther comrades will stand side by side upholding the traditions of John Brown and Nat Turner in resisting slavery. There have always been some whites, like John Brown and Simon Girty, who sided with Black and Red peoples. This truth needs to be told and many more need to be won to stand in solidarity.

The Party unites with the Red Heart Warrior Society (RHWS) and upholds the "Red-Black Alliance" recognizing the long history of solidarity and cooperation between New Afrikan and Native Amerikan peoples. Long before the "Underground Railroad," the path to freedom led to the Indian nations, Red and Black warriors fought side by side in the Seminole Wars and other armed resistance to the expansion of Euro-Amerikan colonialism and slavery. Many New Afrikans have Indian blood heritage and many Indians have Afrikan blood heritage. This shared history and kinship is celebrated by NABPP–PC and RHWS. The Red-Black Alliance is at the core of the struggle against national oppression in Amerika.

The original BPP set a good example in resisting "Cultural Nationalism," building broad unity and inspiring others to "Seize the Time" and "Fight the Power!" We should continue this tradition and take it even further. As one young Black prisoner wrote to me recently, referring to the original BPP: "Whatever somebody in the past did, I can do too, and I can learn to do it better!" This is the attitude of Comrade Rashid, Comrade Shaka and the other young comrades of the NABPP–PC. I, and the other leading members of the Red Heart Warriors Society, are honored to be their comrades.

We don't have a plan for defeat – except to get back up and keep fighting. Time is running out for humanity. The ruling class is set on a self-destructive course and has no hesitation about taking the human race, and all our relations, down with them. They are at war with the universe – they are at war with reality!

The principal contradiction in the world today is between their desire and need to consolidate their global hegemony and the chaos and anarchy they are unleashing by their attempt to do so. Imperialism is, as Lenin pointed out, "The Final Stage of Capitalism." It is capitalism in decline, moribund and decadent capitalism – *capitalism rotten-ripe for proletarian revolution* – and globalization has accelerated this decline and brought the internal contradiction of capitalism to a head. It is objectively growing weaker and thus more fascistic and more insane. The problem is not just George Bush, Jr. – he is the head of a crazy state, where people who believe in the "Rapture" hold the reins of power.

A revolutionary situation is going to present itself, and it is this the NABPP-PC is dedicated to preparing the oppressed masses to be ready for – to spring like a *Panther* at the opportune moment – and bring down the empire. As men condemned to prison, they have no desire or ambition for personal power. Their sole goal is to arm the people with a correct ideological and political understanding of what must be done – to act as a catalyst to others who are free to take the necessary action. As the sage of the *Art of War* – Sun Tzu – pointed out, battles and wars are won or lost *before* they are fought. Preparation is everything!

Comrade Rashid may never escape his solitary confinement. But he is far from being alone. His love for the people connects him to many comrades he may never see or touch. Like Comrade Hasan Shakur, he is uplifted by "Panther Love," and there is no greater calling or purpose in life than to live and die for the people. Using his intellectual and artistic gifts, Rashid is giving his all to the people and to the generations yet unborn.

We have a saying in the Red Heart Warriors that: "The first duty of a warrior is to liberate the ground under his/her own feet." This Rashid does magnificently.

Transforming "Razor Wire Plantations" of oppression into "Schools of Liberation" does not require a riot. The guards can have the gun towers and the keys to every door – except that of the inmates' hearts and minds. The key is "Pantherism!"

The New Afrikan Nation was forged under conditions of slavery and segregation. Its historic destiny is not to constitute itself as a nation of the historic type. In this Marcus Garvey was right, and so was Huey P. Newton. It has become a nation of a new type, a nation without land – a proletarian nation – and its liberation can only be accomplished through proletarian revolution. Its historic destiny is to be the catalyst of an insurrection to sweep monopoly capitalism into the dustbin of history.

We are revolutionary optimists. We believe that the future will be bright – because we shall dare to make it so!

Panther Love! All Power to the People!

PANTHER POWER

AMER IKKA

AFTERWORD

by Sundiata Acoli

Kevin "Rashid" Johnson has put together an outstanding compendium of political essays and letters that addresses many of the critical issues of today.

His intra-prison correspondences with his comrade, Outlaw, is a rewarding study in the determined and ingenious maneuvers that prisoners have to go through to politically educate and organize themselves – and others around them. As a result, just reading the book itself provides one with the basic foundation of a political education.

Rashid's essays covered such seemingly diverse topics as Marxism, the Five-Percenters, Dialectical Materialism, Dead Prez, Mao Tse-tung, Malcolm X, Class Struggle, Revolutionary Nationalism, George Jackson, Marcus Garvey, Guerrilla Warfare, New Afrikan Independence, Machiavelli, the Prison-Industrial Complex, and a host of other subjects. I trust that most readers came away as highly rewarded and enlightened as I did, even though I had minor disagreements concerning certain definitions of "reverse racism/racist." No matter. Minor disagreements are no detraction from this, or any other, excellent work.

But more importantly, Rashid has put his politics into practice to actively "change the world." He is a prime mover of the recently created New Afrikan Black Panther Party–Prison Chapter (NABPP–PC) and the Red Heart Warrior Society (RHWS). Both are much needed agencies with much potential and Comrade Rashid has his work cut out for him. He needs and deserves our full support.

I support his efforts and urge others to do likewise.

386

Zayd
Shakur

Assata
Shakur

Sundiata
Acoli

RASHID
7-J7 '05

www.rashid-art-attack.org

PANTHER VISION

ESSENTIAL PARTY WRITINGS AND ART
OF KEVIN "RASHID" JOHNSON, MINISTER OF DEFENSE
NEW AFRIKAN BLACK PANTHER PARTY-PRISON CHAPTER

"it should never be easy for them to destroy us" GJ

RASHID 7-07

FOREWORD BY JALIL MUNTAQIM
INTRODUCTION BY JARED BALL
AFTERWORDS BY GEORGE KATSIAFICAS AND TOM BIG WARRIOR

Panther Vision
Essential Party Writings and Art of Kevin "Rashid" Johnson, Minister of Defense, New Afrikan Black Panther Party-Prison Chapter

Kevin "Rashid" Johnson • 9781894946766
496 pp. • $24.95

Kevin "Rashid" Johnson entered the u.s. prison system over 20 years ago, one of countless young Black men consigned to lifelong incarceration by the post-civil right policies of anti-Black genocide. While behind bars, Rashid encountered the ideas of revolutionary Black nationalism and Marxism-Leninism, and of the people and organizations who have used and developed these ideas in previous generations, foremost amongst these being the Black Panther Party for Self-Defense. Along with other Black/New Afrikan prisoners, Rashid helped found the New Afrikan Black Panther Party-Prison Chapter, while using both his artwork and his political writings as avenues to advance the cause of liberation for all.

Here, collected in book form for the first time, are Rashid's core writings as Minister of Defense of the NABPP-PC. Subjects addressed include the differences between anarchism and Marxism-Leninsm, the legacy of the Black Panther Party, the timeliness of Huey P. Newton's concept of revolutionary intercommunalism, the science of dialictical and historical materialsm, the practice of democratic centralism, as well as current events ranging from u.s. imperialist designs in Africa to national oppression of New Afrikans within u.s. borders. And much more.

AVAILABLE FROM LEFTWINGBOOKS.NET

Since 1998 Kersplebedeb has been an important source of radical literature and agit prop materials.

The project has a non-exclusive focus on anti-patriarchal and anti-imperialist politics, framed within an anticapitalist perspective. A special priority is given to writings regarding armed struggle in the metropole, and the continuing struggles of political prisoners and prisoners of war.

The Kersplebedeb website provides downloadable activist artwork, as well as historical and contemporary writings by revolutionary thinkers from the anarchist and communist traditions.

Kersplebedeb can be contacted at:

Kersplebedeb
CP 63560
CCCP Van Horne
Montreal, Quebec
Canada
H3W 3H8

EMAIL: INFO@KERSPLEBEDEB.COM
WEB: WWW.KERSPLEBEDEB.COM   WWW.LEFTWINGBOOKS.NET

more of Kevin "Rashid" Johnson's writings can be found on his website:

ww.rashidmod.com